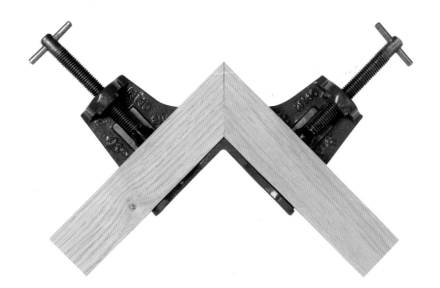

# how to woodwork

# how to woodwork

Phil Davy

hamlyn

First published in Great Britain in 2007 by
Hamlyn, a division of Octopus Publishing Group Ltd
2–4 Heron Quays, London E14 4JP

Copyright © Octopus Publishing Group Ltd 2007

Distributed in the United States and Canada by
Sterling Publishing Co., Inc.
387 Park Avenue South, New York, NY 10016-8810

Phil Davy asserts the moral right to be identified as
the author of this work.

ISBN-13: 978-0-600-61559-0
ISBN-10: 0-600-61559-6

A CIP catalogue record for this book is available
from the British Library

Printed and bound in China

10 9 8 7 6 5 4 3 2 1

**Disclaimer**
In describing all the woodworking practices in this
book, every care has been taken to recommend
the safest methods of working. Before starting any
task, you should be confident that you know what
you are doing, and that you know how to use all
tools and equipment safely. The Publishers cannot
accept any legal responsibility or liability for any
direct or consequential accidents or damage
arising from the use of any items mentioned.

# Contents

# Introduction

It's hard to imagine a world without trees. In fact, there are few natural resources available to us that are so unique. They provide shelter for wildlife, chemicals for medicinal purposes, fuel for heating, fruit to eat, not to mention absorbing carbon dioxide produced by a polluting planet.

But this book concentrates on wood and what you can do with it. Both beautiful and tactile, wood has an incredibly diverse range of uses. Whether employed for house construction, musical instrument making, fine hand-made furniture or delicate decorative marquetry, wood is perhaps the most versatile resource we have. As woodworkers we have a responsibility to ensure that what timber we use is replaced within reason, especially when certain familiar species are becoming endangered.

If you are just getting started in woodwork there are no end of routes to follow, from basic carpentry to fine cabinet-making skills, boatbuilding, carving, woodturning or chairmaking, to name a few. Although techniques may differ in some cases, all disciplines share the common factors of wood and the tools with which to work it. This book aims to guide you through every step in becoming a woodworker, from how to choose and use your tools to buying and preparing timber; from equipping a home workshop to fitting a hinge; from simple design techniques to mastering the joints necessary to build a piece of furniture, we explain step-by-step procedures clearly with drawings and photos. We give you an insight into the more specialist areas of woodwork including turning, carving and bending wood. Final chapters explain what materials you need to finish a project, as well as the necessary adhesives and hardware.

Tips scattered throughout the pages of this book will help make life in the workshop that bit easier, while the Jargon Busters will help you decipher at a glance those words that are unique to woodworking. A glossary provides further definitions. Dimensions throughout are given in metric, while Imperial equivalents are as close as possible.

The woodworker's toolkit can be a curious blend of ancient and modern. While many hand tools are still made from traditional materials and have hardly changed down the years, power tools and machines are constantly evolving. As well as saving valuable time in the workshop, they enable us to attempt techniques that would previously have taken hours to master. Power tools in particular are becoming increasingly sophisticated, with advances in battery technology meaning that frequently cordless tools are preferred to mains-powered versions. New power tools will continue to be invented and developed. Although some may fall by the wayside, with others we'll wonder how we managed to work without them in the future. We give you the most up-to-date information on what woodworking kit is available and how to use it, whether traditional hand tools or state-of-the art machinery. Above all this is a hands-on book, so you can enjoy developing the skills necessary to work with that most amazing of materials, wood.

LEFT Trees are not only objects of great beauty but are one of the earth's most important natural assets. We must learn to treat them with respect.

OPPOSITE Woodworking covers a vast range of disciplines, from mastering hand tools to the efficient operation of machines.

# 1

# Wood
# and materials

There are so many different types of timber and sheet
material available that it can be difficult to choose the
most suitable wood for a particular project. Each has
its own specific qualities, properties and uses. New
species of hardwoods are frequently being introduced,
while the more familiar timbers are becoming
increasingly difficult – and expensive – to obtain.
Selecting the material you want to work with not only
depends on its intended use, but on understanding
how it has been sawn and stored or manufactured.

# Environment

As woodworkers, we have a particular responsibility for the environment. Not only is timber one of the planet's most incredible natural resources but, if forests are properly managed, it is also wholly renewable. A beautiful material, we should consider how we actually use timber as well as ensuring that it always comes from a reliable, sustainable source. We have a responsibility to minimize waste and to recycle materials where we can. Everyone needs to play a part in protecting our fragile environment.

## Deforestation

Many timbers used traditionally in furniture- and cabinet-making are now classified as endangered and are in short supply. As a result, many woodworkers avoid using tropical timbers altogether and buy only temperate hardwoods. It is not always that simple, however. Tropical forests, in particular, provide a vital income for the survival of indigenous peoples. In some of the poorest parts of Africa, for example, rapid deforestation is leading to increased poverty and threatening an environmental crisis. Fortunately, charities such as Tree Aid are involved in establishing and managing tree nurseries, sustainable woodlands and agroforestry.

The intensive logging of temperate and tropical rainforests is not the only cause of deforestation. Global warming means many huge tropical trees are dying due to drought conditions caused by warmer seas, and there is a general rise in forest fires around the world. The Amazonian rainforest has long been referred to as the 'Lungs of the World'. These immense forests absorb carbon dioxide and give off oxygen, vital in reducing the greenhouse effect – the thickening blanket above the earth responsible for increasing our temperatures. If we allow our rainforests to become unsustainable, climate change will increase even more rapidly.

ABOVE Tropical rainforests help reduce the greenhouse effect.

TOP LEFT Intensive logging causes deforestation.

LEFT Forest fires are increasingly common, resulting in soil erosion.

# Sustainability and timber certification

We can help by ensuring that the timber we use, whether from tropical or temperate forests, is from sustainable sources – that is, where trees are replaced with saplings as they are harvested. The Forest Stewardship Council (FSC) is an international organization responsible for the certification of timber and wood products from well-managed tropical and temperate forests around the world. The FSC logo denotes such certified timber and wood products and allows us to make a choice, while at the same time influencing the management of forests. If in doubt, question your timber merchant closely as to the sources of the raw material on sale and his policy on the whole environmental issue. At least this helps to raise awareness of environmental concerns.

The use of veneered boards, such as medium-density fibreboard (MDF) and plywood, not only make certain hardwoods economically viable, but these materials are also likely to be more suitable and stable for many woodworking tasks.

# Alternative species

Great Britain and the United States are two of the world's biggest importers of timber, but with some 30,000 species in the world, we only actually use a tiny minority of what is available. We still tend to favour traditional tropical hardwoods, such as mahogany, for furniture-making and joinery. In an attempt to save what remains of these dwindling forests, however, less familiar timbers are becoming available to woodworkers. Some can be stained to resemble woods like ebony and mahogany, although many species are just as attractive in their own right. If we change our woodworking habits, there will no longer be a need to rely on traditional hardwoods for building, say, a table or set of dining chairs. And there is every reason for substituting endangered tropical timbers for temperate hardwoods, assuming they are certified.

# Recycling

Architectural salvage yards are a good source of reclaimed timber, although you should watch out for nails and screws embedded in the wood, which will snag on saw blades and planer knives. All foreign bodies must be removed before working on reclaimed timber: if in doubt, sweep the surface with an electronic detector.

Old, unwanted furniture can also be a good source of solid timber. Assuming it has no insect attack or rot, it will be fully seasoned and therefore more stable than new wood. Much of it is likely to be veneered, but even plywood panels of cabinets or wardrobes can be used for making perfectly good backs, or even workshop jigs for use with power tools and machines.

BELOW Always carefully examine reclaimed timber for embedded nails or screws before machining.

---

**JARGON BUSTER**

**CITES** Convention on International Trade in Endangered Species monitors woods sold commercially that are at risk.
**FSC** Forest Stewardship Council

# Timber selection

All timber is categorized as either a hardwood or a softwood. The two terms can be misleading since softwoods, such as parana pine and yew, are much harder, denser and tougher than hardwoods such as balsa – a classic example. An extreme comparison, but it demonstrates that you cannot rely on the simplistic view that all hardwoods are hard and all softwoods soft. Fortunately, most species have already been identified for us.

## JARGON BUSTER

**Air-drying** Once a trunk has been converted, logs are stacked 'in stick' in the open air to dry naturally, but protected from the rain.

**Crown-cut** Crown-cut boards display almost flat or slightly curved growth rings in the end grain. Faces show flame effect of growth rings.

**Figure** The grain pattern revealed in a piece of timber, usually when planed. It usually refers to unusual effects characteristic of certain woods.

**Heartwood** Hard, dense cells at the centre of a tree, providing the most stable timber.

**Kiln-drying** The process by which the moisture content of timber is reduced by more than is possible by air-drying. Timber is seasoned in an oven using a mixture of hot air and steam. This is essential for wood destined for internal use.

**Medullary rays** Flecks evident on the face of some quartersawn timber.

**Sapwood** New wood growing furthest from the centre of a tree, providing least stable timber.

**Seasoning** The process of removing moisture from the cell walls of wood.

**Quartersawn** Planks cut from a tree radially, where growth rings are at least 45 degrees to the face. This technique exposes the best figure.

## Growth rings

As a tree grows, a new ring of sapwood builds up around the previous year's growth. The heartwood increases in area, while the sapwood remains much the same thickness throughout the tree's life. A growth ring is the layer of wood produced in one growing period. Rapid growth in spring is called 'earlywood'. Large cells make up this wider, paler part of the growth ring. Denser cells produced in summer ('latewood') form a darker ring, adding support to the tree.

Growth rings in hardwoods are either 'ring porous' or 'diffuse porous' depending on their cell-structure formation. Ring-porous timber has alternating layers of open cells and tightly grouped cells. Open cells are formed as the tree grows during spring and summer, while tighter cells are formed during autumn and winter, as growth slows down. Examples of ring-porous hardwoods are oak and ash. Diffuse-porous timber occurs where there are no clear changes during the growing season, resulting in cells of a more uniform size and formation. Examples of diffuse-porous

ABOVE The trunk, or bole, is the tree's main stem, supporting a crown of branches that bear leaves. A root system anchors the tree in the ground, absorbing water and minerals to sustain it. The trunk carries sap from the roots to the leaves via the cell system.

TOP RIGHT Hardwood trees grow slowly and the broad leaves are usually lost in autumn.

RIGHT Softwood trees generally have straight trunks and needle-type leaves. They include redwoods, the tallest trees in the world.

hardwoods are maple and beech. Ring-porous timbers have a more open grain than that of diffuse-porous hardwoods, which are therefore more consistent when it comes to planing or sanding.

## Characteristics of hardwoods

Broad-leaved trees are called hardwoods, with many species losing their leaves in winter, especially in temperate climates. The hardwood structure relies on each cell or fibre being very long and needle-shaped. Lying side by side, these tend to make the hardwood timbers more elastic than softwoods. Growth rings are often hard to distinguish, especially in diffuse-porous timbers, such as maple. Durability tends to be greater than most softwoods, and the variety of colours offered by hardwood species is vast. Hardwoods grow in both tropical and temperate climates and may be deciduous or evergreen. Common hardwoods include oak, mahogany, maple, walnut, beech and many others.

## Characteristics of softwoods

Coniferous or cone-bearing trees are called softwoods and have needle-pointed leaves. A coniferous tree matures in about a quarter of the time taken by a hardwood tree. The term softwood means that the tree cells are hollow and spindle-shaped. Along the sides of the cells are small holes that act as connecting passages through which food passes on its way to the leaves. Softwoods are generally paler in colour than hardwoods, with clearly visible growth rings. They are generally easier to work than hardwoods, although there are exceptions. Softwoods grow mostly in temperate climates and include spruce, fir, pine, yew, giant redwood and the mighty sequoia.

**The characteristics of hardwood and softwood cells**

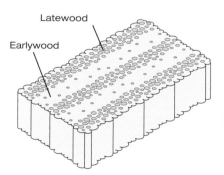

Latewood

Earlywood

Early- and latewood

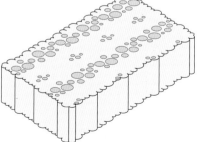

Ring-porous wood – such as oak

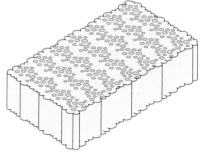

Diffuse-porous wood – such as maple

ABOVE Colour and figure vary widely across different species of timber. From left: marblewood; bird's eye maple; quartersawn English oak and snakewood.

# Colour and grain

Hardwoods range enormously in colour from purples, reds and oranges through greens to browns and blacks. The same cannot be said of softwoods, which are predominantly pale yellows and browns. Apart from colour, grain is probably the primary aesthetic reason for choosing a particular species. Some timbers have large pores or open grain (ring porous), such as oak, chestnut, wenge and teak. Others have a fine grain or small pores (diffuse porous), polishing more easily with a deep lustre (maple, sycamore, holly and tulipwood). Species such as sapele and utile have interlocking grain. This gives a striped effect, with planing tearing the grain on alternate stripes. The ultimate beauty in any species is perhaps that produced from a quartersawn board, revealing the medullary rays. English oak is famous for this figuring.

# Which wood to choose?

There is a greater range of hardwoods available for furniture-making than there are softwoods. Although the latter tend to be much cheaper to buy, they are less dense and durable than hardwoods, and so tend to be used less for woodworking.

When choosing timber, consider the environment to which it will be exposed. For outdoor use, for example, iroko, cedar and European oak are all excellent, although they should still have a protective finish. Not only are teak and greenheart ideal for outdoors, but they can withstand water immersion without detriment to their strength. It is advisable to use teak or cheaper iroko when there is a risk of iron corrosion: ferrous metals can cause nasty black stains in timbers such as oak and chestnut, which have a high tannic acid content. Metal fittings should be plated.

For decorative indoor furniture, walnut, mahogany, yew, oak or maple will look impressive. Sports equipment is often made of ash and willow, whereas balsa is best for making models. Musical instruments frequently use exotic timbers such as rosewood or ebony. Some woods, such as cedar of Lebanon, have a strong aroma and are highly prized for box making.

Timber suppliers tend to refer to a species not by its Latin name but by its general name, such as 'oak'. This one species, however, covers a range of oaks – including American red and white, Japanese and English – each with its own characteristics. Mahogany is a widely used species with many different sources so identification can be difficult. The species includes Brazilian, Honduran, Cuban, American and several types of African mahogany. Besides these, there is also sapele – not strictly a mahogany but widely used as a substitute – meranti from Malaysia, and also lauan, which is stained to look like mahogany. They are used particularly for general joinery work such as window- and doorframes.

There are endless timber characteristics and properties. If a species is new to you, buy a small amount first and experiment before buying more. Some woodworkers find certain timbers can produce an allergic reaction, so purchasing a large quantity could be a costly mistake. Some timbers are also very hard on cutting tools. For example, teak has calcium pockets and grit within its fibres, which can dull a keen edge – even tungsten carbide-tipped saw blades. Dense tropical timbers, such ebony, require exceptionally sharp tools.

# Timber defects

Defects in timber may be obvious – knots and cup shakes on the end of a board, for example – and may occur naturally or be man-made. Some are more difficult to spot than others. Some natural defects are sought-after, as they increase the beauty of the wood.

## Knots

Knots show the emergence of branches in a growing tree. They occur mostly in softwoods, which are often graded by the number and size of any knots present. Small, live knots are not usually a problem, but dead knots are often loose and can drop out. Large knots create weakness and make a board difficult to work. Resin may eventually seep out from knots, especially on timber used externally: seal these before final finishing with a shellac sealer. Small knots in timber such as English oak can be desirable, enhancing the grain's character and increasing the price.

## Checks and splits

Checks and splits in timber are usually the result of poor seasoning, where the timber is allowed to dry too quickly and shrinkage occurs. Major splits tend to occur at the ends and edges of boards, while checks (tiny splits) may appear anywhere across the face. Air-dried oak is particularly prone to this defect. End splits can be reduced during seasoning by sealing board ends with paraffin wax.

## Shakes

Shakes are cracks that occur within the tree, but are longer and wider than checks. Star shakes are radial cracks that appear around the outside of a log, following the line of medullary rays at 90 degrees to the growth rings. They are caused when the outer log shrinks while the centre remains more stable, and are the result of a log being left too long before conversion. Heart shakes result from internal shrinking and radiate outwards from the centre of the log. These may be caused by over-maturity of the tree or disease. Cup or ring shakes occur when growth rings separate. They form in the growing tree when subjected to high winds or a lack of food.

## Cupping, twisting and bowing

Cupping is a common problem in crown-cut softwood. Boards tend to cup away from the curve of the growth rings as the timber dries out, both faces contracting at different rates. Twisting and bowing often result from bad sawing or poor stacking once the log has been converted. Some trees grow in a natural spiral, leading to twisting. Bowing along the length is usually the result of stacking boards badly. Stresses resulting from these distortions can make machining the affected timber difficult.

## Burrs

Sometimes formed when the bark of a tree is damaged, growths are produced when the wound heals. Known as burrs, or burls, they can grow on the trunk, the

roots or individual branches. Characterized by dense, swirling grain, burrs are highly prized and generally cut into veneers or used for woodturning. The wild interlocking grain makes burrs extremely difficult to use for furniture-making.

## Insect and fungal attack

Sapwood in new timber is prone to insect attack and bark should be removed before boards enter the workshop. Old buildings with poor ventilation and heating can lead to damp conditions that give rise to fungi and wood-boring insects. Constructional timbers are susceptible to attack from both wet and dry rot. Furniture stored in these conditions is also prone to attack from various beetles and must be treated with a suitable preservative.

BELOW European oak is susceptible to defects after felling. Star shakes occur if the trunk is not converted soon enough.

BOTTOM Burrs may grow on the outside of a tree when it has been damaged in some way.

**Further information**
Environment  pages 10–11
Timber seasoning and conversion  pages 16–19
Buying and storing timber  pages 20–23
Timbers of the world  pages 30–37
Timbers for turning  page 176
Timbers for carving  page 188

# Timber seasoning and conversion

When a tree is felled, the majority of its weight is water. To 'convert' a trunk into usable timber, the sawmill cuts it into various board thicknesses. This method involves starting on one side of the trunk and, as each pass of the saw cut is complete, the next cut is made, and so on, until the entire trunk has been sawn.

TOP The most economical way to convert a log is by through-and-through sawing.

ABOVE A plank being sawn on a large vertical band resaw. The log moves forward on a tracked carriage through the blade.

## Sawing methods

Different methods of sawing timber yield different types of board with regard to stability, appearance and cost. There are several questions to ask yourself when choosing and buying wood: what method of sawing has been used to cut the log?; and how are the boards stored in the yard while the timber stocks are air-drying? Has the timber also been kiln-dried?

### Quartersawing

Many years ago, when labour costs were far lower than they are now, timber merchants were prepared to saw a log in half lengthways, and in half again to give a quadrant, or quarter circle, at the end of the each length. The reason for this 'quartersawing' was to reveal the medullary rays that would otherwise be lost. These highly prized rays, or flecks, are present in all trees to a greater or lesser extent, although they are most often seen in oak boards. Quartersawing is very wasteful, because it involves turning the timber frequently before the next saw cut, and it is now rare to find a sawmill converting a tree to boards in this way. For this reason, it is worth buying a board displaying medullary rays should you see one.

### Through-and-through sawing

The most common cutting method, through-and-through sawing simply involves the trunk being sawn from one edge. As each saw cut is complete, the log is moved the required distance to produce another cut until the trunk is sawn into a number of boards. Logically, the centre boards show the medullary rays and are produced without the cost of quartersawing. This method also produces the widest boards, although the heart is prone to splitting.

## Tangential sawing

In some countries a log is sawn to produce the maximum wood from the trunk, regardless of whether or not the resulting boards have an attractive figure. This system of sawing around the log is known as 'tangential' cutting because each cut forms a tangent to one of the annual rings. It is not unusual for one face to include sapwood. It is advisable to reject any sapwood in your finished cabinetwork: it is prone to beetle attack, it shrinks badly, and its immature fibres do not accept glue or polish as well as the heartwood section.

BELOW Logs usually arrive at the sawmill by truck, although in some countries they may be transported by water.

### Sawing methods

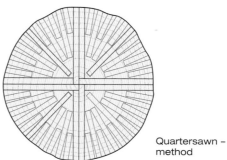

Quartersawn – traditional method

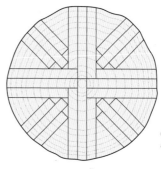

Quartersawn – less intensive and wasteful method

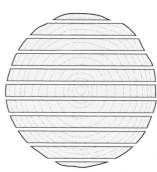

Common through-and-through sawing

---

## JARGON BUSTER

**Crown-cut** Another term for through-and-through sawing (see left). Crown-cut boards display almost flat or slightly curved growth rings in the end grain. Board faces show the flame effect of the growth rings.

**In stick** Air-dried boards are stacked as they come off the log with spacer battens, or 'stickers', spaced evenly between them.

**Seasoning** The process of removing moisture from the cell walls of wood.

**How figure is produced by different sawing methods**

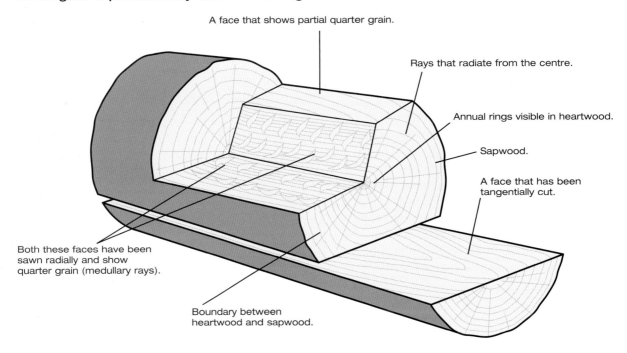

A face that shows partial quarter grain.

Rays that radiate from the centre.

Annual rings visible in heartwood.

Sapwood.

A face that has been tangentially cut.

Both these faces have been sawn radially and show quarter grain (medullary rays).

Boundary between heartwood and sapwood.

LEFT Boards from several logs stacked vertically after kiln-drying at a small sawmill. They are more often stacked horizontally where there is space.

# Drying timber

Green timber has a moisture content of about 30 per cent, known as fibre saturation point. Once sawn, individual boards are stacked in the open air, using small strips of wood called 'stickers', to separate them from one another. Air flowing over each board draws the water to the surface by capillary action; this then evaporates, reducing the moisture content to about 25 per cent. The time required to 'season' the wood in this way depends on the thickness to which the boards have been cut. A rough guide is one year per 25 mm (1 in) thickness of board.

## Kiln-drying

Air-drying worked reasonably well before the advent of central heating and air conditioning. However, the climate in many countries means that even the best air-dried timber retains about 16 per cent moisture content, no matter how long it has been dried, which is too high for most modern homes. Today, any wood used indoors must be able to remain stable, even when the central heating system is full on. In order to achieve this, air-dried timber is placed in a kiln to extract more moisture until it reaches an average of 15 per cent moisture content.

Always ask whether the wood you buy has been kiln-dried: the letters 'KD', which conform to most trade description acts, should be printed on your receipt. In the event of subsequent extreme movement in your timber, it may be necessary to prove that your timber was sold as kiln-dried. Most timber merchants are conscientious and will replace the odd board that appears to have too high a moisture content despite being kiln-dried.

## Kiln- or air-dried timber?

The best moisture content for timber in today's well-heated homes is around 10 to 12 per cent. This is difficult if the sawmill supplies only timber averaging 15 per cent! Most good cabinet-makers will rough-machine their wood and then expose it to a well-heated workshop prior to finishing a piece to its final dimensions.

Air-dried timber is usually cheaper than kiln-dried, but the moisture content is unlikely to be lower than about 16 per cent. This level makes it suitable for external use such as constructing garden sheds, outdoor structures and timber framing. Timber with a moisture content of more than 20 per cent is susceptible to dry rot, however.

Do not assume that you can reduce the moisture content of this less expensive timber by leaving it in a warm room. You cannot, and if you use the timber for furniture-making, your work will suffer from bad shrinkage and distortion.

Kiln-drying timber takes a few days, as opposed to the months or years required for air-drying. For furniture and internal joinery items, timber should be kiln-dried down to about 11 per cent. Timber in close proximity to heat sources, such as radiators or fireplaces, should ideally be as low as 9 per cent. Sometimes, the kilning process leaves surface splits across the board face, which can cause problems. They indicate that the drying took place too rapidly, leaving the inner part of the board wet with the outer part too dry. This is called 'case-hardening'. Avoid such boards: once you have machined the surface, the wet inner fibres will distort the board when subjected to the heat in your workshop.

## Moisture content

Sawn timber is rarely bone dry: it gains or loses moisture depending on the surrounding atmosphere, and expansion or shrinkage occurs as it adapts to humidity and temperature.

Moisture content is the weight of moisture shown as a percentage of the timber's dry weight. For example, in a board with 20 per cent moisture content there is actually 2 kg (4½ lb) of water for every 10 kg (22 lb) of dry wood. Moisture content is usually measured with an electronic meter, its pin electrodes detecting electrical resistance. Alternatively, a small timber sample can be weighed before and after being dried in an oven, then a simple calculation carried out.

When you are buying timber beware of claims like 'average moisture content 15 per cent.' This could mean some boards retain as much as 19 per cent, while other boards from the same kiln could be as low as 12 per cent.

BELOW A stack of timber emerging from a kiln after drying for several days. The moisture content is checked using an electronic meter.

**Further information**

# Buying and storing timber

Timber yards can be intimidating places for the woodworker making a first visit. Although buying softwoods is fairly straightforward, hardwoods can be another matter. If possible, find a more experienced woodworker who will be willing to guide you through some of the pitfalls. If buying timber from a large supplier, check whether they have a minimum-quantity purchasing policy.

## Buying timber

There are two ways of buying hardwoods, depending on the facilities available at the timber yard. The cheapest way is to select boards yourself at the yard, checking for defects and roughly marking out what you need. If you can transport the timber home so much the better, although most yards will deliver for an extra fee. You can then saw the boards up to the required size at your workshop, although you will probably be left with some offcuts.

If you have limited machining facilities, some timber yards will cut – and even plane – boards to your cutting list, charging per saw cut or by the hour for machining. This is obviously a more expensive method and you are unlikely to be able to make decisions regarding grain patterns or defects.

Some hardwoods have a much higher wastage factor than others (see below), and you should take this into

TOP A log sawn through-and-through prior to being put 'in stick' to air-dry. Boards are stacked in sequence as they are sawn.

ABOVE The selection at the timber yard can be daunting. Ask advice from experienced staff or a woodworking friend.

### TIP

• Try to establish a rapport with your timber merchant. It is amazing how a good relationship can yield special offers or invitations to inspect a new delivery of wood.

account when estimating the quantity required for a project. For example, English walnut and yew have as much as 400 per cent wastage while others, such as beech and mahogany, have less than 100 per cent.

Buying softwoods is generally easier, as most imported timber is square-edged, sometimes even planed to size. Rather oddly, softwoods are usually sold by the cubic metre in Britain, while hardwoods are traditionally priced by the cubic foot or foot run. When timber is priced by the metre or foot run, width and thickness are ignored, although this will already have been taken into account by the timber merchant. This is often the case with wood sold in narrow strip form.

## At the timber yard

Before buying wood for your own use, it is wise to inspect how boards are stacked at your chosen timber yard. Most timber merchants are conscientious in spreading the load evenly when stacking half a dozen fully sawn logs on top of one another. Others are careless, however, and you may be surprised to see trunks with such uneven weight placed on them that the entire log bows considerably at one end or in the centre. Be aware that stresses introduced as a result will eventually cause a board to try to revert partly to its original form, which could cause problems later on.

Generally speaking, much of the movement of each sawn board will have resolved itself in the air-drying

ABOVE Careless stacking leads to degradation in board quality, giving poor performance and greatly reducing its value. Avoid such timber unless it's for firewood.

BELOW A board with a serious shrinkage split which cannot be closed up. Most splits are less obvious but planks should be examined carefully.

process. Although timber yards place cleats on the ends of boards to reduce splitting, wood should be allowed to move in whatever direction it wants to go. Very little can stop a growth line shrinking if it wants to, and it has been known for 152 mm (6 in) nails to snap in half owing to the force of shrinkage.

The majority of wood with splits and shrinkage defects will be marked with a wax stick or marker pen, or removed from the stack altogether. It will be to your cost if you fail to spot any such defects in the length of a board. Often a split will continue, following a growth line, and can even reappear on the opposite face or

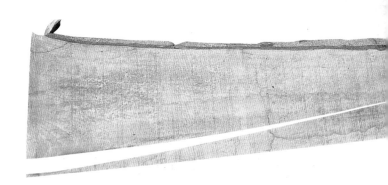

# CALCULATING CUBIC CONTENT

The easiest way to calculate the cubic content of a piece of timber is to multiply its length by its width and multiply that figure by its thickness. Once you've done that it is easy to estimate the total cost of the boards. Simply multiply the quantity of timber by the price given by the timber yard, either per cubic foot or cubic metre. When drawing up a cutting list you will now be able to estimate how much timber you need, allowing extra for waste, depending on the species of timber. Bad defects, such as knots, splits and shakes, should be marked out and deducted from the calculation. Make sure that you always use either the imperial system or the metric system, but do not mix the two. With metric it is easier to calculate in metres, as millimetres will create so many zeros it becomes confusing.

## Calculating cubic content for different pieces of timber

1 cubic metre can consist of any size timber that makes up the same volume:

A = 1 piece at 500 x 500 x 1,000 mm
= 0.5 x 0.5 x 1 m = 0.25 m3

B = 25 pieces at 100 x 100 x 1,000 mm
= 0.1 x 0.1 x 1 m = 0.01 m3

C = 10 pieces at 50 x 500 x 1,000 mm
= 0.05 x 0.5 x 1 m = 0.025 m3

D = 4 pieces at 250 x 250 x 1,000 mm
= 0.25 x 0.25 x 1 m = 0.0625 m3

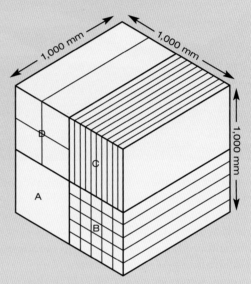

**1 cubic metre = 1m³ = 1,000,000,000 mm³**

## Calculating cubic content in cubic feet

There are 1,728 cubic inches in a cubic foot. How many cubic feet are there in six hardwood boards, each 10 ft long, measuring 6 in wide and 2 in thick?

Working in inches, each board contains:
120 x 6 x 2 = 1,440 cubic inches

Multiply this figure by six for the number of boards: 6 x 1440 = 8,640 cubic inches

Now divide this by 1,728 to convert cubic inches to cubic feet: 8,640 ÷ 1,728 = 5 cubic feet

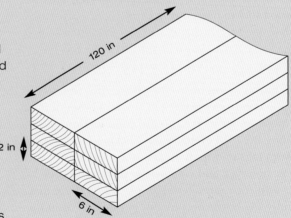

**Cubic content of six identical boards**

edge, making the board worthless for part of its length. Always check both faces of a board carefully. Often the best face is presented, but a closer look at the opposite side may reveal larger, additional knots and wild grain, which means that some parts cannot be used for structural purposes. These defect areas are often marked out in the calculations, but if you feel that the potential saving is not worth the inherent problems later on, choose another board. Do not buy distorted boards: the fibres will have been distorted in the drying process and the cell walls will remain permanently damaged.

The basic rule when inspecting timber is that, the more parallel the grain, the less it will shrink. This is not to say you should not buy a board with flowery and wild grain, as this may be more exciting visually. It does mean, however, that you may have to saw a wide, figured board into narrow widths of perhaps 152 mm (6 in) and re-glue them. This will give you a wide board with much of the tension removed. If you buy your wood with two waney edges and the board is not the same width at each end, the timber yard will measure both ends, plus the middle of the board, and calculate an average width. Unless you will have boards delivered, it is a good idea to take a handsaw when visiting a timber yard.

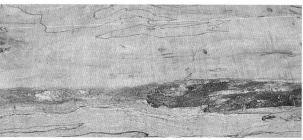

TOP Stack timber carefully in your own workshop. Use stickers between each board, spaced vertically above each other.

ABOVE A board with a dead knot, part of which will fall out. This is caused by a branch dying before the tree is felled.

## Storing timber in the workshop

In your workshop, stack long boards flat on the floor rather than propped at an angle against a wall. Do not expose them to direct sunlight, as this will cause the natural colour either to fade (as in mahogany) or to darken (as in cherry). Brush melted paraffin wax on the end grain of all boards to prevent the ends drying too quickly in a heated workshop. A good maxim is 'to keep a long piece of wood as long as you can for as long as you can': many woodworkers have workshops full of timber that is too small to use! Finally, keep all wood storage areas well ventilated and avoid damp conditions. A dehumidifier is recommended.

---

**JARGON BUSTER**

**PAR (planed all round)** The term refers to softwoods that have been planed on all four sides.

**Waney edge** The natural edge of a plank, which may still have a covering of bark.

---

### Further information

# Veneers

Virtually every figured hardwood and many softwoods can be obtained in the form of veneer – a thin sheet of the solid timber. Decorative veneer is normally glued to a 'groundwork' of timber or sheet for stability and strength, while constructional veneer is used for laminating and producing plywood and other sheet materials.

The range of veneers available is enormous – from exotic burrs to three-dimensional ripple and figured veneers. Many of the world's most unusual and magnificent trees are converted into veneer, as are fine examples of less exotic timbers. Common thickness is 0.6 mm (approximately ¹⁄₆₄ in), although constructional veneers for laminating are thicker, between 1 and 3 mm (¹⁄₃₂ and ⅛ in).

## Veneer production

To produce a veneer, a log is either cut square or rotary-cut. When cut square it is soaked for some time in hot water before being placed on a massive guillotine, which cuts a 1-mm (¹⁄₃₂-in) thick slice of wood along the log's entire length. As the blade retracts, so the log moves foward by 1 mm (¹⁄₃₂ in) and the process is repeated. As each veneer leaf falls onto the previous one, the figure is visibly repeated on each leaf. Quartersawn slicing produces more figured grain in the veneer than normal, flat slicing. Once the leaves have been dried and stacked – generally in bundles of 24 leaves – each bundle is taped so that the sequence of cut leaves is not disturbed. This way the entire solid log is rebuilt in bundles or parcels.

With rotary-cut veneering, the log is first de-barked and steamed. It is then mounted on a large lathe-like machine. The log revolves and a continuous sheet emerges as the cutting knife reduces the radius of the log. Mounting the log in several different positions results in various grain patterns. When positioned off-centre, the veneer's figuring is similar to that obtained by flat slicing. Back cutting is used to exaggerate the effect of curl veneer (from a fork in the tree's trunk), which produces a feathered effect.

ABOVE Veneer leaves are stacked in bundles or flitches. Exotic and valuable woods are usually covered over to prevent discolouration by daylight.

**Veneers cut by slicing method**

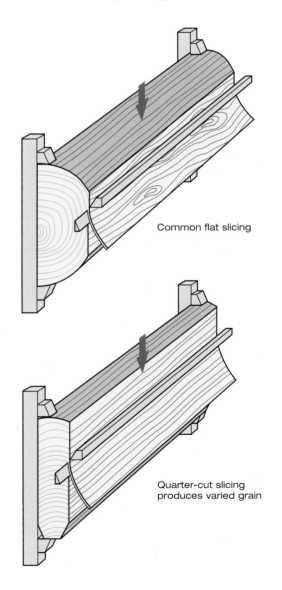

Common flat slicing

Quarter-cut slicing produces varied grain

# Types of veneer

Veneers fall into two categories. The first comprises leaves produced from good, clean boards, but that are not necessarily highly figured. For example, rotary-cut veneers are economical to produce and are used in the manufacture of plywood. Other slice- or guillotine-cut veneers are clean and representative of a species but without the highly prized figure. Suitable for areas inside a carcase, for example, these straightforward veneers are often crown-cut, which gives a wider leaf than the straight grain of a quartersawn log.

The second category comprises exotic or highly figured veneers, which can range from fiddleback rays that dance across the surface to quilted maple, where the surface literally appears to have the texture of a satin quilt. Often the figure and real beauty of a species can only be found in veneer form and, although most hardwoods and softwoods can be converted into veneer, it is an expensive process, ideally reserved for a good commercial log.

# Tips for buying and storing veneer

- Always check that the bundle has not been disturbed. Look through the leaves and any loss of sequence will be apparent.
- Hold a random leaf up to the light. If it has been badly cut daylight will appear through all or part of the leaf.
- Check that the leaf edges have not discoloured with ultraviolet light. The centre of the leaf should match the colour of the edge.
- Always store veneers away from direct light. Tape the ends to prevent splitting and store in a cool dry place, preferably flat.
- Once you have bought your bundle of veneers, number each leaf in sequence. Do this before spreading them out. Once they are scattered around the workshop it is easy to mismatch when trying to establish the original order.

**Further information**

**Veneers cut by rotary method**

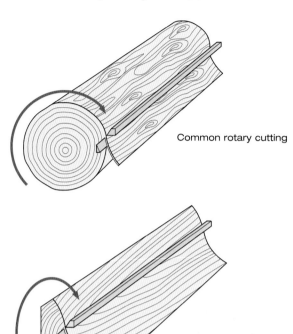

Common rotary cutting

Back cutting for curl veneers

---

## JARGON BUSTER

**Burr or burl**  Wild grain revealed when a growth on a tree is cut off and sliced.

**Caul**  A stiff board, flat or curved, for cramping groundwork and veneer together.

**Crown-cut**  Another term for through-and-through sawing. Crown-cut boards display almost flat or slightly curved growth rings in the end grain. Board faces show the flame effect of the growth rings.

**Flitch**  A bundle of veneer leaves.

**Groundwork**  Sheet material or timber to which veneer is glued.

**Laminating**  The process of gluing several layers of veneer together to form a stable, curved shape without steaming and bending. (Plywood is a form of laminating, using constructional veneers.)

**Quartersawn**  Planks cut from a tree radially, where the growth rings are at least 45 degrees to the face. This technique exposes the best figure  and timber is most stable.

# Sheet materials

There are various benefits to using sheet materials: they are generally more stable than solid timber, thickness tends to be uniform, and quality is fairly consistent if bought from the same supplier. Veneered boards enable you to utilize natural timbers – sometimes with quartersawn or exotic figuring – reasonably economically. There is also less impact on the environment than when using certain solid timbers. Plastic coatings are widely used on sheet materials used for kitchen manufacture and other mass-produced furniture.

ABOVE Sheet materials come in several sizes and thicknesses. They can be cut with power tools or hand tools.

## JARGON BUSTER

**Fillers** Substances used to fill small holes and defects in timber. Usually chemicals, although sawdust mixed with glue is sometimes used.
**Melamine** A durable, hard plastic coating applied to sheet materials during manufacture.
**Quartersawn** Planks cut from a tree radially, where the growth rings are at least 45 degrees to the face. This technique exposes the best figure and timber is most stable.

## TIPS

• Before sawing a veneered board, score the underside of the cutting line with a craft knife and straightedge, or stick masking tape along the line. Either method prevents the veneer from splintering. Man-made boards, MDF and chipboard in particular, require very sharp saws for cutting. High resin content will blunt saw teeth and planing edges at twice the rate of real wood.
• It is essential to wear a good dust mask when machining these materials, especially MDF, as breathing in the fine dust is harmful.

## Medium-density fibreboard

Medium-density fibreboard (MDF) consists of minute particles of wood mixed with a heavy-duty resin. It is the most versatile man-made board of all, used extensively for furniture-making, toys and shop fit-outs, as well as joinery and carpentry projects. More stable than other boards, it is also relatively cheap. It comes in wide range of thicknesses from 2 mm ($\frac{3}{32}$ in) up to 51 mm (2 in) and a variety of surface finishes. An excellent surface for veneering, painting, staining or polishing, the edge can be shaped and spindle-moulded like solid timber. It can be routed easily to provide unique 3D textured surfaces, although the router should be hooked up to a dust extractor. Moisture-resistant (MR) and fire-resistant (FR) grades are available, while melamine-faced MDF is used extensively for building kitchen units and office furniture. Edges of veneered MDF boards are commonly finished with hardwood lippings that match the veneer. Increasingly, MDF is replacing softwood in the construction industry for joinery items such as skirting and door architraves.

Contemporary designers and furniture-makers can now benefit from coloured MDF. The colours are created using organic dyes mixed with the wood fibres before the boards are pressed. They can be machined in the same way as normal MDF and the colour is consistent throughout the board thickness. Only a clear finish is needed to seal the surface.

# Plywood

Originally the most widely used board, plywood is now somewhat overshadowed by MDF. It consists of a number of layers of constructional veneers, each laminated together to the previous layer with the grain at 90 degrees. Generally, the more layers of veneer the more stable the board. Outer leaves may be hardwood or softwood. Much plywood today is made from veneer leaves that have been poorly dried and result in distorted boards, which means you may have to search for undistorted boards.

There are several grades of plywood, varying enormously in quality and cost. The cheapest is 'shuttering ply', used extensively in the construction industry for building formwork for concreting and other temporary structures. A release agent is first applied to the plywood's surface to prevent the concrete sticking as it cures. 'Birch ply' is regarded as the best quality for both internal and external use, while 'marine ply' is water-resistant and used widely for boat building. This is commonly made from Douglas fir or larch.

Thickness ranges from model-makers' 'aero ply' at 1 mm, up to 25 mm (approximately ⅟₃₂–1 in). A more recent development is moisture-resistant flexible plywood, which enables instant curves to be formed easily in furniture and joinery projects. Thickness ranges up to 8 mm (⁵⁄₁₆ in). Flexible MDF has almost identical properties to this plywood and is available in similar thicknesses. Fire-retardant plywood is used widely in the construction industry.

# Blockboard

Blockboard consists of an inner core of softwood strips – about 22 mm (⅞ in) wide – veneered over at right angles to the grain in a rotary-cut veneer, such as gaboon. Good-quality blockboard is not always easy to find: the inner softwood core is often not dried thoroughly. When it eventually does dry, a pattern showing the core strips is revealed through the polished surface, sometimes referred to as 'telegraphing'. On poorer quality blockboard the softwood strips of the inner core do not always butt up tightly against each other. This may not be apparent until you saw through the board when gaps can appear. Veneered blockboard is often used for carcases and cabinets, as well as internal joinery, shop fitting and screens.

Laminboard is a higher quality blockboard, but is rarely used nowadays because of its cost. The inner core strips are about 6 mm (¼ in) wide, creating a more stable material than blockboard.

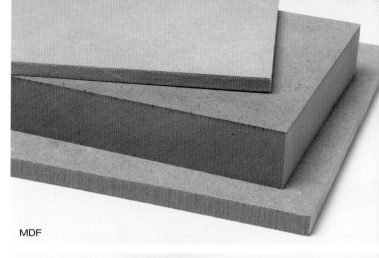
MDF

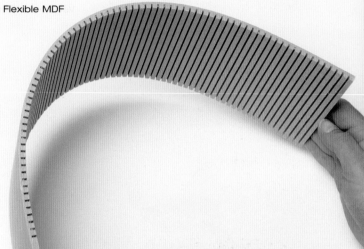
Flexible MDF

Coloured MDF

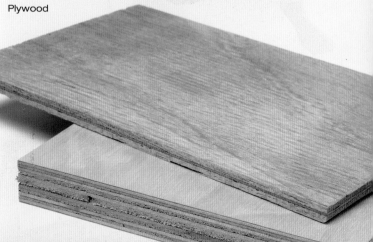
Plywood

Veneered MDF

# Chipboard

Also known as particle board, chipboard comes in several grades. It consists of wood chips mixed with synthetic resin, which are placed in a heated press. Different layers in the thickness are visible. For smooth-surface chipboards, finer particles of chip are compressed on the outer faces with a coarser, looser wood chip used for the middle. A favourite with the construction industry, chipboard is also used extensively for shelving and lower grade furniture. Some variants are made for exterior use, while others are specifically designed for kitchen worktops – up to 51 mm (2 in) thick. Decorative chipboards are available with resin, paper-coated, plastic or wood-veneered surfaces.

Chipboard has little strength unsupported, and tends to sag under its own weight. Various types of edge lipping are available in plastic, metal and wood. Many require either a sawn or routed groove for attachment, or are glued with cramps. A chipboard edge without protection is not only unsightly, but leaves the edge vulnerable to chipping.

Flooring-grade chipboard is tongued and grooved on all four edges, although it can also be square-edged. A tongue simply locates into a matching groove, adding to the overall strength and preventing sagging when

LEFT Blockboard (top) is still used for furniture, shop fitting and joinery. Chipboard (middle) and hardboard (bottom) are more popular in the construction industry.

BELOW Sheet materials are cut most accurately on a dimension or panel saw.

stepped on. Where panels are sawn to length or width, the resulting butt joints should be positioned over a joist or have a supporting batten nailed underneath. Narrow boards are useful for flooring in attics, as they are designed to pass through a ceiling hatch easily.

## Hardboard

Hardboard is a fibreboard, similar to MDF, consisting of tiny wood particles mixed with a resin. Sugar-cane pulp is also traditionally used in its manufacture. Hardboard is often laid on uneven flooring before laminate wood or carpet is laid. Perforated hardboard, or pegboard, is useful for tool storage panels. Special hooks are simply inserted into the holes. Oil-tempered hardboard is impregnated with resins and oils, making it weather resistant. Hardboard comes in thicknesses from 2–6 mm (approximately ³⁄₃₂–¼ in) and is available in a limited range of colours as well as the more common original brown finish.

Hardboard should be conditioned before being nailed rigidly to a framework; if not, it will buckle after fixing. A sheet should be laid down and water brushed or sprayed on the back. This ensures that the sheet expands and will pull tightly when dry. Allow to dry before nailing in place.

## Veneered boards

There was a time when you could buy plywood and blockboard veneered on both sides with pine or a hardwood such as oak. Now, however, this option only really exists with MDF. For interior use, the thinnest boards may have a decorative veneer on just one side, with an inferior balancing veneer on the reverse. Above 6 mm (¼ in), boards may have a quartersawn veneer on one side, with crown-cut veneer on the reverse. Typical veneers are ash, white and steamed beech, sapele, cherry, maple, oak, birch, American black walnut and pine. A stable material for making furniture, these boards should be cut very carefully to prevent the veneer breaking out underneath. Thickness ranges from 4–26 mm (⅛–1½ in), with panels reaching 3,050 mm (10 ft) in length.

## Working with sheet materials

Sheet materials are best cut with a circular saw fitted with a fine-tooth TCT blade. At least 40 teeth are recommended for sawing veneered boards. If using a portable saw, run the tool against a straight guide batten cramped across the board, checking for alignment with a large try square. Always use dust extraction when sawing any man-made material.

Where you see defects in a board's face, try not to use fillers. These shrink in time and show below the surface. Always use the actual veneer material – birch for birch ply, gaboon for gaboon ply and MDF for repairs to MDF, and so on.

Although small-section, solid-wood lippings can simply be glued to the edges of sawn boards without problems, do not rely on doing this for heavy lippings. Rout a groove in both the back of lipping and the board edge for a loose tongue of plywood or solid timber. This should be a snug fit and will increase the strength of the gluing surface.

When planing solid-wood lippings level with the surface of a veneered board, be careful not to break through the face. The same applies to ordinary chipboard, where planing too deep will reveal a coarser chipboard which is very noticeable under a coat of paint.

Hardware and fasteners have been developed specifically for jointing sheet materials and assembling carcases built from them. These include everything from simple plastic corner blocks and chipboard screws to sophisticated concealed hinges and dowel connector systems. For most hardware, holes should be bored precisely at 90 degrees for professional results. Use a pillar drill or stand-mounted power tool for this.

### SHEET SIZES

Most sheet materials conform to a standard size of 2,440 x 1,220 mm (8 x 4 ft). Some MDF boards are produced in lengths of 3,050 mm (10 ft), with widths of 1,200 mm or 1,525 mm (4 or 5 ft). Melamine-faced MDF can be purchased up to 3,660 mm (12 ft) in length, and widths of up to 2,050 mm (approximately 81 in). These industrial-sized boards are really only suitable for converting on a vertical wall saw before final dimensioning on a panel saw.

**Further information**
Environment  pages 10–11
Veneers  pages 24–25
The work environment  pages 66–67
Drills  pages 104–105
Veneering  pages 178–182
Laminating wood  pages 184–185

# Timbers of the world

Before selecting timber, consider the advantages and disadvantages of the wood. Over the following pages you'll find a helpful introduction to a wide range of soft- and hardwoods.

## Softwood

The term 'non-porous' is sometimes applied by botanists to softwood species, many of which grow in the northern hemisphere. Instead of moisture passing through open cells throughout the tree's length, as in hardwoods, each individual softwood cell relies on moisture passing through its cell wall. This often causes softwoods to perform quite differently to hardwoods when used in the workshop.

### Parana pine: *Araucaria angustifolia* (1)

**Sources** Brazil, Argentina, Paraguay
**Sustainability** tropical softwood, with risk of illegal logging
**Typical uses** internal joinery, stairs
➕ close-grained, wide boards; easy to machine, with low wastage
➖ cupping a problem with wide boards
Denser than most softwoods, parana pine often grows above 21 m (70 ft) in height. Unlike most softwoods, this hard pine is generally knot free, and can be obtained virtually free from knots in wide boards. Honey-coloured, its reddish streaks are regarded as a feature. Growth rings are hard to distinguish.

### Cedar of Lebanon: *Cedrus libani* (2)

**Sources** Middle East, Europe
**Sustainability** unlikely to be certified
**Typical uses** drawers and box linings
➕ wide, stable boards; strong aroma repels insects
➖ brittle; quite expensive
A general term, as there are three or four different cedars with similar characteristics. This timber is known for its strong fragrance, which deters moths, and is often used as a drawer lining. Very light with little constructional strength, it is available in very wide boards, some of which are quartersawn.

### Larch: *Larix deciduas* (3)

**Sources** Europe
**Sustainability** not endangered, though available from certified sources
**Typical uses** external joinery
➕ straight grain; durable outdoors
➖ splits and knots a problem
A wonderful timber for outdoor use, it not only grows to a great height, but also produces really wide boards. Often seen in the form of fencing, garden sheds and even flooring. Traditionally used for pit props in mines and telephone poles. Unlike pines and spruces, which are evergreen, this species loses its leaves in winter.

### European redwood: *Pinus sylvestris* (4)

**Sources** Europe, northern Asia
**Sustainability** not endangered
**Typical uses** household furniture, joinery, house construction
➕ cheap and plentiful; easy to work
➖ can be knotty
Also known as Scots pine, in western Europe redwood abounds as furniture and structural members in house building. Prone to movement, its wide spring growth is quite soft, making the harder summer growth pronounced. It changes colour with ultraviolet light, which can be unattractive if the exposure is uneven.

### Douglas fir: *Pseudotsuga menziesii* (5)

**Sources** North America, UK
**Sustainability** not endangered, though available from certified sources
**Typical uses** house construction and joinery
➕ water-resistant; straight grain, fairly strong and can be knot free
➖ can be brittle and susceptible to splintering
A giant of a tree, often growing in excess of 85 m (280 ft). Generally reddish in colour, the sectional sizes available are enormous, so its uses are vast, from large timber structures to interiors. Not only very tough, but water-resistant. Also known as British Columbian pine and Oregon pine.

### Yew: *Taxus baccata* (6)

**Sources** Europe
**Sustainability** often found in churchyards and parks, certification is rare
**Typical uses** furniture-making, musical instruments, bows, veneer
➕ beautiful colouring and grain; straight-grained timber bends well
➖ very high wastage (up to 400 per cent), so very expensive

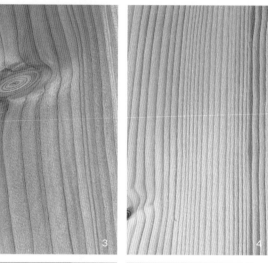

Some trees exceed 1,000 years in age. Yew has extraordinarily elastic properties, hence its historical use for long bows and the finest Windsor chairs. Boards have a high proportion of sapwood and its branches make beautiful oysters. The foliage is poisonous to many animals, including cattle.

## Western red cedar: *Thuja plicata* (7)

**Sources** North America and Europe
**Sustainability** certified timber available. Not easily regenerated, supplies of best stock low
**Typical uses** roof shingles, musical instruments
✚ easy to work; naturally durable
➖ dust can cause respiratory problems
Western red cedar is available in wide boards and very easy to work. The lovely aroma can remain in the wood, especially when used in confined spaces. Very durable and much used for internal joincry. It withstands almost any climatic condition, so is particularly good for houses.

## Western hemlock: *Tsuga heterophylla* (8)

**Sources** North America and Europe
**Sustainability** not endangered, though available from certified sources
**Typical uses** internal joinery, stair balusters, plywood, sheds and greenhouses
✚ straight grain, stable; easy to work
➖ poor durability, soft
Although a good general-purpose timber for interior work such as panelling, western hemlock is prone to movement in enclosed, temperature-variable conditions. It grows fast, is clean and even in grain, but should not be used externally. Also called fir or spruce.

# Hardwood

From early experimentation, it has been discovered which woods are durable and perform well for tool-making, boat building, furniture-making, even wheel-making. In these categories hardwoods generally perform better than softwoods. This is partly owing to the different composition of the cell structure in hardwoods, which allows much greater flexibility than in most softwoods.

## Sycamore: *Acer pseudoplatanus* (9)

**Sources** Europe, western Asia
**Sustainability** not endangered, though some timber is certified
**Typical uses** furniture-making, musical instruments, woodturning, kitchen utensils
✚ fine grain, few defects; easy to bend
➖ surface can burn when machining; not as hard as maple
Although almost white when converted, in time it turns yellowish-brown. In quartersawn boards the medullary rays are beautiful and subtle. Rippled figuring is prized for musical instruments. Seasoning and workshop drying can still result in distorted boards; they must be stood on end to season or the colour is lost forever. A superb wood once tamed.

## Sugar maple: *Acer saccharum* (10)

**Sources** North America

**Sustainability** not endangered, though certified timber easily available

**Typical uses** furniture-making, tool handles, butchers' blocks, woodturning, flooring

➕ cuts well, retaining sharp edges when machined

➖ hard on edge tools; poor durability

Also known as rock maple, sugar maple is a versatile, close-grained, dense temperate timber that finishes well. The wood ages and discolours less than sycamore and its grain can be straight or very wavy. Bird's-eye, rippled and quilted maples are exotic variations, often displaying stunning figuring. Sugar maple is prized by cabinet-makers.

## Red alder: *Alnus rubra* (11)

**Sources** North America

**Sustainability** not endangered, fast growing

**Typical uses** furniture-making, joinery, carving, woodturning

➕ stable, straight grain

➖ bland appearance; fairly soft

Used more than anything as a utility timber, red alder grows quickly and is widely available as a result. Easy to season and very stable, this temperate hardwood makes a good substrate for veneering. A relatively soft timber, you will need sharp edge tools to produce a decent surface.

## Boxwood: *Buxus sempervirens*

**Sources** Europe

**Sustainability** rare, but not certified

**Typical uses** tool handles, woodturning, musical instruments, printing blocks

➕ fine, smooth, close grain; attractive colour

➖ restricted to small diameter branches; limited quantities make it expensive

Unlike most hardwoods, boxwood is sourced from hedgerows and mature trees, making it quite rare. It is sometimes available from specialist timber suppliers. A favourite of woodturners, it is capable of retaining detail cuts well. Often used for chess pieces, chisel handles and stringing for inlay work.

## Sweet chestnut: *Castanea sativa*

**Sources** Europe and Turkey

**Sustainability** not widely available, though not endangered

**Typical uses** staircases, coffins

➕ strong, durable, inexpensive

➖ slow to season

Sweet chestnut is a handsome tree with a large crown. Also known as Spanish chestnut, this resembles flat-sawn oak, although few medullary rays are seen. Softer and lighter than oak but found in larger sections, this wood is delightful to work. Its high tannic acid content stains fingers very easily. Sweet chestnut trees are harvested for their nuts.

## Iroko: *Chlorophora excelsa*

**Sources** Africa
**Sustainability** possible low risk, but difficult to find certified timber
**Typical uses** external joinery, garden furniture, boat building
⊕ strong and fairly stable; oily and durable
⊖ interlocking grain; unpleasant to work and dulls blades quickly
A pale to dark brown tropical timber, iroko is similar to teak in appearance. It is unpleasant to machine without good extraction as its pungent smell irritates the nasal passages and many woodworkers refuse to work with it. A good outdoor wood for garden furniture and situations in which humidity levels can fluctuate widely.

## Rosewood: *Dalbergia* (12)

**Sources** Central and South America, India, Indonesia
**Sustainability** endangered, some Indian timber plantation-grown
**Typical uses** musical instruments, cabinet-making, tool handles, veneer
⊕ dense, beautiful colour and figure
⊖ some endangered; prone to fine surface splits
There are several different rosewoods including Brazilian, Indian, Rio, Honduran, Mexican, Madagascan, each with its own beautiful colour and grain. Export bans imposed by South American countries mean that most are now virtually impossible to obtain, except in veneer form. Plantation-grown Indian rosewood is most common. One of the most sought-after exotic timbers.

## Kingwood: *Dalbergia cearensis* (13)

**Sources** Brazil
**Sustainability** not listed as endangered, but still scarce
**Typical uses** cabinet-making, inlay, veneer
⊕ dramatic colour and grain
⊖ splits are common; very expensive
A beautiful timber that is difficult to obtain in large sizes sections. Contrasting pale yellow sapwood, which is often incorporated into furniture for decorative effect. Heart shakes are common. Often sold by weight rather than cubic content, kingwood is a dense timber, which polishes well. Also known as violetwood.

## Cocobolo: *Dalbergia retusa* (14)

**Sources** Central America
**Sustainability** vulnerable, with certified timber rare
**Typical uses** musical instruments, woodturning, cutlery handles, inlay, veneer
⊕ Amazing colour and grain; water-resistant
⊖ interlocking spiral grain is common; very expensive
This dense, exotic tropical timber has irregular grain but is stable when dry. Its colour is stunning, with alternating orange and red streaks with darker lines. From the rosewood family, cocobolo contains oils, so gluing can be a problem. Its durability makes it valuable for cutlery handles. Also known as granadillo.

## Macassar ebony: *Diospyros celebica* (15)

**Sources** Indonesia
**Sustainability** vulnerable, with certified timber rare
**Typical uses** musical instruments, cabinet-making, woodturning, inlay
⊕ extremely hard and dense
⊖ seasons slowly, risk of splitting; blunts tools rapidly; rare and very expensive
Varies greatly in colour, from dark brown with black stripes to mostly black with yellow stripes. It is particularly streaky in veneer form. Prized for fingerboards on guitars and the violin family, it is sometimes dyed to create a uniform black colour. Difficult to work, with edge tools needing frequent honing.

## Sapele: *Entandrophragma cylindricum*

**Sources** Africa
**Sustainability** certified timber is scarce. Status varies
**Typical uses** doors, windows, furniture-making, flooring, plywood, veneer
⊕ wide boards; not too expensive
⊖ interlocking grain can tear
Owing to the size of the tree, sapele is available in very wide boards. Rather stripy and not too exciting visually. Used for commercially produced joinery and as a substitute for mahogany, although not the most stable timber. Quartersawn timber can be highly figured, with fiddleback figure common.

## Jarrah: *Eucalyptus marginata*

**Sources** Australia
**Sustainability** status uncertain, and uncertified timber rare
**Typical uses** house construction, furniture-making, woodturning, carving
⊕ naturally durable, strong; can be figured
⊖ dulls edge tools quickly; grain can be interlocking
Much of Western Australia is built of jarrah; it is used in bridges, railway sleepers, flooring and many outdoor situations where strength and durability are essential. This temperate hardwood is an even reddish-brown colour, but the grain often lacks character. Used for internal cabinet-making, it is tough to work with hand tools.

## Beech: *Fagus sylvatica* (16)

**Sources** Europe

**Sustainability** not endangered, though some certified timber

**Typical uses** woodwork tools, workbenches, commercial furniture-making

- good for bending; inexpensive
- shrinkage a problem

Huge beech trees mean wide and thick boards are available. Renowned for being unstable, shrinkage is 400 per cent greater than any other European hardwood, although it is one of the cheapest temperate timbers. It can work beautifully when dry and glues well. Diseased beech has dark veins, called spalting, prized by woodturners.

## Ash: *Fraxinus excelsior*

**Sources** Europe

**Sustainability** not endangered

**Typical uses** sports equipment, boat building, furniture-making, veneer

- strong and flexible, ideal for bending
- grain can tear when planning; prone to splits

Ash is a tough, temperate, ring-porous timber with attractive grain. As well as being one of the best woods for steam bending, it has excellent shock-absorbing properties, making it ideal for tool and cricket bat handles. When the white heart turns to a streaky colour it is known as olive ash. Rippled ash generally in veneer form.

## Ramin: *Gonystylus macrophyllum* (17)

**Sources** Southeast Asia

**Sustainability** not endangered

**Typical uses** plywood, furniture-making, carving

- fine, straight grain
- bland appearance

Ramin is one of a family of similar trees from Southeast Asia. It has a very open, featureless grain, which is difficult to cut to a crisp finish. It is often used in furniture where components are hidden, such as framework. The splinters are poisonous and must be removed from the skin immediately.

## Lignum vitae: *Guaiacum officinale* (18)

**Sources** Central America

**Sustainability** endangered and CITES listed

**Typical uses** marine components, bowling bowls, woodturning

- heavy, durable and self lubricating
- very difficult to work; interlocking grain

Lignum vitae ('tree of life') is naturally oily, making it ideal for boat bearings and clock movements, though gluing can be tricky. One of the world's densest tropical hardwoods, it is extremely strong and durable, with beautiful colour and grain. Very expensive, and often sold by weight rather than board size.

## Bubinga: *Guibourtia demeusei* (19)

**Sources** West and central Africa

**Sustainability** not endangered

**Typical uses** tools, musical instruments, cabinet-making, veneer

- striking colour, can be highly figured; stable when it is dry
- grain can be interlocking; blunts edge tools easily

A dense reddish-brown wood with thin dark lines giving an interesting pattern. The vibrant colour darkens with exposure. It glues and finishes well, making it an attractive timber for high-quality tools. It is sometimes used as a cheaper alternative to rosewood (also known as African rosewood). In veneer form it is called kevasingo.

## American black walnut: *Juglans nigra*

**Sources** North America

**Sustainability** not endangered, certified timber readily available

**Typical uses** furniture-making, musical instruments, gunstocks, joinery, veneer

- fairly straight-grained, easy to work
- dents easily

A beautiful, cheaper alternative to European walnut, American black walnut is magnificent for furniture-making. Relatively lightweight, it is easy to work with hand and machine tools, though gives off an unpleasant smell. Stable once seasoned, its gorgeous deep-brown colour can have a purple tint. This temperate hardwood polishes beautifully.

## European walnut: *Juglans regia* (20)

**Sources** Europe, parts of Asia

**Sustainability** not endangered, though timber is sparse and not certified

**Typical uses** furniture-making, woodturning, box making, veneer

- beautiful grain, figure and colour; easy to work
- very expensive; risk of insect attack

Walnut trees often die before reaching a good size, although boards can be fairly wide. Ease of use, colour, texture, figure and sheer depth of beauty combined with its stability make this species unique and highly prized. In veneer form, crotch and burr are especially sought-after.

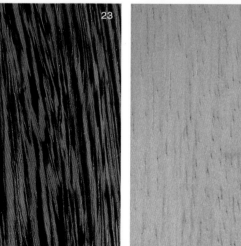

## American whitewood: *Liriodendron tulipifera* (21)

**Sources** North America, Europe
**Sustainability** not endangered, grows fast
**Typical uses** toys, painted furniture, pattern making, joinery
➕ straight grain, medium strength; seasons well; stable and inexpensive
➖ rather bland appearance; not durable
American whitewood is confusingly also called yellow poplar or tulipwood. It is second-rate timber for making furniture, but is excellent as a good stable subbase for veneering or for hidden carcases, or where painted furniture is required. American whitewood is sometimes used for plywood. It machines easily and is excellent for making jigs.

## Zebrano: *Microberlinia brazzavillensis* (22)

**Sources** West Africa
**Sustainability** vulnerable, so veneer preferable to solid wood
**Typical uses** furniture-making, woodturning, carving, inlay, veneer
➕ beautiful figure when crown-cut; stable once seasoned and durable
➖ interlocking grain difficult to work; veneer can buckle
Zebrano is an exotic tropical timber with a range of colours in the form of contrasting striped lines, which can vary in density. This timber is often used as a detail in marquetry, but its initial lustre can fade when it is exposed to too much ultraviolet light. Its boards may be rather limited in size. Zebrano is known as zebrawood in the United States.

## Wenge: *Millettia laurentii* (23)

**Sources** Central Africa
**Sustainability** endangered, with no apparent certified timber
**Typical uses** woodturning, flooring
➕ durable, dense and strong; distinctive colour and straight grain
➖ splinters easily; finishing can be a problem
When planed, wenge changes from a straw colour to almost black. Open-pored, but with a good grain filler, replaces rosewood admirably. Lacks figure, but for small areas like turnings it has a wonderful grain distinction. Brittle and very splintery, finishing wenge can be problematical owing to grain's absorption variation. Similar to panga panga.

## Balsa: *Ochroma pyramidale* (24)

**Sources** Central America, West Indies
**Sustainability** not endangered
**Typical uses** model making, carving
➕ excellent to carve with sharp tools; buoyancy aids
➖ very soft and weak, will crush easily; expensive
The lightest and softest wood in the world, yet it is a hardwood. One of the few timbers where the sapwood is utilized. Trees grow rapidly, but are very susceptible to damage. A marvellous timber for model making and for containers requiring buoyancy. Tends to be available only in small sizes.

## Plane (lacewood): *Platanus acerifolia*

**Sources** Europe

**Sustainability** not endangered

**Typical uses** furniture-making, veneer

➕ stunning figure when quartersawn

➖ roupala and silky oak may be confusingly sold as lacewood

One of the few species which, when the medullary rays are seen in the quartersawn board, changes its name, from plane to lacewood. The tree is predominant in cities and is distinguished by its continuously peeling bark. A good furniture wood with great subtlety and finishes well.

## European cherry: *Prunus avium* (25)

**Sources** Europe

**Sustainability** not endangered, but timber not widely available

**Typical uses** woodturning, veneer

➕ grain can be attractive

➖ boards limited in size and seasons poorly

Often a difficult timber to obtain, as trees do not live that long. Cherry can be awkward to plane without breakout, especially on quartersawn boards. Equally, it is worth persevering, as the close grain can polish beautifully.

## American cherry: *Prunus serotina* (26)

**Sources** North America

**Sustainability** not endangered, plenty of certified timber

**Typical uses** musical instruments, furniture-making, woodturning, carving, boat building

➕ straight, fine grain and attractive colour

➖ high degree of sapwood on each board

Also known as black cherry, it can be difficult to obtain the best quality outside North America, as this is rarely exported. Board conversion for maximum volume means most exported timber has excessive movement and wastage is high. Some boards can yield good figure. It can be stained to imitate mahogany reasonably well.

## Padauk: *Pterocarpus dalbergiodes* (27)

**Sources** Andaman Islands (Indian Ocean)

**Sustainability** certified timber doubtful, but not yet endangered

**Typical uses** furniture-making, boat building, flooring

➕ stunning colour, durable

➖ interlocking grain difficult to work, blunting tools

Padauk is difficult to work owing to its interlocking grain, but persevere and the reward will be a beautiful rich, deep-red timber with dark streaks dancing over the surface. Beware of this colour fading somewhat when exposed to ultraviolet light. African padauk is similar in colour and texture and easier to use.

## American white oak: *Quercus alba*

**Sources** North America

**Sustainability** not endangered, certified timber readily available

**Typical uses** furniture-making, joinery, construction work, flooring

➕ durable, strong, straight grain; inexpensive

➖ grain lacks character

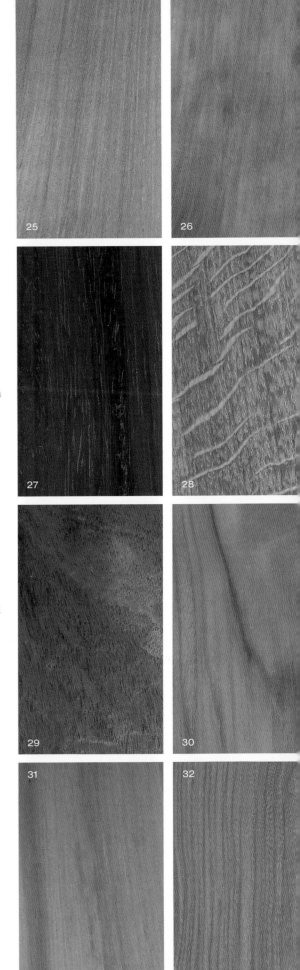

This oak is regarded by many as adequate in that it is durable and tough, has good sectional sizes and length, but is prone to having sapwood included in sawn boards. White oak is, however, dull and must rank as a functional oak rather than one with character. A useful all-round temperate hardwood that can be used externally.

## American red oak: *Quercus rubra*

**Sources** North America
**Sustainability** not endangered, certified timber readily available
**Typical uses** furniture-making, joinery, flooring
⊕ deeper colour than white oak; inexpensive
⊖ less figure than most oaks; not durable
Although there is a greater depth of colour in red oak it cannot be used externally. Very similar in working properties to white oak, the quartersawn boards may display some rays, though not as extensively as European oak.

## European oak: *Quercus robur* (28)

**Sources** Europe
**Sustainability** certified timber available, but not under threat
**Typical uses** furniture-making, high-class joinery, timber framing, boat building, veneer
⊕ durable, hard and strong; distinctive grain and colour
⊖ natural defects mean wastage can be significant; expensive
European oak is a majestic timber, with quartersawn boards displaying fantastic medullary rays, for which this wood is famous. Of all the oaks, this one is the most spectacular for furniture-making. Burr oak is prized by woodturners and by cabinet-makers in veneer form. A gorgeous surface is virtually guaranteed, whatever the finish.

## Brazilian mahogany: *Swietenia macrophylla* (29)

**Sources** Central and South America
**Sustainability** endangered tropical timber, although certified timber widely available
**Typical uses** furniture-making, cabinet-making, quality joinery, veneer
⊕ plain-sawn boards can produce flamed figure
⊖ grain can tear easily; prone to insect attack
The only true mahogany now commercially available, and the reason for much debate surrounding rainforest issues. Used as a substitute for prized Cuban mahogany, which is virtually extinct. Brazilian mahogany produces grain with many variations, including crotch pattern, the result of intersecting branch and trunk.

## Teak: *Tectona grandis* (30)

**Sources** Southeast Asia, West Africa
**Sustainability** not endangered, though plantation-grown or certified timber preferable
**Typical uses** boat building, flooring, garden furniture, decking
⊕ water-resistant and naturally durable
⊖ very expensive; blunts edge tools rapidly
A timber that exudes a natural oil from its pores, enabling it to withstand exceptional conditions. Difficult to de-grease for gluing purposes, but still a joy to work, despite its calcium pockets and grit particles blunting edge tools. Excellent for furniture-making, both indoors and out. Substitutes include afrormosia and iroko.

## European lime: *Tilia vulgaris*

**Sources** Europe
**Sustainability** no problem, grows abundantly in Europe
**Typical uses** woodcarving, woodturning, toys, musical instruments
⊕ fine, even grain cuts easily; not expensive
⊖ slight movement when dry; board ends can split
Arguably the best timber for woodcarving, it is a real delight to work with sharp edge tools. Lime is not really suitable for furniture as its appearance is rather bland, although it is often used for children's toys. Freshly machined timber darkens to pale brown with exposure.

## Obeche: *Triplochiton scleroxylon* (31)

**Sources** West Africa
**Sustainability** not endangered, readily available
**Typical uses** mouldings, hidden furniture components
⊕ stable; easy to work
⊖ bland appearance; grain can be interlocking
A good ground timber, used for drawer bases, rails that require veneering, and so on. It is useful as a stable base for incorporating with other timbers. It is often stained to improve its appearance. Also known as linden.

## Elm: *Ulmus hollandica* (32)

**Sources** Europe
**Sustainability** some certified timber, increasingly rare
**Typical uses** tabletops, chair seats, boat building, flooring, veneer
⊕ dramatic grain and colour variation
⊖ grain pattern makes it difficult to work; needs careful seasoning
Thousands of trees have died from Dutch elm disease across Europe. When available, however, this magnificent species provides durability, depth of beauty and exotic figure. The burrs and knots of this timber make its character unique. Quite soft for a hardwood, the grain is fairly coarse. English elm is not as tough as European.

# 2

# Woodworking design

Design in woodworking can be extremely simple or incredibly complex, and may be influenced by a range of factors, including purpose, timescale, materials and budget. This section outlines the basic principles that apply and illustrates the importance of a good design brief. Design ideas may be realized via computer programs or through sketching and drawing: both skills are fairly easily acquired, as explained here, and mastered with practice. The techniques involved enable you to produce working drawings for your projects as well as cutting lists – important when buying and preparing timber and materials.

# An introduction to design

This section concerns the concept of 'design' – exploring what is actually meant by the term, and demonstrating a simple step-by-step breakdown of a 'design method'. This will provide you with an overview of the design process, and enough information to start designing for yourself.

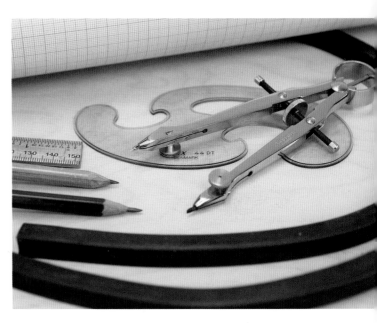

## What is design?

Design is essentially about meeting requirements, proposing solutions and solving problems. The process involves a whole range of intellectual and practical skills, including structural, aesthetic and conceptual thinking, in addition to economic, environmental, production and cultural considerations. In practical terms, all of this information has to be communicated through concept sketches, working drawings, graphics, models and prototypes.

A good designer is an informed person, who takes account of all these factors and uses his or her creative ability to give an end result that reflects the needs of the producer and user. Designers therefore need to be acutely aware of their market and to use an appropriate mix of skills for each problem.

What follows serves as an introduction to basic design. The principles described here apply whether you are designing a jewellery box, a chair or a large cabinet. Additional information may be required in certain cases: with a chair, for example, there may be ergonomic factors, such as the angle of the back, the height of the seat and whether arms are required; with a cabinet, the important issue is volume and various criteria for storage or display. One thing common to all furniture, however, is that both the structural requirements and the safety of users are primary considerations.

TOP Simple drawing instruments such as compasses, flexible and French curves are invaluable.

LEFT Side and three-dimensional views of a bedroom chair using computer-aided design (CAD). This has replaced the traditional drawing board for many woodworkers.

# The design process

Think of the design process as a funnel: all the available information and known requirements are poured in, and filtered through as one, to result in a solution. The result is a process that involves many separate elements interacting together.

**1 Definition of the problem:** You identify, or someone approaches you with, a problem that needs to be solved.

**2 Research:** You gather and collate as much information as possible about the problem.

**3 Identification of constraints:** You consider and highlight any constraints that may affect your progress – safety, materials, timescale or cost, for example.

**4 Concept and exploration:** You start to propose conceptual solutions, based on your knowledge of the problem. This refined information is commonly known as a 'brief'. The brief is used as a guide, so that when proposing solutions you do not stray too far from the problem and its constraints.

**5 Design detail and development:** You choose one or two of the best concepts and develop them by working to more detail, checking your ideas against the noted constraints as you go along. Once you have found a suitable solution you can produce working drawings.

**6 Realization:** You produce the design to scale or as a full-scale prototype. The quality of the result depends largely on how thoroughly the design phases were undertaken and how carefully the model or prototype is made.

**7 Evaluation:** You compare the proposed solution to the original brief. At this stage, you can decide on final improvements to the design before committing yourself to the production of the finished piece.

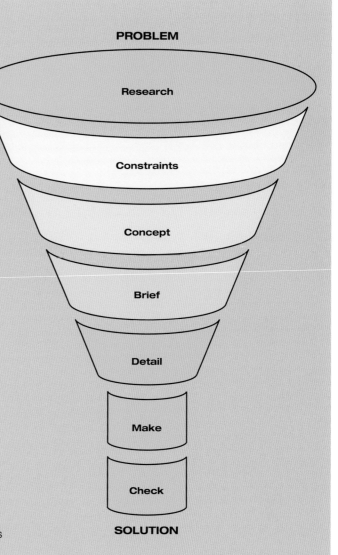

PROBLEM

Research

Constraints

Concept

Brief

Detail

Make

Check

SOLUTION

---

## JARGON BUSTER

**Design brief** A written plan identifying a problem and how it can be solved, within certain criteria and constraints, by a designer.
**Ergonomics** The study of people's relationship to their working environment – particularly relevant in the design of furniture.

**Further information**
Drawing and sketching techniques  pages 42–44
Timber and cutting lists  pages 45–47
Computer-aided design  pages 48–49
Furniture gallery  pages 50–53

# Drawing and sketching techniques

Once you have successfully worked through the first three phases of the design process, and have derived the brief (see page 44), you are in a position to communicate your initial ideas – usually done through sketches. Start with general ideas and develop your concept sketches gradually, adding more detailed information such as tone, texture and shading as you progress.

ABOVE A flexible curve has a lead core, which stays put when bent to shape. It has two ruling edges, for pencil and ink.

## Freehand drawing

Everything you see can be drawn or represented well by fitting its shape into one of the following: a cube, a sphere, a cylinder, a cone or a rectangular box. As with any other skill, this takes practice and, as you begin to master the technique, it becomes easier and more enjoyable. There are a few simple things you need to learn to improve your drawing skills – the emphasis here is on 'freehand', because there is a natural tendency to turn to a ruler, which actually takes longer and does not, in fact, improve your skill: freehand parallel lines (vertical and horizontal); freehand rectangles, squares and parallelograms; freehand circles (usually inside squares) and freehand ellipses (inside parallelograms and rectangles).

**TIP**

• Get into the habit of keeping your sketches in a hard-backed sketchpad with non-removable pages, as this removes the temptation to scrap the bad drawings and keep only the good ones. By retaining all the early sketches you can chart your progress, which is very instructive and also helps to show where best to concentrate. This invaluable practice will help you to draw with some degree of accuracy relatively quickly.

**Solid shapes**

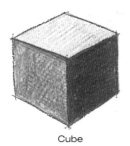

Cube

Sphere

Cylinder

Cone

Rectangular box

## Exercises to improve your drawing skills

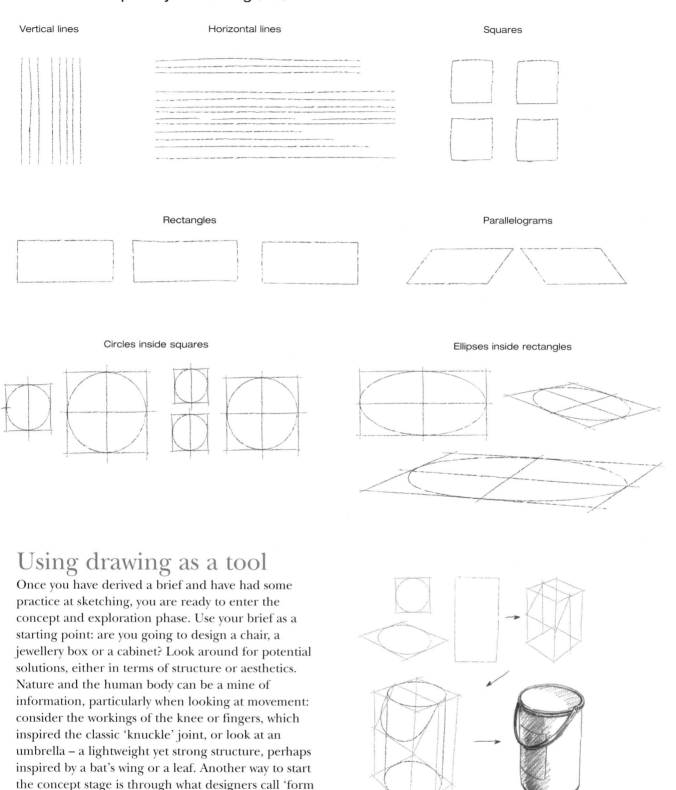

Vertical lines

Horizontal lines

Squares

Rectangles

Parallelograms

Circles inside squares

Ellipses inside rectangles

# Using drawing as a tool

Once you have derived a brief and have had some practice at sketching, you are ready to enter the concept and exploration phase. Use your brief as a starting point: are you going to design a chair, a jewellery box or a cabinet? Look around for potential solutions, either in terms of structure or aesthetics. Nature and the human body can be a mine of information, particularly when looking at movement: consider the workings of the knee or fingers, which inspired the classic 'knuckle' joint, or look at an umbrella – a lightweight yet strong structure, perhaps inspired by a bat's wing or a leaf. Another way to start the concept stage is through what designers call 'form generation'. This can start with simple sketches of squares, rectangles, circles and so on. By adding to them, subtracting from them, subdividing and rearranging the subdivisions, you can create a whole series of potential new paths to explore.

ABOVE First draw a circle in a square, then a parallelogram with an ellipse inside and a rectangle. Then put them all together and you have the outline of a paint tin. Add depth by hatching in shadows.

## Sample design brief

**The brief:** to design a low table that can act as a whole, or as a set of separate tables.

**1** Apply the 'form generation' technique. Start with squares, triangles, circles and rectangles and explore various options by adding, subtracting and subdividing. Each shape created is a potential tabletop (or tops).

**2** Consider the elements as a whole and as a set, and pick one or two ideas to work with. Here, legs are added to each quarter and the concept as a whole is fine. As separate tables, however, each top and leg is unstable.

**3** Explore your designs further, solve any new problems that arise and sketch in more detail. Consider additional possibilities for legs that work separately. Draw a sketch of the proposed solution.

By adding two more legs to each quarter, each section can stand alone, but there are too many legs.

By adding boxes underneath each section, again, each quarter can stand alone, but it will look very 'boxy' or heavy.

By adding an 'L' to each quarter, the separate tables become stable. Because the 'Ls' are open at the outer faces, they are visually less heavy. They follow the natural split lines, and are therefore less obtrusive.

From your information and a few exploratory sketches, you now have one potential solution that can be further detailed and developed. Since it is a circular table, you know it fits into a square; it therefore follows that if the height is the same as the width and the length, it can be represented three-dimensionally by putting it in a cube.

### Further information

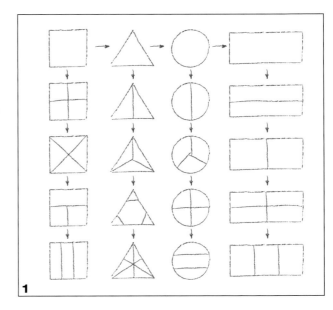

1

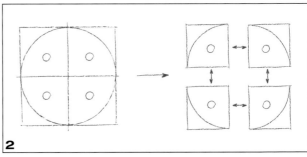

2

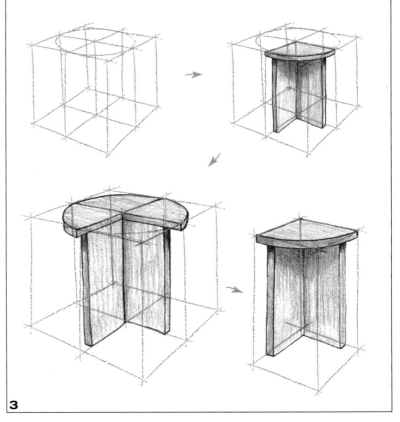

3

# Timber and cutting lists

There are several points to bear in mind when considering timber selection: what is the piece you are making and how will it fit into the home? What final effect do you wish to achieve? Are colour and grain pattern important factors, and so on. You also need to see what is available from your timber supplier, so you can buy boards that allow you to cut components economically and use wood of suitable stability for the task. A cutting list helps when planning both the selection and preparation of the timber for any project, showing timber sizes and quantities.

ABOVE A chalk line is a useful tool for marking out rough-sawn boards prior to sawing them to size. Lines can easily be erased.

## The cutting list

In the excitement of starting a new project it always pays to remember that you can save a great deal of time and money by planning what you are going to do before buying any timber. Make up a list of all the components you require for the project, stating against each item its length, width and thickness. (It may also help to have separate columns for sawn sizes as well as finished dimensions.)

This 'cutting list' is a great help when buying and selecting timber. It is also necessary when machining components back in the workshop, as you can see at a glance, both the rough-sawn size of an item and the finished dimensions after planing.

A good maxim is to design your components so that they can be planed easily from 25 mm (1 in) or 51 mm (2 in) rough boards. It is common practice for timber yards to saw wood to about 28 mm (1³⁄₂ in), which dries down and shrinks to slightly over 25 mm (1 in). A board of this thickness will give you a finished component of roughly 19 mm (¾ in) when planed on both sides. A 51 mm (2 in) board will give a finished thickness of about 45 mm (1¾ in).

Consider carefully whether you need particularly stable components, such as drawer sides or the loose leaf for a drop-leaf table. In both these cases you should use quartersawn timber, which is particularly stable and less likely to cup or warp. Consider, also, whether you are buying kiln-dried or air-dried timber. If air-dried, then you must allow a period of at least one to two weeks after your initial planing of the timber for the material to settle and acclimatize to your workshop's humidity. If you are using kiln-dried timber you can expect any temporary movement owing to acclimatization to happen much more quickly, but for shorter periods.

## Marking and cutting the timber

Once you have selected your timber and brought it back to the workshop, select which board will give you which component on your cutting list. It helps to stand the boards on end so that it is easier to check both faces. The first crosscut is critical: although shorter boards are much easier to handle, once a plank is, say, 1,219 mm (4 ft) long instead of 2,438 mm (8 ft), the options for using that plank for lengthy components are obviously reduced.

## CUTTING LIST FOR TABLE

| Item | Quantity | Material | Finished sizes (length x width x thickness) |
|------|----------|----------|---------------------------------------------|
| Legs | 4 | oak | 750 x 45 x 45 mm (29½ x 1¾ x 1¾ in) |
| Side rails | 2 | oak | 1,950 x 70 x 25 mm (76¾ x 2¾ x 1 in) |
| End rails | 2 | oak | 950 x 70 x 25 mm (37⅜ x 2¾ x 1 in) |
| Top* | 3 | oak | 2,000 x 336 x 35 mm (78¾ x 13¼ x 1⅜ in) |

### Notes

*The solid wood top is glued up from three narrower boards. Allow 5 mm (³⁄₁₆ in) extra on component width and thickness for sawn sizes, plus an extra 25 mm (1 in) for length.

**Alternative timber:** Any tough, close-grained hardwood.

**Suggested finish:** Oil or lacquer.

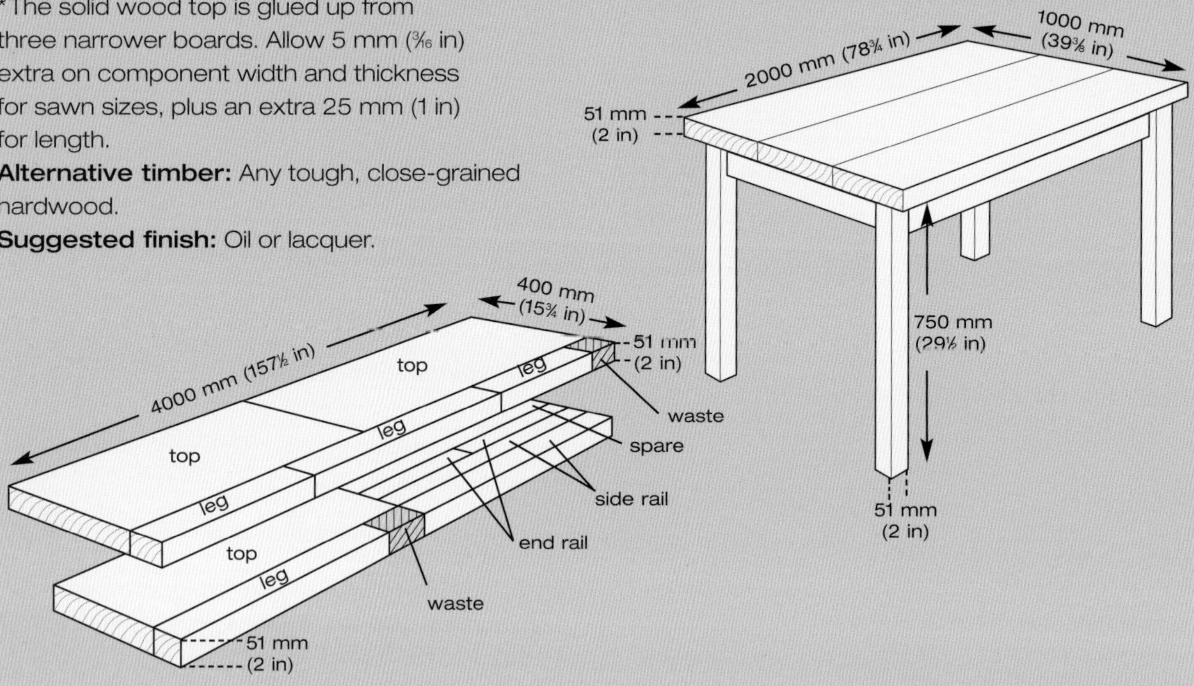

### JARGON BUSTER

**Chalk line** Hand tool for marking lines using chalk dust.

**Cutting list** A chart on which all the different components and sizes for a project are listed. This is very useful when you need to buy or select timber for a project.

**Laser line** Electronic tool that emits a laser beam. Fitted to some power saws to give cutting line.

Use a chalk line to mark cutting lines down the length of the rough-sawn board as shown. Do not attempt to cut to your finished sizes at this stage, but cut each component 5 mm (³⁄₁₆ in) or so oversize.

Sawing along the chalk lines is best done on a band saw, although it is quite manageable with a jigsaw. Use the band saw freehand without any fence or guides, and simply guide the saw down the chalk line. A steady hand and good lighting around the band-saw table help accomplish this task. Make sure that your band saw is fitted with a sharp blade and is properly tensioned. Also check that the upper blade guide is set so that no more than 10 mm (⅜ in) of teeth are exposed above the timber. Keep your hands well back from the blade: although the band saw is a relatively gentle machine to use, it is still capable of inflicting very painful and damaging cuts.

# Laser line

It is possible to use a simple laser device to project a line along the timber, although this can be more work than using a chalk line. It involves using a pencil to mark the path of the beam on the board, connecting up the marks with a straightedge.

Lasers are also used for levelling, so shelving, cupboards, dado rails and so on can be aligned horizontally or vertically on a wall before drilling. In the construction industry lasers have many uses, from setting out buildings to lining up timber roofs. They can also project lines at any angle – useful for marking out stair handrails. More sophisticated laser devices include digital measurement of length, area and volume at the press of a button. Distance range on professional models can measure up to 200 m (approximately 650 ft).

ABOVE The disadvantage of using a laser is that it's impossible to see the line in bright daylight.

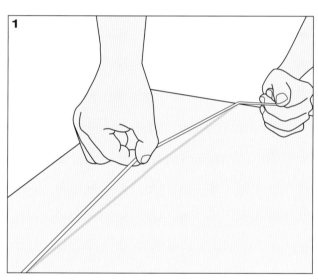

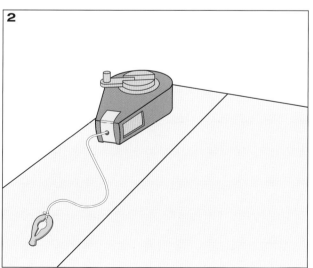

## How to use a chalk line

The chalk line is a hand tool that consists of a case filled with chalk dust and, typically, 30 m (approximately 98 ft) of 1 mm ($\frac{1}{32}$ in) braided cotton or synthetic line. You hook one end of the line over the board at your first measuring point and stretch the line to your second measuring point – in this case at opposite ends of the board. By flicking the taut line against the surface, you mark a chalk line. The tool is frequently used in the construction trade and is available from builders' merchants.

**1** First brush the boards you have selected with a wire brush to remove all dirt, grit and foreign material that may blunt your tools. Pull the line out of its case, through the chalk, and down the length of the board.

**2** Snap the line against the board to leave a straight, clean chalk line on the timber.

### Further information

Timber selection  pages 12–15
Timber seasoning and conversion  pages 16–19
Buying and storing timber  pages 20–23
Drawing and sketching techniques  pages 42–44
Computer-aided design  pages 48–49
Band saws  pages 152–154
Machine safety  page 169

# Computer-aided design

With access to a computer it is possible to design items of furniture without the skills of the draughtsman. With an appropriate computer-aided design (CAD) program you can learn how to develop ideas, change proportions, even view a piece in different timbers before starting to build a project. There is no doubt that CAD is becoming an increasingly affordable and desirable tool for the modern woodworker.

ABOVE Laptops are increasingly common in workshops, enabling you to produce an accurate three-dimensional drawing fairly quickly.

## Using CAD

While you may be happy copying woodworking projects from books and magazines for a while, there comes a point when you will want to make something for which there is no existing drawing. If you go straight into the workshop and start cutting up wood without a proper plan or design, a successful outcome is not very likely.

Traditionally, drawings were produced on paper, using a T-square, draughting squares and protractors. This can be rather time-consuming, with any alterations requiring a new drawing. With CAD, you can develop an object on screen, view it from any angle and even make it look real with the addition of surface textures, lights, reflections and shadows. You can make

**Development of a chest of drawers in CAD**

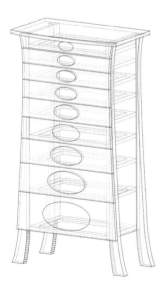

X-ray chest

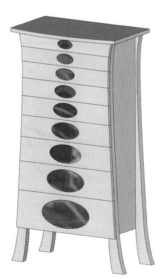

Solidity with colours

Rendered to show textures

changes by copying the original and modifying just one area; and you can save parts that tend to feature most often, to use them again for other models.

There are two main types of CAD: two-dimensional (2D) and three-dimensional (3D), although nowadays even simple CAD software has some 3D functionality. Most packages have their own strengths and weaknesses, so you may find yourself using different programs for different sorts of tasks. In CAD, reference points are defined by their X and Y components, much like a grid reference. In 3D programs they also have a Z component which gives them depth. You can indicate points with the mouse, or type them in on the keyboard. Menu options determine how the points are joined together – maybe a straight line, a curve or a dimension, for example. Lines may be solid or dotted, black or coloured, fine or broad.

CAD can be a great aid when selling a design to a customer. Many people have difficulty visualizing a finished piece from a flat drawing and will respond much more positively if you are able to show them a model. Another advantage is that you can achieve the look you want before buying any timber.

## CAD software

CAD software is available in a wide range of price bands, from prohibitively expensive to free. Surprisingly, some of the free programs are excellent as tools for the home woodworker, and you will find various packages available on the Internet – try entering 'free CAD' in a search engine.

Those packages that are not free are often available with a free trial, so you can try them out before spending any money. Some have two versions available, usually a free version with limited functionality, and a paid-for version with greater functionality and customer support.

The image above was modelled in Google SketchUp and the chest of drawers opposite was rendered in Kerkythea. As with any tool there is a learning curve, but not all CAD programs are difficult to use. Many people find SketchUp particularly easy to grasp; even complete beginners can produce something quite useful in a short space of time. There are on-line tutorials to help you get going and on-line forum groups for those who want to exchange ideas.

Once you get used to producing models in CAD, you will find that it becomes increasingly valuable as a design tool, reducing the likelihood of mistakes and increasing the chance of making something that looks right, not just nearly-right.

**The X, Y, Z coordinates**

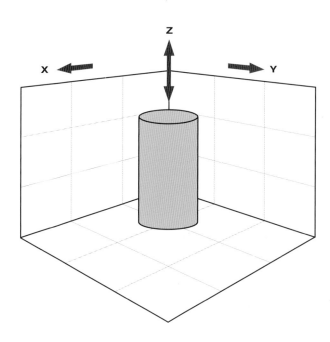

### JARGON BUSTER

**Axes** Three mutually perpendicular directions, usually called X, Y and Z axes.

**CAD (computer-aided design)** Software replacing the traditional draughting board, paper and pencil.

**CAM (computer-aided manufacture)** Machines (lathes, milling machines, and so on) controlled by a computer rather than directly by an operator. They often take their geometry information directly from a CAD model.

**Coordinates** Numbers that define positions in space using the X, Y and Z axes.

**Rendering** The process of putting colour, texture, lights, shadows and reflections on to a model, in order to make it look realistic.

**Further information**
An introduction to design  pages 40–41
Drawing and sketching techniques  pages 42–44
Furniture gallery  pages 50–53

# Furniture gallery

Furniture design has always been influenced by a complex range of interrelated cultural, economic, social and technological factors. Before the 16th century most furniture was heavy and utilitarian. With growing political and military stability, however, it began to take on a new social significance. The forms that we know today began to emerge from 1500, at which time British furniture was developing in the wider western European context. Both were later to influence American styles. Design and development are now global and IKEA is but the latest in a long line of leading influences on an international scale.

ABOVE Cherry highboy made in Connecticut, USA about 1750. It has three flame finials, carved shell and fan decoration, plus cabriole legs.

Many historians focus on the development of fine furniture – historically dominated by city-based cabinet-makers and the preserve of the rich. Equally significant, however, are the regional variations and 'country' furniture that existed at the same time – the everyday furniture of the masses. The 18th-century design classic, the Windsor chair, cannot be ignored, for example, neither can the inspirational furniture produced by the Shaker community in the United States.

Fine furniture is important historically because it was innovatory, and everyday furniture developed in its wake. There was often a considerable time lag in this development, and the resulting forms were far less sophisticated; sizes were often reduced to fit less spacious living conditions, and timbers tended to be cheaper, native hardwoods such as ash, beech, elm and, later, pine, instead of the more exotic mahogany and ebony. Such furniture is also important because of the extraordinary skill of the ordinary men and women who designed and made it.

Towards the end of the 17th century, fine furniture became an object of fashion and increasingly flamboyant and expensive, reaching a peak during by the 1830s. Growing prosperity, industrialization and the rise of democracy then began to blur the boundaries – a process that accelerated during the 20th century. Fine furniture is now much more widely available, and where rich patrons of artisan furniture-makers do exist they are more likely to be rock musicians than aristocrats.

## Furniture construction

The evolution of furniture design is dependent on developments in construction methods. Most furniture has a common origin in the simple plank chest whose construction relied on oak pegs and iron nails. Although the mortise-and-tenon joint was known at the beginning of the 16th century, furniture was still relatively crude.

More sophisticated joinery emerged with the advent of framed panelling from Europe and the development of the 'true' mitre, as opposed to the 'mason's', mitre – its rudimentary predecessor. Not only did this innovation make furniture lighter and therefore more portable, it counteracted the natural tendency of timber to split, warp, twist and shrink. The dovetail and drawer developed together, initially in court cupboards. At first, the dovetail pins were crude and widely spaced on the drawer sides but over the next 200 years they became finer and closer. Drawer runners also became more efficient: initially nothing more than a groove for a runner in the drawer side they gradually evolved so that the drawers ran on their bottom edges, supported on a strip of wood glued to the carcase.

Contributing to an explosion in furniture design from the end of the 17th century, the dovetail enabled the development of larger flat surfaces in cabinet furniture. This facilitated the rise of veneering, where increasingly exotic timbers and other materials were applied to the flat substrate of oak or pine. An unprecedented amount of decoration and colour emerged, none of which would have been possible without improvements in animal-based glues earlier in the century.

Most basic furniture forms, including the chest of drawers and the longcase clock, had evolved by 1700, and became the basis for subsequent improvements. Knuckle joints replaced iron hinges; brass castors developed from original wooden and leather versions; and the half-round, cross-grained mouldings attached to chests to protect expensive veneers were replaced with protruding cock-beading on the drawers themselves. In chairs, two significant design elements emerged: the raked rear legs for greater stability and the cabriole leg, which did not compromise strength for elegance.

# Early influences

Furniture has always been subject to outside influences, often architectural. The modernzing influence of the 15th- and 16th-century Italian Renaissance spread throughout Europe, where heavy medieval Gothic prevailed.

Another significant surge of development came in the early 18th century, the result of three primary influences from: the advent of the lighter Baroque styles from mainland Europe; the migration of skilled Flemish and French craftsmen; and the growth of European trade with the East. The taste for all things oriental lasted periodically well into the 19th century.

By the time fine furniture had become a fashion statement in the late 18th century, influences came in quick succession, often as a reaction to existing styles. British architect, William Kent (1685–1748), took Italian Palladian architecture as his model, in stark contrast to

BELOW The classic English Windsor chair (left), traditionally built with steambent ash bow and arms, plus an elm seat. The cherry Shaker rocker (centre) has mushroom armrests and dates from about 1820. Designed by Hungarian architect Erno Goldfinger in the 1930s, this minimalist chair (right) consists of steel and plywood.

the French rococo style that dominated much of Europe, with its flowery, asymmetrical designs, and by the end of the 18th century, a reversion to classical forms was spreading through Europe, and on to the United States.

Early 19th-century, Regency, furniture was heavily influenced by the French Empire style which itself included elements of ancient Egyptian styles. Indeed, the term French polish, a characteristic finish of the Victorian and Edwardian eras, derives from a fashion that originated in France.

## Timbers and other materials

Oak was the predominant native hardwood during the 16th century, because it combined strength with availability. It remained the staple timber for furniture well into the 17th century, with walnut gradually becoming more popular. The early 18th century witnessed the importation of mahogany in large quantities and it became the mainstay of much European and American furniture. In fact, mahogany later superseded both oak and European walnut as the favoured timber. Other tropical hardwoods, notably satinwood and rosewood, became fashionable during the late 18th century and 19th century, while the more sombre American black walnut was a favourite towards the end of the 19th century.

Over the same period, contrasting veneers, such as padauk and tulipwood, and various inlays were used to increasingly stunning effect. Bone, ivory, mother-of-pearl and marble were all included at some time and cocus wood, cut by slicing diagonally through the branch of a tree, created 'oyster' veneer. But perhaps the most exotic technique was 'Boullework': developed in France during the late 17th century, the technique employed tortoiseshell (actually turtle) and silver, pewter or brass to produce the most intricate patterns on surfaces for the very richest of patrons.

Wrought iron hinges, straps and studs gave way to more elaborate cabinet brassware and ormolu decoration. Other forms of surface decoration evolved, too. The popularity of expensive ebony in the late 17th century led to the use of cheaper ebonized finishes well into the 20th century. Gilded gesso was employed lavishly at times, particularly for picture and mirror frames and glazed panels; 'japanned' lacquer was popular in the late 18th century; and paint has always been used extensively, both as a general finish and for specific designs.

TOP A fine example of the rococo style, this ornate Dutch marquetry bureau bookcase dates from the early 18th century.

RIGHT A Gothic lacquered dresser from the Red House, home of William Morris, one of the founders of the Arts and Crafts Movement.

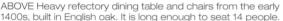

ABOVE Heavy refectory dining table and chairs from the early 1400s, built in English oak. It is long enough to seat 14 people.

TOP RIGHT A rare Italian virginal from 1680, housed in an elaborate ebonized cabinet.

RIGHT Fragments of animal bone were used as decorative inlay on this stunning marquetry table from the 17th century.

Art Nouveau furniture of the late 19th century attempted to break away from the 'hotch-potch of eclecticism' of the mid-19th century, but furniture design was not thoroughly revolutionized until the 20th century with the widespread use of tubular steel, moulded plastics, formed plywood and laminates and composites.

# Technological developments

Most modern hand tools existed in basic form at the beginning of the 16th century and, by the time of England's Great Exhibition in 1851, most modern woodworking machinery existed at least in principle, including a (not very successful) carving machine.

In between, there were numerous technical and technological developments. Although perhaps small in themselves, these had a significant cumulative effect. For example, improved steel allowed the crisp carving of the new hard mahogany in the 18th century, while the development of metalwork lathes in the early 19th century enabled the mass-production of cheap screws. Industrial advances in the late 19th and early 20th

centuries – including the emergence of railways – had a vital impact on furniture. It enabled the demands of a mass market to be met by mass production, blurring the distinction between fine and ordinary furniture.

The Arts and Crafts Movement of the late 19th century in Britain and the United States was a response to the demise of the skilled craftsman in the face of technological progress and a perceived decline in standards. Today, however, artisan furniture-makers and new technology are quite compatible. There has been a resurgence of skilled craftsmen and -women since the 1970s, while technology continues to have an impact with computer-aided design (CAD).

And just as improvements in tea-clipper sailing ship technology led to the development of new furniture forms such as the tea table and tea caddy, so modern innovations have the same effect. We now have a whole new range of traditionally made wooden furniture to store CDs and other computer-related equipment. Furniture and technology will continue to develop in tandem.

# 3

# The workshop

If you aspire to being a fine craftsman, it is certainly possible to achieve this working in a garage or on the kitchen table. However, it is far easier if you set aside a place for concentrated work. Your workshop is a special place that reflects the standards you aim to reach: tools are always sharp and close at hand; the air is tinged with the smell of timber; and a good, sturdy workbench encourages you to develop your skills. A workshop is a place of reflection, planning and building projects to ever-higher standards.

# Workshop location

Many woodworkers dream of a custom-built, fully-equipped workshop, but most of us do not have the budget or the space. Your workshop size and location will be determined primarily by budget, personal circumstances and the kind of woodwork you intend to do there.

Someone using mostly hand tools making relatively small pieces of furniture can create a workshop from a spare room or a basement. A woodturner may not have much more than a lathe, a bench grinder and band saw – particularly if turning small timber blanks – so a compact shed may be sufficient. On the other hand, if you plan to buy machines and prepare your own timber, you will need considerably more space. Not only do you need room for equipment and a bench assembly area, but somewhere to store wood as well.

## Garage or outbuilding

If a garage is the only option consider whether it still needs to accommodate a vehicle. If it does, a folding workbench at one end may be the answer, particularly if yours is a single garage. Storage space will be limited to the walls, and machines will probably need to be compact, so they can be stored away after use. If your garage does not need to house a car, a compact but very reasonable working area is immediately possible, with good access for timber and sheet materials. Make sure you insulate the door against noise and heat loss.

A benefit of having a garage or outbuilding close to the house is that a power supply may already be connected. Many garages have few windows or none at all, which is good for security but poor for daylight, which means relying on artificial lighting. Adding a roof light to a pitched or flat roof will make a big difference and can also improve ventilation. Most garages will have a hard concrete floor, which is ideal for positioning machines but tiring when standing for long periods of time. A timber subfloor or rubber matting is recommended around the bench area.

## Shed

A timber shed in the garden may be all that is feasible as a workshop, but there is no reason why this cannot be made into an efficient workspace. On a tight budget, it is possible to buy a basic shed fairly cheaply and erect it in a day. Unfortunately most of these are of quite flimsy construction, and may have a relatively short lifespan. You will probably need to improve windows, doors and general weatherproofing, but with a shiplap or tongue-and-groove construction this is generally straightforward.

When it comes to positioning a shed workshop, the closer it is to the house the better, although one built from combustible materials must be at least 2 m (6 ft) away. Unfortunately, timber buildings are poor when it comes to providing good security. There can also be problems with damp or condensation, so attach a plastic membrane to the interior walls before adding insulation.

### TIP

• Unless you have very understanding neighbours, a noisy workshop will not be appreciated in most residential areas. Always tell them before erecting a new workshop in the garden, and pay attention to their views to iron out any potential problems. It is also wise to check with your local government to see if you need to comply with any regulations.

It is a good idea to clad walls with medium-density fibreboard (MDF) or plywood, to add rigidity to the structure and provide a solid backing for fixing shelves and cupboards.

## A room in the house

Certain interests – musical-instrument making or woodturning – often require little in the way of space and it is quite feasible to turn a spare room into a small workshop. Heating bills will be relatively low, insulation should not be a problem and daylight should be plentiful. Security will also be less of a problem than for a workshop that is physically separate from the house.

## Custom-built workshop

If you have the space, designing and building your own workshop is a highly satisfying project, and ensures that you get what you want from the start. This is the ideal scenario, but it is also the most expensive option. You may decide to use an architect to draw up plans, although this is not essential. Here, you have the choice of using blocks, bricks, stone or timber or a combination of all three for construction, and to decide on the number and configuration of doors, windows and internal walls.

LEFT A suitable workbench is vital for most forms of woodwork, no matter whether the workshop is located in a spare room or a garage.

BELOW Heavy machinery will need to be positioned on a solid floor. In most locations it will be necessary to insulate the workshop against noise.

---

### JARGON BUSTER

**Shiplap** Prepared softwood boards that overlap each other when used horizontally. A rebate on the lower edge sits over the top edge of the next board. Often used for cladding timber sheds.

**Tongue and groove** Prepared softwood boards that interlock, with a projecting tongue along one edge and matching groove along the other. Also called matchboard.

## Renting

If you hope, eventually, to turn your hobby into a business, it may be worth considering renting a small workshop. Once you start making money you may be forced to take this step anyway. However, rental costs will be out of the question for most part-time woodworkers, unless you can share the space with another craftsperson to reduce overheads.

**Further information**

# Workshop essentials

Remember that if you are budgeting for a new workshop, then building or converting an existing building is only the first stage. After completion it must be equipped, although this can take place over a period of time as funds allow. And, of course, there will be running costs. An unheated workshop in winter is not a pleasant environment in which to work.

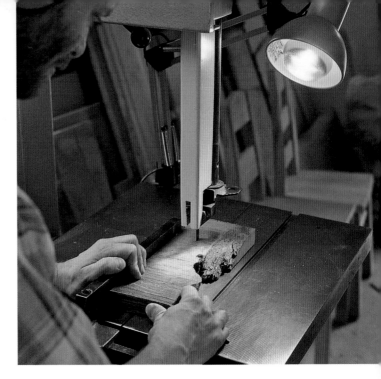

ABOVE Good lighting is essential for accurate work, whether using machinery or hand tools.

## Planning your work

When choosing your workspace, there are several points to consider. Firstly, do you need to install your own machines or could you get time-saving timber preparation done by a local wood machinist or joinery firm? If you are prepared to acquire skills with a relatively small kit of hand tools, you could manage without the noise, dust and generally unpleasant working conditions created by machines and power tools, not to mention the expense.

Once you know the sort of woodwork you intend to do, make a list of the equipment you're likely to need. Include in this hand and power tools, plus possible machines. It's useful to draw up two lists: one of essential kit that you cannot do without, and a second one of potential equipment you may need to buy in the future. This will help you when planning the basic layout of the workshop.

## Heating and humidity

Heating and humidity control are both very important. Timber is sensitive to changes in atmosphere and an unheated workshop will invariably be damp. This will result in warped timber and your tools and machines may rust, too. Outdoor workshops should be heated carefully with a form of dry heat. Mobile gas heaters may be convenient but they also emit moisture. Think about installing an electric low-output background heater that runs all the time, and a dehumidifier. This

not only extracts moisture from the air but also keeps the air warm. If you are likely to work for long periods of time, consider installing a woodburner or a stove that runs off sawdust. Garage and garden-shed workshops should have insulated walls, ceilings and floors. You should also add a damp-proof membrane to internal walls and ceilings to reduce condensation.

## Noise and insulation

Most forms of woodwork entail noise at some stage. Routers and planers are among the worst offenders, although some hand tools are not quiet, either. Unless you live in a remote area away from other people, always consider your neighbours. If in doubt about noise levels, ask a friend to listen outside the workshop while you operate the noisiest equipment. If using power tools or machines, make sure you set a reasonable time each evening when you shut these down. When considering materials for heat insulation, polystyrene may be cheap, easy to fit and effective, but it does little to deaden noise: rolls of fibreglass are a better option.

---

### JARGON BUSTER

**Catenary wire**  A steel wire stretched overhead between two points, usually buildings. Used to suspend a power cable.

# Power and lighting

If connecting an outbuilding or shed to a power supply, check with your local government regarding any likely regulations. All electrical work must comply and be installed, or checked, by a qualified electrician. If running an electric cable underground from the house, use the armoured type, which has a protective sheathing. A cable can be suspended overhead, although there is a greater risk from accidental damage. It should be a minimum distance from the ground and attached to a tensioned catenary wire. This wire must be earthed to the main earthing point of the house, and any external joints should be made with waterproof connectors.

Install more electric sockets than you think you will need and position them around the workshop to avoid cables trailing across the work area. Good lighting is essential, with overhead fluorescent strip lighting the easiest to install. If possible, situate your bench alongside a window and use an anglepoise lamp to illuminate bench work. Although daylight is best, watch out for direct sunlight on timber components, which can warp and twist as a result.

# Security

Workshop security is a major concern. Location is important, and a workshop at the far end of a long garden is more at risk than one close to the house. When evaluating the risks, consider how you would get into your workshop if you lost the only key. This will highlight weaknesses, such as padlocks that can be cut, external hinges that could be prised off and windows that could be forced.

Simple alarm systems are inexpensive to fit and may well act as a deterrent. Outdoor security lighting with movement sensors can be installed relatively cheaply. Padlocks with built-in alarms are another option.

If you do not want to fit steel bars to your windows, make simple shutters from plywood that can be fixed in position easily and secured from within.

Sadly, portable power tools are stolen to order these days. You only need add up the cost of a few items to see what it would cost to replace them if lost through theft. Mark all power tools with your postal code using electronic chips or invisible ink, so they can be identified if recovered by police after a break-in. If possible, make sure the contents of your workshop are insured. If woodworking is your hobby, it should be possible to add an inventory to your household insurance policy. If you intend to make money from woodworking, business insurance may be an option.

TOP A dehumidifier extracts moisture from the air, so controlling the humidity level.

ABOVE For a shed workshop a padlock with built-in alarm is a good choice. If tampered with, a loud siren sounds and LEDs flash.

**Further information**

# Workshop layout

Having decided on the overall size and shape of your workshop, it is essential to plan the layout before you begin building benches, fitting shelves or buying machinery. It is easy to underestimate what you need and how this could change in the future.

ABOVE Hand and power tools can be stored in wooden boxes or in purpose-built cupboards. Old kitchen units can be useful for this.

## Planning on paper

The classic way to plan the layout of a workshop is on graph paper using a suitable scale – 1:25 is easy to work with. Draw a plan of the floor area to scale, marking door and window positions. Then draw all intended equipment including benches, machines and cupboards, also to scale, on separate paper or card and cut them out. You can then move these around your floorplan, considering the pros and cons of various positions, until you are satisfied with the layout. With appropriate software, planning a layout is faster on a computer, particularly if you have a simple drawing program. You can produce several different models, each as sophisticated as your skills and the software allows.

## Planning for machines

When planning the positions of machines, make the best use of any diagonals, doors and openings: for example, aligning a planer with a doorway increases maximum capacity. Work out if you can afford to bring full-sized 2,440 x 1,220 mm (8 x 4 ft) sheets of MDF or plywood into the workshop, or whether you will need to saw them into smaller sizes outside. Remember, also, that a small pile of timber components may take up very little room, but the resulting assembly of half a dozen dining chairs will need a lot of space!

Some machines need space at each side, as well as in front and behind. A table saw should be positioned in the centre of a workspace, while a planer thicknesser and a band saw are fine against a wall, for example. For each you will need enough room to feed long lengths of timber in at one end and out at the other. A radial arm or mitre saw needs an equal amount of space either side, although if used mainly for cutting boards to length, should ideally have greater capacity at its left side.

Make sure that tables of individual machines do not interfere with one another when feeding timber through. If they do, either tilt machines slightly, or jack up equipment on timber blocks, so tables are at the same height. Make use of the fact that a band saw has a much higher table than most other small machines. If stuck for space, position the band saw so that you feed timber above and across an adjacent machine. You can also use doors and windows to your advantage. If the windows are low enough, you can feed timber across a band saw or planer table and out through an adjacent window.

If you have the space, group the machines in the middle of the workshop. Assuming only one machine will be used at a time, their timber feed directions can run at 90 degrees to each other. The power supply can also be located centrally, avoiding the need to run cables down walls in several positions.

You will need an auxiliary bench area that can be set up as a sharpening station. This should house a bench grinder plus honing stones and accessories. Make sure this is well away from the bench, so equipment cannot get contaminated by sawdust.

## Planning your workshop layout

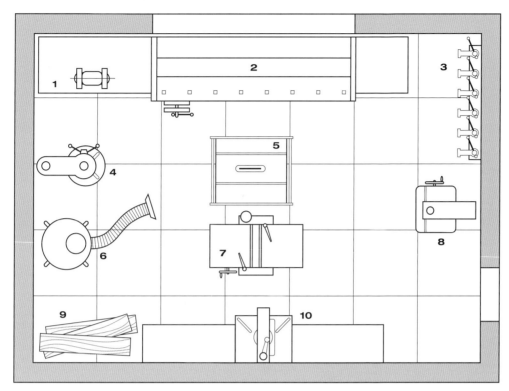

1 Sharpening station
2 Workbench positioned under window
3 Cramps stored on wall
4 Pillar drill
5 Table saw
6 Portable dust extractor
7 Planer-thicknesser
8 Band saw
9 Timber storage
10 Mitre or radial arm saw

## Planning workflow

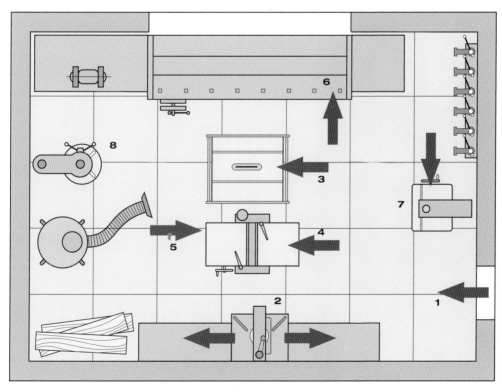

1 Rough-sawn timber enters workshop
2 Boards sawn to length on mitre saw
3 Timber cut to width on table saw
4 Face side and edge prepared on surface planer
5 Planed to width and thickness on thicknesser
6 Prepared timber marked out on bench
7 Curves cut on band saw
8 Holes bored on pillar drill

# Storage

Even the most basic workshop needs to be well organized if you are to work efficiently, and the smaller the workshop, the greater the need to be tidy. Make sure every tool has a home – even if it is no more than a humble plastic toolbox – and get into the habit of clearing up and putting away tools at the end of each working session.

## Storage solutions

Try to store as much as possible up and away from the workshop floor. Make good use of all available wall space to add plenty of shelving, which does not need to be particularly deep. Adjustable shelving systems mean you can alter the spacing whenever necessary, or add more shelves to the existing brackets. Use 19 mm (¾ in) MDF, chipboard or shuttering ply for shelving. It does not need to be of the best quality, so this is a good opportunity for recycling materials.

You can use old kitchen cabinets to support machines such as mortisers, pillar drills and bench grinders. They also provide storage for power tools, abrasives and tooling. Add a work surface of thick MDF if the worktop is missing and anchor the cupboards to the wall to provide rigidity. Unless you have a very low ceiling, make use of the roof space. In a shed you can stow boards between the support trusses, although be careful of the weight. Support slender lengths of timber along their entire length, to prevent bowing and twisting. Joists can be used for hanging jigs and templates, or small hand tools, but remember to add insulation first.

## Tools and equipment

Chisels can be held vertically in a rack alongside the bench, placed in a tool cupboard or in drawers. Keep frequently used hand tools close to the bench, and those receiving occasional use in drawers under the bench, cupboards or toolboxes. Place small packets of silica gel or rust-inhibiting paper in drawers or toolboxes to preserve expensive metal tools. Shadow boards are a clever way of organizing tools, where you can see immediately if one is missing.

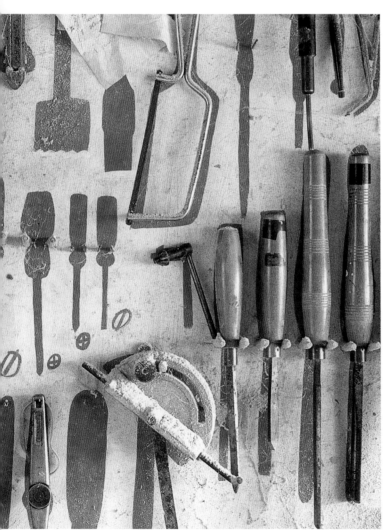

TOP Store timber offcuts according to species in bins or on shelves. Anything under a certain length should be thrown out or used as fuel.

ABOVE Where hand tools must be accessible a shadow board is a simple way of storing them.

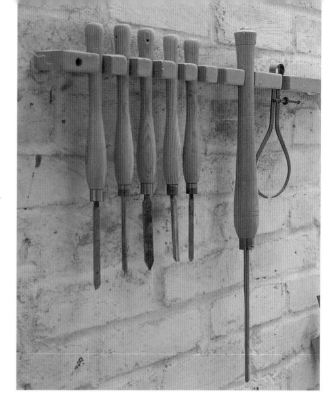

Most power tools do not take up much space, so you can store them in cupboards. Pigeonholes for individual tools are better, preventing cables from tangling. Keep cutters and blades with their appropriate tools. Most power tools now come in plastic storage cases, in which case you can leave them on open shelves without attracting dust. Store router bits in holes drilled into a block of wood so you can always find the cutter you want.

Place sash and G-cramps on racks along the wall or on short pieces of dowel glued to boards. If you have many cramps, consider building a mobile trolley on which to store them. Keep different types of cramp together and always replace them after use.

Screws, nails and items of hardware can be housed in storage cabinets with clear plastic drawers, or in glass jam jars with screw lids. Label everything so you can see at a glance where a specific size or type of screw is kept, for example. If possible, store all flammable products, including polishes, stains and lacquers in a steel cabinet for safety. If there is a risk of children entering the workshop, keep chemicals under lock and key. Make sure you have a suitable fire extinguisher close by.

## Timber and sheet materials

Although heavy boards will need to be stacked horizontally on the floor, try to store smaller lengths of timber on shelving above. Make sure shelves are very sturdy, using either a heavy-gauge steel system, or making your own support brackets from wood or plywood. Keep boards separate from one another with evenly spaced sticks, to allow air to circulate.

Build a small area, or use a plastic dustbin, for storing offcuts. Arrange exotics and hardwoods by timber species if possible. You need to be quite ruthless about what you keep and what to give away or use in the woodburner. Try to avoid storing lengths of softwood vertically, as they will bow easily.

Wherever possible, store sheet materials flat to prevent them warping. The alternative is to build a simple storage rack to keep the sheets vertical, making them easy to slide out when required. Wedging them together with offcuts will restrict them from bowing.

TOP Chisels and turning tools can be hung on racks mounted on the wall, in a cupboard or along the back of the workbench.

ABOVE Cramps should be housed together according to pattern and size. Smaller G- and F-cramps can be stored on racks near the bench.

---

### JARGON BUSTER

**Shadow board** A white-painted board fixed to the wall for hanging hand tools. The shape of each tool is outlined in a contrasting colour.

---

**Further information**

# The workbench

A solid workbench is the heart of any workshop and is a worthy investment whether you buy one or build it yourself. A good workbench is a large-scale cramping device that enables you to hold a piece of timber or project securely while working, whether it is gripped vertically, horizontally or tilted. A decent bench should be heavy, rock solid and should not suffer from vibration when using a mallet.

## Basic criteria

A traditional cabinet-maker's workbench is usually made from beech, although other close-grained hardwoods, such as maple or birch, are more stable. If building your own bench you can economize by making a framework of softwood, where members are a minimum of 75 x 75 mm (3 x 3 in) PAR. The top, however, should be hardwood for strength, durability and above all weight, and should be at least 51 mm (2 in) thick. It is important that the top of your workbench is dead flat, clean and free of damage. Check it periodically with a long straightedge and, if necessary, true up the surface with a bench plane, the longer the better.

Adding a lower shelf increases rigidity and provides storage space; a drawer is also handy. It is common to enclose the space beneath the top as cupboards, with doors at the front or the end. You can also incorporate a simple slotted rack along the back for storing hand tools, such as saws and chisels. A carpenter's bench has a recessed tool well running lengthways along the top, so tools do not interfere with timber or projects placed on the bench surface. A bench too low can be raised on wooden blocks fixed under each leg.

TOP A workbench does not have to be huge, but it should be sturdy. It is the ideal first project for many beginner woodworkers.

ABOVE A traditional bench with front and tail vices. Holes along the top for dogs enable work to be cramped.

---

### JARGON BUSTER

**Bench hook** A small rectangular work board with stops on top and underneath, held against the edge of the bench. It enables small pieces of wood to be gripped while sawing.

**Holdfast** A metal arm inserted in a collar in the bench top for holding timber flat. It may have a threaded screw adjuster or simply be tapped in place with a hammer.

**PAR (planed all round)** A term referring to softwoods that are planed on all four sides.

**Winding sticks** A pair of identical hardwood strips with parallel edges. Placed at opposite ends of a board, they are used to check for twist by sighting along one strip and aligning it with the other. Coloured edges make this easier.

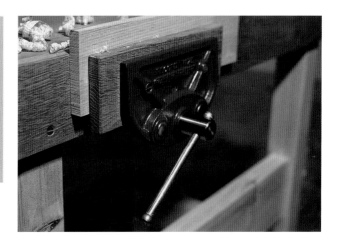

## Vices

Most benches have two vices for cramping. The face, or front, vice is usually placed on the left side of the bench if you are right-handed. The end, or tail vice, is situated at the opposite end. Both are used for cramping work in the conventional way. The tail vice can also be used in conjunction with a pair of bench dogs. These are square, or shaped, movable pegs used for gripping a work piece flat on the surface of the bench while you work on it. They enable you to plane, use a router or carve, or can be used for cramping up boards when gluing edge to edge. Dogs are inserted in two rows of evenly-spaced mortises cut into the top of the bench. If there are no holes for dogs in the top of the bench, consider fitting a bench stop. This simple device is used to prevent timber moving when planing, and is recessed below the surface when not required.

Vices on shop-bought benches tend to be of continental pattern and from hardwood, while English pattern, bolt-on, cast-iron vices are more popular when building a bench. A quick-release vice is preferable, enabling you to open or close the jaws rapidly before tightening. Inner faces of metal vices should be lined with hardwood to prevent marking the work piece and damaging tools.

## Holding tools

A simple, yet very useful, holding device is the bench hook. This tool enables you to grip a piece of wood securely while cutting it with a back saw. A holdfast can

TOP A vice is essential for cramping timber. A quick-release cast-iron vice should be fitted with wood jaws to prevent it marking the work.

ABOVE Where space is tight a portable folding bench is invaluable. It can also be used outdoors and as an extra work surface.

be fitted anywhere on the bench top, the lower lip meaning it can be held in a vice or against the edge of the bench. Usually made from cast metal, it fits into a collar recessed into the surface and enables timber to be held securely for carving or other work.

## Portable benches

Auxiliary benches can take the form of portable mini-benches, folding trestles or carpenters sawhorses, all of which can be erected and dismantled as necessary. They all enable you to work outside, whether cutting up sheet materials or using power tools. Horizontal slats can be moved in and out to grip the workpiece. A folding bench that is attached to, and drops down from, a wall provides useful assembly space and may be essential in a garage workshop.

**Further information**
Workshop location  pages 56–57
Workshop essentials  pages 58–59
Workshop layout  pages 60–61
Storage  pages 62–63
Health and safety  pages 68–69

# The work environment

A comfortable, safe working environment leads to greater efficiency. If temperature and humidity are right, timber is more likely to remain stable and you will be able to concentrate on producing quality work. Machines and power tools produce a lot of waste, so make sure extraction is effective so dust is kept to a minimum.

## Dust extraction

Power tools and machines can create an extremely uncomfortable and potentially harmful level of dust. Make it a priority to install adequate extraction equipment that collects dust before it has a chance to get into the air and empty extractor bags or containers outside the workshop, so that fine dust does not become airborne again. Not only is dust harmful, it will interfere with your work when applying a finish to a project. Consider a separate finishing room if space permits.

## Vacuum extractors

Power tools that produce dust or chippings – sanders, saws, routers and planers – have an outlet for attaching the flexible hose of a compact portable vacuum extractor, which contains a replaceable paper cartridge to filter fine dust particles. Such a unit can easily be moved around the workshop, and is quick to swap between tools. Many extractors have a mains socket allowing you to plug in a power tool directly, automatically activating the unit at the same time. The unit remains running for several seconds after switch-off, to collect residual dust.

## Extraction systems

Larger extractor units, suitable for machines such as planers and table saws, use disposable plastic sacks for collecting the waste – some designed specifically for fine dust and others for coarse dust and chippings. These extractors may be either mobile units with a flexible hose or part of a built-in system with duct pipes that remove the waste from individual machines. Ducting may be either galvanized steel or plastic, and

is designed to attach permanently to walls and ceilings. Lengths are simply clipped together, with various bends and adaptors for changing the pipe direction or reducing its diameter. Common diameters are 63, 100 and 150 mm (approximately 2½, 4 and 6 in).

## Filtration units

Filtration units hang from the ceiling and absorb airborne particles that escape collection by the above methods. They are typically used with a timer and can operate for several minutes after you have left the workshop, switching off automatically.

---

### JARGON BUSTER

**COSHH** Control of Substances Hazardous to Health Regulations
**Ducting** Pipework through which sawdust or chippings pass on their way to an extractor unit.

---

### WARNING

Plastic (PVC) ducting is cheaper than its steel equivalent but tends to accumulate static electricity, with the potential for sawdust becoming ignited by sparks. It is essential that such systems are correctly earthed.

# Face and ear protection

Power tools and machines not only produce a lot of fine sawdust and coarser chippings, they can cause chips to fly off at any moment. They are also noisy, although hearing loss is gradual and may not seem a problem initially. It is essential to protect yourself from these potentially serious health hazards, especially if exposed to them for extended periods of time.

## Eye protection

Your eyes are at considerable risk when using power tools or machines that can create flying debris. Clear, rigid plastic visors or toughened safety glasses are comfortable to wear, even over spectacles. A powered respirator combines a fine dust mask and visor, giving full facial protection. These are particularly good for woodturning and routing, where your face can be close to the work piece. A built-in fan provides a constant stream of filtered air across your face and ensures the visor does not fog up. A rechargeable battery enables you to wear the device for several hours at a time.

## Ear protection

Hearing loss due to prolonged exposure to machinery noise used to be common in the woodworking industry. Tighter health-and-safety regulations mean this is now less of a problem, but there is still a danger in the home workshop. Avoid this by always wearing ear protection, either in the form of ear defenders or disposable foam earplugs, when using any power tool or machine. Keep a pair of ear defenders next to a machine so there is no excuse not to wear them.

## Face masks

It is always wise to wear a face mask, even if using a dust extractor. The dust created when machining some sheet materials and certain hardwoods can cause severe throat irritation and discomfort. In Europe, disposable masks are identified by a dust-rating system, with a 'P2' protection level suitable for woodworking (MDF in particular). If the code is not displayed on a mask it probably does not reach the required standard, so avoid using it. Better-quality respirator masks feature disposable filters, which last longer than disposable versions and give better protection. For spray finishes, a dual-cartridge respirator mask will give protection against lacquers, paints and toxic dust.

## Foot protection

You can cause damage by dropping a length of timber on unprotected toes. Wear boots with steel toe caps, or at least wear a sturdy pair of leather shoes, even if you change into them at the workshop door on hotter days.

TOP Hang ear defenders and safety glasses within easy reach of power tools or machinery.

ABOVE A portable vacuum extractor can be hooked up to power tools such as sanders and routers.

LEFT Wear a face mask when using powered sanders, or hook power tools up to a dust extractor.

# Health and safety

Although woodworking can be very relaxing and rewarding, it can also be quite dangerous. Every workshop contains a number of hazards, some potentially greater than others. It is important to be aware of these in order to minimize the risk of injury to yourself or anyone else entering the workshop. Always treat machines and power tools with the greatest respect, and never operate them with safety guards removed.

ABOVE Chisels, gouges and similar sharp edge tools can be stored in a tool roll. This protects edges as well as making them safe.

## Edge tools

Sharp-edged chisels and plane blades can slip and cut you badly, so minimize the risks by learning how to handle these tools carefully. For example, always keep both hands behind the cutting edge when using a chisel. Store chisels in a tool rack or in a canvas, or leather, tool roll so that edges are covered when not in use, or slip plastic blade guards over the ends. Cheap to buy, they come in different sizes to fit individual tools.

## Power tools and machines

Always plug a power tool into a residual current device (RCD). In the event of the cable being cut, this will switch off the power supply in a fraction of a second, preventing electric shock. When replacing a blade in a circular saw, wear strong gloves to prevent injury. Gloves are also essential when changing the knives on a surface planer, which are often spring-loaded and need to be pushed downwards. Keep the floor around machines such as table saws and planers, free from timber offcuts. It can be easy to trip up when handling large boards.

## Fire risks

Timber, offcuts, sawdust, shavings and finishing materials are all potential fire hazards that need to be controlled and kept away from naked flames. Fit at least one fire extinguisher near the workshop door and have it checked at recommended intervals. Water, foam and powder extinguishers are all designed for use on different types of fire. It is a good idea to fit a battery-operated smoke alarm to the ceiling of the workshop. Clean and check the battery regularly.

You should store finishing materials in a steel cupboard or cabinet, ideally outside the workshop, although this may not be feasible. Dispose of cloths used for applying finishes carefully: do not throw them in a waste bin where they could ignite. If using a room in the house, or an adjoining garage as a workshop, inform your insurance company of the change of use. If not, you may find the house is not adequately covered in the event of fire.

### TIPS

- Keep a torch just inside the door where you can reach it in the event of a power cut. A large workshop may need one at either end.
- If you are working alone in the workshop, fit an intercom system between it and the house. In an emergency, you will be able to summon help.
- Keep a mobile phone with you with important contact numbers stored.

## JARGON BUSTER

**NVR (no volt release)** A type of safety switch.
**Pushstick** A wooden or plastic safety device used to push narrow or small components past the blade on a saw. Prevents fingers getting too close to the moving blade (see also page 169).
**RCD** Residual current device.

# Chemicals

Chemicals, such as varnish and paint stripper, will burn your skin if splashed. Always wear durable protective gloves and eyewear when working with such products, and read the manufacturers' instructions on containers carefully. If you do get a burn, wash your skin under running water for 10 minutes, then cover it with a sterile dressing. If you need to make a hospital visit, make a note of the chemical responsible.

Keep a box of disposable latex gloves in the workshop and wear these when applying a finish with a cloth or pad, especially stains and oils. Many chemicals should only be used with adequate ventilation. If this is not possible in your workshop, consider using an alternative procedure. Contact the local authorities to find out what chemical disposal provisions have been made in your area. Never dispose of them down the drain. Applying finishes to projects outdoors may be better for your health, but the end result may be more difficult to control owing to temperature and humidity.

# First aid

Even the smallest workshop should have a basic first-aid kit, which should be positioned in a prominent place and not hidden away in a cupboard. Contents should include: plasters, dressings, alcohol cleaning pads, tweezers, scissors, safety pins, adhesive tape and eyewash. Always replace any items used from the first-aid kit as soon as possible.

**Further information**
Workshop location  pages 56–57
Workshop essentials  pages 58–59
Workshop layout  pages 60–61
Storage  pages 62–63
The work environment  pages 66–67
Machine safety  page 169

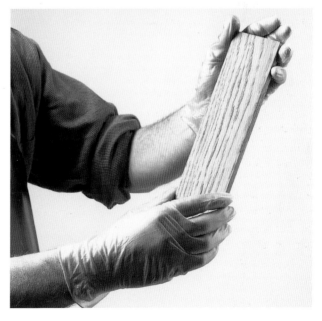

TOP When handling large, heavy timber wear durable gloves to prevent splinters.

ABOVE Thin, disposable latex gloves are ideal when applying finishes or using chemicals generally.

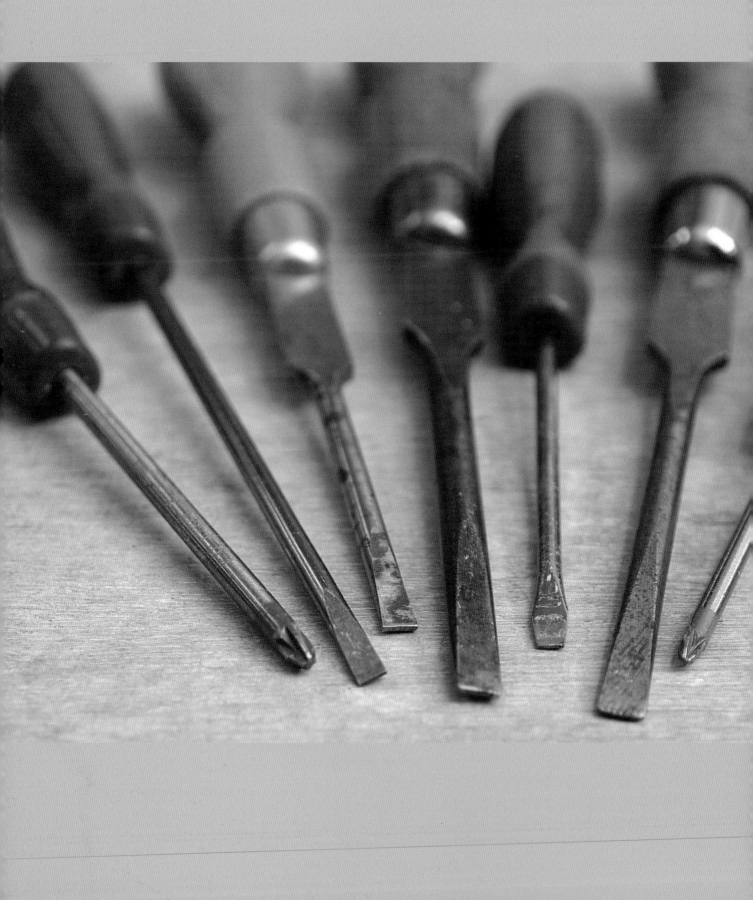

# 4

# Tools: the basics

Tools are necessary for even the most basic woodworking tasks. Treated with respect, they will enable you to develop your hand skills with accuracy and precision. An essential item for the woodworker, your toolkit should be well maintained and never allowed to deteriorate. It is worth spending time getting your tools to work properly, whether they are brand new or second-hand. It goes without saying that you should keep them in a secure workshop or garage. Expensive to buy, tools can be even more costly to replace.

# Buying tools

There has never been such variety when it comes to buying woodworking tools. Some purchasing methods may seem risky, but all have their merits. Gone are the days when you had to rely on the local hardware shop for tools and materials. Increasingly, it is possible to buy items over the Internet or by phone without even having to leave the workshop. Whatever the method, remember that tool quality is more important than its cost.

## Specialist tool shops and DIY stores

Although smaller, independent tool shops find it hard to compete with big chain stores, they are usually difficult to beat for specialist knowledge and after-sales service. They may not have the vast range of brands that a DIY shed can offer, but chances are they will stock the odd hand tool you thought had ceased to exist. Furthermore, if they do not have the tool you want in stock, they will normally be happy to order it.

The bigger DIY stores, or sheds, offer a good opportunity to see what is new on the market, and often carry a huge variety of hand and power tools. Most allow you to shop during the evening and at weekends, which is unlikely at specialist retailers, and prices are generally very competitive. If you are looking for budget power tools, most DIY stores sell their own brand, which can offer good value.

## Internet and mail-order

No matter where you live, as long as you have access to the Internet, you can browse the websites of relevant manufacturers and retailers and check out the latest power tool or time-saving gadget. Within reason – and for a price – delivery to remote areas is no longer the problem it once was: many woodworkers live in Europe and buy from suppliers in America, and vice versa.

There are other advantages to buying on the Internet: assuming the supplier has the goods in stock, delivery is usually prompt; and prices can often be lower than in the stores, although retailers are increasingly aware that they have to compete with on-line sellers. It helps if you know what tool you want, as this makes price comparisons easier. Bigger retailers tend to have their own tool catalogues in print too, which you may find less tiring to read than a computer screen.

One disadvantage to mail-order or on-line shopping is returning a tool, say if you are not happy with the quality or it is faulty. Although this can also be a problem when buying over the counter, it is generally quicker and easier to return a tool to a store then having to mail it back to the seller.

## Woodworking shows

The best place to see tools and machinery in action is at a woodworking show. Aimed at the enthusiast, these offer many bargains. Check magazines and the Internet to see if there is likely to be such an event near you, or when the major shows take place during the year. These shows also offer an opportunity to talk to tool specialists. In many cases, this may be the only place you can try a tool before you buy.

## Woodworking magazines

Specialist magazines can be a good source of used tools and machinery, as well as timber. Most have a page where readers advertise unwanted tools. Often these items are in good condition and have been well cared for, but be aware that good, well-priced tools are likely to sell fast. It makes sense to take the usual precautions when paying

for goods: it is quite reasonable to ask a seller to post or email a photograph of the tool you are interested in purchasing. That way you can judge its condition before committing yourself.

ABOVE Woodworking shows are the ideal place to see power tools and machinery being demonstrated and ask questions.

LEFT If you are prepared to spend time using abrasives and steel wool, it is possible to restore old tools to their former glory.

BELOW Beautiful hand tools of the highest quality are produced by a number of smaller manufacturers.

## Old tools vs. new tools

Tools do not necessarily have to be brand new to work efficiently, and there are definite advantages in buying old tools. Many experienced craftsmen are adamant that the steel quality of old tools, particularly chisels, is higher than in modern equivalents. Although there may be some truth, there are an increasing number of new hand tools of exceptional quality to tempt the woodworker. Many have price tags to match, but there is a hand tool renaissance.

It is possible to pick up perfectly good hand tools in junk shops or at car boot sales, but it helps if you know what you are looking for. You may stumble upon a bargain or find yourself paying too much for a tool of dubious quality. Never be tempted to buy a power tool from a stallholder, no matter how cheap it seems. There is no way of knowing whether it works, and worse, it could be dangerous.

A number of outdoor festivals take place around the country during the summer months. With timber and woodland crafts as a theme, these can be valuable sources of used hand tools, providing the collector with an opportunity to sift through boxes of planes, chisels, saws and related items. You can usually buy timber at these events, often from trees having grown in the vicinity.

## Further information

Essential toolkit  pages 74–75
Hand tools  pages 82–117
Power tools  pages 118–141
Machines  pages 142–169

# Essential toolkit

Even if you intend to do most of your woodworking with machines, you will still need a certain number of hand and power tools. It pays to buy the best tools you can afford, but this does not mean you have to buy everything at once. Buy as and when you need a particular tool.

ABOVE Hand tools should be kept in cupboards, drawers or toolboxes when not in use.

## Measuring and marking tools

**2H pencils** Used for drawing precise lines. Marks from harder grades will be difficult to see and those from softer grades too wide. Traditional carpenter's pencils are too thick for fine woodwork.

**Marking gauge** One with brass inserts in the stock will last much longer than a cheaper version without.

**Marking knife** For scribing shoulder lines of joints. A knife may be ground and sharpened on one face or both. Only the tip is used.

**Sliding bevel** Used for measuring angles other than 45 or 90 degrees.

**Steel rule** Essential for accurate marking out, this should be 300 mm (12 in) in length and of good quality. A hole in one end enables you to hang it up close to the bench.

**Steel straightedge** An excellent engineer's tool for drawing, cutting veneer and checking timber surfaces when planing.

**Tape measure** Minimum length 5 m (16 ft). Shorter tapes have narrower blades, which are flimsy.

**Try square** A blade length of about 230 mm (9 in) is best, preferably with brass facing to the stock to reduce wear. A small engineer's square can be indispensable for fine work.

## Saws

**Coping saw** For making curved cuts in timber and sheet materials.

**Gents saw** For finer cutting work, this is a smaller version of the dovetail saw.

**Handsaw** For cutting both sheet materials and solid timber, this can either be the traditional type that can be re-sharpened or hardpoint. Crosscut teeth are preferable for general sawing work.

**Tenon saw** For cutting joints, a blade length of 254 mm (10 in) will be sufficient. Alternatively, use a large dovetail saw.

## Planes

**Block plane** For trimming end grain, applying chamfers and other fine planing work.

**Jack plane** The best all round bench plane in terms of size, this is used for preparing rough-sawn timber or working edges of sheet materials.

## Edge tools

**Bevel-edge chisels** A set of four initially: 6 mm (¼ in), 12 mm (½ in), 19 mm (¾ in) and 25 mm (1 in). Handles may be hardwood or plastic.

**Cabinet scraper** Often provides the best way to finish timber with wild or interlocking grain.

## General tools

**Centre punch** To mark hole positions before drilling.

**Cork sanding block** For use with abrasive paper when sanding by hand.

**Cramps** For gluing work and holding it down on the bench, traditional G-cramps are sturdy and hard to beat. You will need at least four: two at 203 mm (8 in) and two at 254 mm (10 in).

**Cross pein hammer**  A heavier claw hammer will be useful for general maintenance and carpentry work.

**Files for metal**  Flat, half-round and circular patterns are useful.

**Hacksaw**  With 305 mm (12 in) blade. Even though working with wood, it is surprising how often you may also need to cut metal.

**Honing guide**  To help you get a perfect edge when sharpening.

**Mallet**  For striking chisels and assembling projects, this can be made in the workshop.

**Nail punch**  For driving nails below a surface, ready for filling.

**Pin hammer**  For driving panel pins and tacks.

**Rasp**  Used for shaping wood.

**Sash cramps**  Use at least two for gluing up panels and boards.

**Screwdrivers**  For both slotted and cross-headed screws, you will need at least two sizes of each type.

**Sharpening stone**  For honing chisels and plane blades.

Marking gauge

## Power tools

**Cordless drill**  More convenient than a mains-powered tool, this is essential for boring holes, unless you choose a hand drill. A set of lip-and-spur bits is the best choice for wood, although flat bits are good for larger holes where accuracy is not crucial.

**Jigsaw**  Ideal for cutting sheet materials down to size and for crosscutting solid timber.

**Random orbit sander**  A good all-round finishing tool, this will save hours of tedious sanding by hand.

**Router**  A small, lightweight 6 mm (¼ in) collet machine is indispensable for moulding edges, making joints and lots more. A basic set of router bits will get you started.

Cordless drill

## Follow-up toolkit

Sooner or later you will probably want to add one or two more specialist tools to the basic kit. These are the most useful hand tools:

**Cutting gauge**  With a knife blade, this is particularly useful for dovetail shoulders.

**Mitre square**  For marking and checking 45-degree angles.

**Mortise gauge**  Although you may only need a marking gauge initially (with one pin), a mortise gauge (with three pins) can be used for both scribing tasks.

**Smoothing plane**  For finishing a timber surface.

**Spokeshaves**  For forming curves in timber. Both a convex and a concave sole are necessary.

Cross pein hammer

### Further information

# Fettling tools

Fettling is the process of preparing and upgrading a tool before sharpening. Edge tools, in particular, can be made to perform more efficiently, tuning them to a level of precision and function that a manufacturer cannot provide economically. Fettling is usually done once in the lifetime of a tool, although old tools may need a second treatment if not well maintained. Although other hand tools can be fine-tuned, steel bench planes and chisels are most noticeably improved by fettling. More expensive, high-quality hand tools made by small, specialist toolmakers offer greater accuracy and require little, if any, fettling.

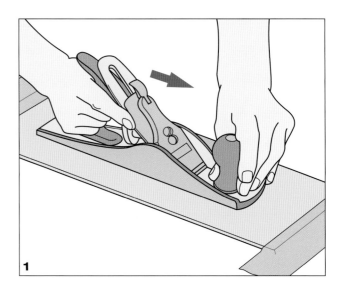

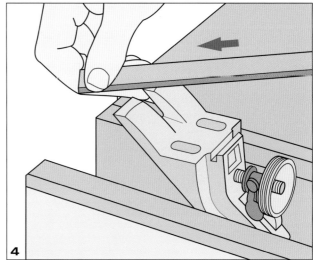

## Preparing planes

The sole of a new, steel plane is unlikely to be completely flat and true. This is because a mass-produced casting does not always have long enough to settle down before it is machined, so will continue to move for some time after the tool has been made. The longer the plane, the more likely the inaccuracy, so check its sole with a steel straightedge.

A correct-fitting and -positioned frog and blade assembly will help the plane cut more effectively, reducing tearout on hardwoods with wild or irregular grain. For a bench plane to work properly, the blade should be slightly curved across its width. This is to encourage the bevel to cut a shaving width of about 25–35 mm (1–1⅜ in) from the centre part of the blade. After fettling a plane, experiment with different settings on scrap pieces of wood.

## How to fettle a bench plane

**1** To flatten the sole, stick a sheet of 60-grit abrasive paper to a piece of flat glass or a cast-iron machine table with strong tape. Remove the blade assembly and push the plane firmly across the abrasive paper, holding the tool at both the back and the front. A sole that is badly distorted will take some time to flatten. Work from coarse through to fine grades of abrasive paper. Carborundum powder may be used instead of abrasive paper and should be sprinkled on to the glass.

**2** Check the sole frequently with a straightedge or steel rule. As high points become polished, hollow areas will diminish. Holding the plane up to the light will highlight uneven areas. Use finer grades of abrasive to polish the sole to a fine finish.

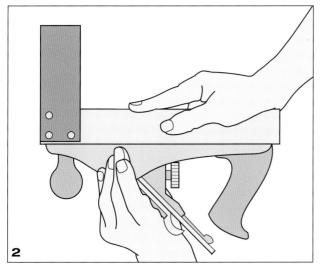

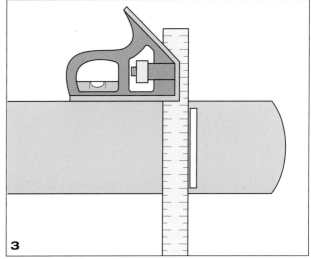

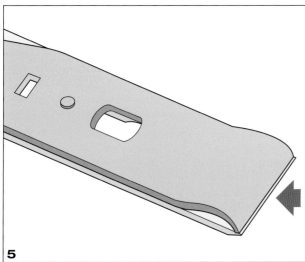

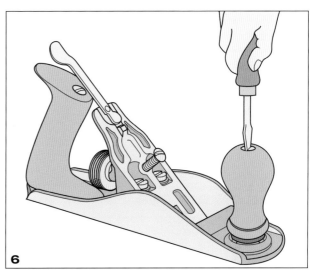

**3** The mouth of the plane must be square to the sides of the plane. Check this with an engineer's square and use a fine file, if necessary, to remove unwanted metal.

**4** Adjust the frog – the cast block on which the blade assembly is seated. The frog should bed tightly into the plane body. If not, remove it and use a fine file on mating surfaces or the plane casting itself. The blade assembly should also fit snugly against the frog. Slide the frog and blade assembly (with the rear screw) until the gap in front of the cutting edge is about 2 mm ($\frac{3}{32}$ in) wide. Tighten the frog locking screws.

**5** To prevent chatter when planing, and shavings jamming underneath the cap iron, make sure this fits tightly against the blade. If necessary, file the edge of the cap iron flat and finish off on an oilstone. Check,

when reassembling the cap iron and blade, that there is no gap between them. Polish the front curve of the cap iron with steel wool to create a smooth surface for shavings to pass over.

**6** The front knob and rear handle should fit tightly against the plane casting and remain solid when tightened with a screwdriver. On old tools, hardwood handles can shrink and become loose, in which case you may need to add a washer under the fixing screw or reduce the length of the threaded steel rod with a hacksaw. Check that the lateral adjustment lever moves easily and lightly oil the pivot. Do the same with the blade depth-adjuster wheel.

# Preparing chisels

The back of a chisel blade must be perfectly flat to perform properly and can be checked with a steel rule. Although laborious work, flattening the blade only needs to be done once. The best method is to use a steel lapping plate with carborundum powder as the abrasive. Aim to get a finely polished surface right across the back of the blade, bearing in mind that the corners do the most effective cutting. A polished surface enables you to cut with less effort needed to push the blade through the wood.

# Fettling a back saw

Back saws invariably need some fettling in order to perform properly. Remove the layer of lacquer usually coating the blade, using fine steel wool and white spirit. Also remove some of the set applied to the saw teeth also, using either a small slip stone or a tiny hammer, tapping very gently against a small anvil or steel block. Set is added to the teeth to make the saw cut a groove or kerf wider than the blade itself. By reducing the kerf of a new saw you are reducing the energy and work required to use the tool, so increasing your control over it.

---

### JARGON BUSTER

**Carborundum powder** An abrasive powder used on a lapping plate to surface a tool. Lubricate with water or oil.

**Fettling** The process of preparing a tool before sharpening, to make it work more efficiently.

**Lapping plate** A dead-flat piece of steel on which tools can be ground flat.

**Mating surfaces** Two flat metal surfaces that should bed together firmly, without movement.

**Set** Saw teeth are alternately bent slightly to one side of the blade, then the other. The resulting cut (kerf) is wider than the blade itself.

**Tearout** The lifting and breaking of wood fibres when planing timber against the grain.

---

**Further information**
The sharpening process  pages 79–81
Saws  pages 88–93
Planes  pages 94–99
Chisels  pages 100–103

## How to fettle a chisel

**1** Sprinkle coarse carborundum powder onto the lapping plate and add a few drops of water. Place the back of the blade flat on the plate and apply pressure with both hands. Rub the chisel up and down the plate, until you get an even grey colour right out to the edges and corners of the chisel. Be careful to incorporate all the carborundum as you work since this abrasive breaks down with use to give an even finer finish. Any coarser grains that remain will scratch the surface of the blade you are trying to true.

**2** It should take about 15 minutes to get a 12-mm (½-in) wide chisel flat. Once a true surface has been created, check your work by polishing the back of the chisel on a 1,000-grit Japanese waterstone or a diamond stone, lubricated with water, and taking care not to get carborundum paste on the waterstone. Finish on a 6,000 grit-polishing stone. If an even polish does not appear quickly, go back to the lapping plate.

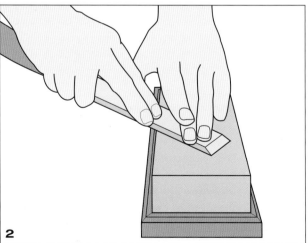

# The sharpening process

Sharpness is essential in controlling a cutting edge effectively, whether it is a plane, a chisel or a saw. The sharper the tool, the less force required to push the edge through the timber. The more power needed to push a chisel through the wood, or a plane across its surface, the less control you have. A razor-sharp edge will slice through with the minimum of effort.

ABOVE Woodturning tools are sharpened on a vertical bench grinder. Adjust the toolrest so that it is close to the wheel.

## Grinding

Most plane and chisel blades are ground at an angle of 25 degrees. New tools will be ground already, but after repeated honing you will need to regrind the bevels. The easiest method is to use an electric wet-stone grinder, which cools the blade edge with water. This prevents the steel overheating during the grinding process, which could lead to the temper of the steel being lost and the hardness of the cutting edge reduced. For this reason, high-speed bench grinders are not recommended for woodworking tools, apart from those used for woodturning. A wet-stone, or water-cooled, grinder may have either a vertical or horizontal stone, which rotates slowly and you usually clamp the blade of the tool in a jig that you move across the revolving surface.

## Sharpening saws

It is possible to sharpen handsaws in the workshop, although this takes considerable skill. Saw doctors (located in specialist tool stores) have the equipment and expertise to sharpen bench saws much more accurately than even a skilled woodworker can. If you do want to try sharpening a saw, obtain a cheap, secondhand tool to practise on first. You can sharpen the very small saws, however. Dovetail saws are best sharpened using a 102 mm (4 in) precision saw file at right angles to the blade. The technique is to settle the file into the gullet of each tooth, then to give one stroke per tooth. Sharpen saws like this little and often, rather than waiting for them to become dull and useless.

## Sharpening stones

Whatever type of stone you use for sharpening, it will need a lubricant. This suspends the steel particles as they are ground from the blade and prevents them clogging the grinding surface as you push the tool across it.

Oilstones may be natural or synthetic and are used with a thin oil. Synthetic stones are either made from aluminium oxide or silicon carbide particles. They are hard-wearing but limited in the grades offered. More expensive, natural, Arkansas stones are generally available in three grades (fine, medium, coarse). Combination oilstones have a different grit on each

### JARGON BUSTER

**Burnisher** A straight, hardened steel blade set into a handle for raising the burr on a scraper. It may be oval or circular in section.

**Gullet** The valley between two teeth points.

**Honing** After grinding, edge tools are honed (sharpened) on an abrasive stone to produce a cutting edge.

**TCT (tungsten-carbide tipped)** Circular saw-blade teeth and router bits are usually tipped, remaining sharp longer than high-speed steel (HSS) versions. Better for sheet materials.

**Temper** The process of hardening the cutting edge of a tool by heating and cooling the steel.

Shaped slipstones for curved edge tools

Diamond stone

Oilstone in hardwood box

Japanese waterstone in adjustable holder

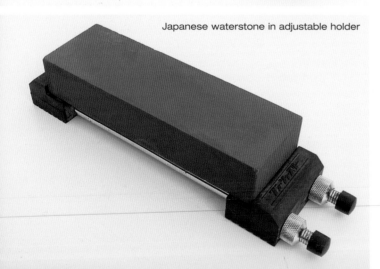

side, either fine/medium or medium/coarse. Messy to use, the blade should be wiped carefully after honing, so the timber is not contaminated by oil.

Japanese waterstones are softer and relatively fragile. Made from both natural and synthetic materials, they wear rapidly so need to be flattened regularly on abrasive paper. They must be soaked in water for several minutes before use, and can also be stored under water. They cut quickly and come in a wide range of grades. Finer stones are used to polish blades and are capable of producing a superb edge. Grades start at around 800 grit (coarse) and go up to 8,000 grit (very fine). A 1,000-grit medium grade is a good choice if buying one stone only. Before honing, a waterstone should be prepared with a Nagura stone, a piece of chalk-like mineral. Adding water, this is rubbed across the surface of the waterstone to produce a slurry. This acts as a fine abrasive paste to give a polished edge to the tool.

Diamond stones are an expensive investment, but hard-wearing and very efficient. The particles are bonded to a plastic base and water is used as a lubricant, although special cutting fluids are more effective. Thin diamond slipstones are ideal for touching up TCT router bits and circular-saw teeth. Slipstones are smaller, shaped, stones for honing gouges and carving chisels. They come in several shapes, including cone and tapered patterns.

Edge tools can also be sharpened on abrasive sheets stuck down to a flat surface such as plate glass or metal. The most suitable abrasive is silicon carbide paper, with water used as a lubricant. Grades of 220 grit and finer are most appropriate.

### TIP

• A blunt edge is also more dangerous: a chisel is more likely to slip when blunt than when sharp. Never allow your tools to become blunt, but hone a plane or chisel blade as soon as you start to feel slight resistance when cutting.

**Further information**
Saws  pages 88–93
Planes  pages 94–99
Chisels  pages 100–103
Spokeshaves and scrapers  pages 113–115

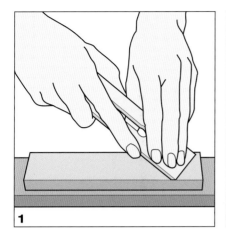
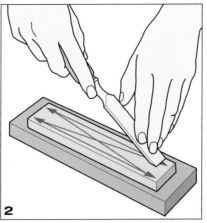
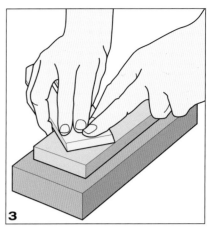

**1**

**2**

**3**

## How to hone a chisel or plane iron

Once a chisel is ground it must be honed before use. Although the 25-degree bevel may be sufficient for cutting softwoods, the edge formed is too weak for hardwoods. A steeper angle of 30 to 35 degrees is required, known as a secondary bevel.

**1** Apply a lubricant to the stone. Holding the chisel or plane blade in your right hand (or vice versa if left-handed), place the bevel down flat on the stone. With two fingers of your left (right) hand, press down on the back of the blade.

**2** Lift the blade slightly and push it forwards along the stone, making sure you keep the angle constant.

Make several circuits around the stone with a figure-of-eight pattern. Aim to hone the front 1 mm (1/32 in) of the cutting edge. After a few strokes you will find a wire burr has formed on the rear edge of the chisel.

**3** Lay the back of the blade completely flat on the stone and press down on it with two fingers. Push the tool along the stone a couple of times, then turn it over and make a couple of strokes with the bevel face down again. Repeat, with the back of the blade flat, to remove the burr.

**Grinding and honing angles**

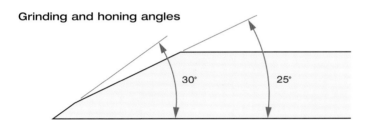

30°    25°

## HONING GUIDES

A honing guide clamps the blade at the correct angle to the stone, enabling you to move the tool backwards and forwards to obtain a precise bevel edge. Most honing guides can be used for plane blades as well as chisels, and can be adjusted to a variety of angles. With enough practice you will be able to master the sharpening technique without needing a guide.

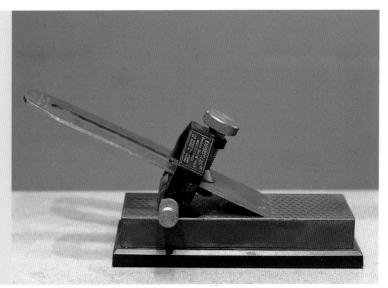

# 5

# Hand tools

Every woodworker needs at least a few basic hand tools. Although many are still made using traditional materials, such as brass and rosewood, plastics are now used for various components, such as handles – particularly at the budget end. Quality has never been better at the upper end of the hand-tool market, however, and beautiful tools from smaller manufacturers become more attractive as woodworkers discover the shortcomings of working with inferior products. Combined with technological advances in metallurgy, these tools are welcome in an age of mass-production, where declining standards in quality are commonplace.

# Measuring and marking tools

Accuracy in woodwork is a fundamental requirement, relying on precision measuring and marking equipment. This simple process determines the quality of subsequent work and it pays always to mark out timber components exactly to size and cut to the marked lines. Most European measuring tools are marked in both the metric and imperial systems.

## Pencils

Pencils are graded according to hardness. A medium grade (HB) is too soft for the accurate marking of joints, and needs frequent sharpening. For most woodwork a 2H grade pencil is more suitable. The lead in a carpenter's pencil is too thick and is unsuitable for furniture-making except, perhaps, for tasks such as the identification of sawn boards.

ABOVE Accurate measurements are essential for most forms of woodwork.

BELOW A marking knife creates a finer line than a pencil. It is normally used against a try square or steel rule.

## Marking knives

A marking knife is often preferred to a pencil for marking out. Where a pencil line has a certain thickness, a marking knife is bevelled on one side only and is therefore capable of producing marks of absolute accuracy. To use the knife, hold it at 90 degrees to the timber with the bevel side facing the waste side of your component or joint. The line struck denotes the exact position of your cutting line. Buy the knife with the best-quality steel available, as it has to be rubbed constantly against the blades of steel squares. Sharpen a marking knife as carefully as you would a chisel.

# Rules and tapes

You should always check the dimensions of your projects against a workshop rule. Most useful is a 305-mm (12-in) long steel rule, although a 610 mm (24 in) version is valuable when making drawings. A 152 mm (6 in) rule is very handy when checking timber sizes and can be slipped into a pocket. A steel rule with 1 mm ($\frac{1}{32}$ in) graduations is easier to read than one marked with 0.5 mm ($\frac{1}{64}$ in) increments.

A retractable tape measure is indispensable when marking out sheet materials or checking long boards. It is unlikely to be as accurate as a long steel rule over a distance, however. Most tapes have a locking button for the blade and a length of 5 m (16 ft) will be more than adequate. To compensate for both internal and external measurements, the end hook is designed to be loose and so will move slightly.

Another essential tool is a straightedge – about 1,000 mm (39 in) in length. This is used to check components and other tools for flatness. Do not rely on the edge of a rule to do this job, as it may not be as straight as you need it to be.

---

## JARGON BUSTER

**Face edge** This is the second surface to be worked when preparing timber. The face edge and face side are always at 90 degrees to each other. Both are used as reference faces for marking tools.

**Face side** When preparing timber this is always the first face to be planed. It must be perfectly flat and straight.

**Stock** On a square, the component into which the blade is fixed; on a gauge, the hardwood component through which the stem slides.

---

Japanese laminated steel marking knife

English pattern marking knife

European pattern marking knife

Retractable tape measure

Imperial 6 in steel rule

Metric 300 mm steel rule

Steel bevelled straightedge

# Squares and sliding bevels

A try square is one of the woodworker's essential tools. A traditional square has a rosewood stock, sometimes faced with brass, plus a steel blade. Cheap plastic versions are available, but the most accurate is the all-steel engineer's square. A blade length of 228 mm (9 in) is fine for most work, although a smaller 76 mm (3 in) version is good for setting out intricate joints.

Combination squares are heavier and can be cumbersome for fine work. However, the adjustable blade means you can measure the depth of rebates and grooves accurately, as well as set out 45-degree mitres. For frequent marking out of 45-degree angles, a fixed-mitre square is useful. This usually has a hardwood stock.

When using a try square to check that a board edge is at 90 degrees, place the stock against the face side and slide it along so that the blade is just touching the edge of the timber. When squaring a line across timber, put the marking knife or pencil tip on the mark first and slide the blade of the try square up against it. Mark the line across, holding the stock firmly against the timber. Always mark on the outside of the blade.

A sliding bevel is essential for marking out and checking an angle that is not 90 degrees or 45 degrees. The adjustable blade is locked with a lever or thumbscrew. For setting out dovetails, a template will save you having to adjust a sliding bevel each time. Buy in pairs or with a different slope angle along each edge (1:6 for softwoods, 1:8 for hardwoods).

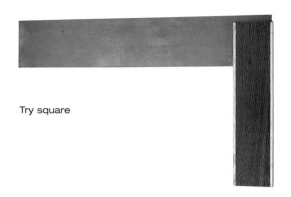

Try square

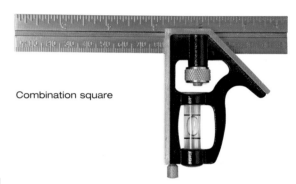

Combination square

Mitre square

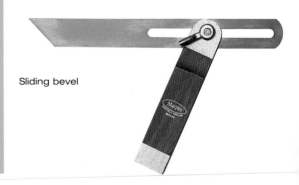

Sliding bevel

## HOW TO CHECK A SQUARE

It is essential that a try square is exactly 90 degrees or your work will be inaccurate. Check the tool by placing the stock against the planed edge of a piece of sheet material or a wide board. Draw a fine pencil line along the blade's outer edge and turn the tool over. Both line and blade edge should match exactly. A square can become inaccurate if dropped. If this happens, it is possible to file the outer edge of the blade until it is square again. However, the inner edge is extremely difficult to restore and is best left alone.

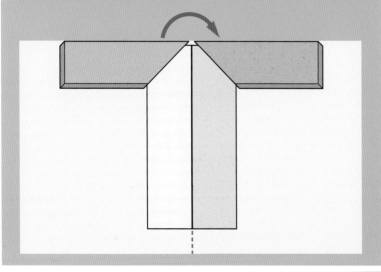

# Gauges

Marking and cutting gauges are used to scribe dimensions with the grain and across the grain respectively. A marking gauge has a small sharp pin, while a cutting gauge is fitted with a scribing knife, sharpened with a bevel on one side only, like a marking knife. You may need two or three gauges as it may be necessary to keep one set to a particular dimension. You can fettle a standard marking gauge to work well both with the grain and across it.

A marking gauge is a simple tool, primarily used to scribe a line along the grain of the wood. File and adjust the pin so that it cuts a neat, clear line. Push a gauge away from you to mark. When setting a gauge, slightly tighten the adjuster screw. Check the measurement and, if necessary, tap the end of the stem on the bench to fine-tune. Once set, fully tighten. A cutting gauge is set in the same way. Use a cutting gauge so the bevelled side of the blade is always on the waste side of the cut.

A mortise gauge is fitted with two pins – one is adjustable – to enable you to scribe mortise-and-tenon joints with parallel lines. Set the two pins to the exact width of the chisel you are using to chop the mortise. This is an important tool and it is worth buying the more expensive version where the second, movable, pin is adjusted by a screw thread.

### Further information

Timber and cutting lists  pages 45–47
Buying tools  pages 72–73
Essential toolkit  pages 74–75
The sharpening process  pages 79–81
Joints  pages 190–219

Marking gauge with single pin

Cutting gauge with brass knob

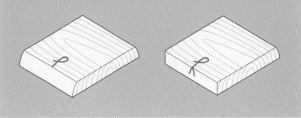

Mortise gauge with screw adjustment

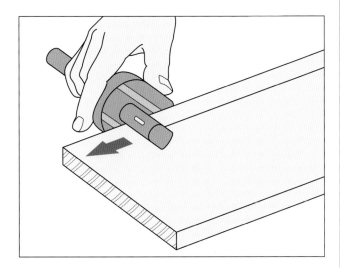

ABOVE Hold the marking gauge firmly against the edge of the timber. Push it away from you, with light pressure on the pin.

## FACE MARKS

When preparing timber, the first face to be planed is known as the 'face side'. This is usually the most attractive side of the board regarding grain pattern and defects. It is essential to identify this face with a pencil mark, the loop of which should run to one edge – the next surface to be planed. When this, the 'face edge' has been planed true, mark it with an upside down 'V'. Both marks should align. You should use all subsequent marking and measuring tools from either the face side or the face edge.

# Saws

The bench saw family is incredibly versatile, with tools capable of everything, from slicing a heavy, rough board to length to cutting the most precise dovetail joint. Straight and curved cuts are possible, with teeth cutting on the push stroke, or the less common pull stroke in the case of Japanese tools. There are several categories, the main ones comprising handsaws, back saws, frame saws and special saws. A confusing subject to the novice woodworker, you only really need a couple of saws to get started.

ABOVE A dovetail saw fitted with a heavy brass back. Here it is in use with a bench hook supporting the work.

## Handsaws

Designed for crosscutting timber, ripping along the grain and sawing sheet materials, handsaws vary in length from about 400–660 mm (approximately 16–26 in). The main differences are in teeth shape and pattern. A ripsaw will have 4 or 5 tpi, while a crosscut saw is finer at about 7 or 8 tpi. A panel saw is finer still with 10–12 tpi. This is more suitable for cutting joints and sheet materials. With the exception of hardpoint versions (see below), most saws have teeth that you can sharpen, although you are less likely to file the finer blades.

Traditionally, handles are hardwood, with the steel blade screwed or rivetted in place. Lacquered beech is most common, while expensive saws may use rosewood or maple. Plastic is a cheaper alternative and may have a soft grip for comfort. A traditional, top-quality handsaw will have a taper-ground blade that is thicker near the teeth and thinner near the top edge. This gives relief to the cut and helps to guide the saw.

Sometimes frowned upon by traditionalists, hardpoint saws are the best tools for cutting sheet materials. Man-made boards like MDF and chipboard will dull a handsaw very quickly, while the heat-treated teeth on an inexpensive hardpoint saw will remain sharp far longer. These teeth cannot be sharpened, however.

## Back saws

Shorter than a handsaw, a back saw has a stiffened blade. A strip of brass or steel is folded along the back, adding weight to the saw as it cuts. The most common back saws are tenon and dovetail saws, used for cutting joints and other fine sawing work. Traditional back saws have decorative, open or closed hardwood handles, designed to fit the hand comfortably. Although most back saws have teeth that you can sharpen, you can also buy hardpoint versions of tenon saws in popular sizes.

Tenon saws have blades from 250–350 mm (approximately 10–14 in). Teeth are typically 12–16 tpi. Dovetail saws are smaller, with blades from 200–250 mm (approximately 8–10 in) and teeth typically as fine as 20 tpi. Smaller still are gents saws, whose blades vary in length from 100–250 mm (4–10 in). These are used for precision cutting, with teeth typically 20 tpi. Jeweller's saws are similar in size, with even finer teeth.

Most woodworkers have two or three back saws: a tenon saw for general work and larger joints; a small 200 mm (approximately 8 in) dovetail saw for small joinery work (with very little set); and a 250 mm (approximately 10 in) dovetail saw or smaller tenon saw for larger carcase work.

Ripsaw with resharpenable teeth

Hardpoint saw with hardened teeth

Crosscut saw with resharpenable teeth

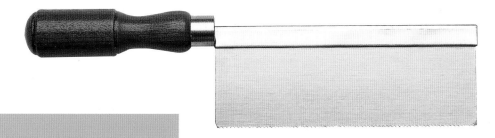

Gents saw

## TIP

• Protect the teeth of your saws with clip-on plastic covers when not in use; slide-on strips can be dangerous when teeth are razor sharp.

# Frame saws

Frame saws consist of a narrow blade suspended in a steel frame, which enables you to rotate the blade through 360 degrees for cutting curves in timber and sheet materials. Blades are tensioned either by adjusting a threaded handle or flexing the frame and tightening turnscrews.

The most common frame saws are coping and piercing saws, indispensable for smallscale curved cutting. A coping saw has a standard blade length of 150 mm (approximately 6 in) and about 14 tpi. You unscrew the handle to remove the blade, which fits over pins at each end of the frame. A piercing saw has an even finer, shorter blade at 130 mm (approximately 5 in). It is used for marquetry, model making and cutting soft metals. Fret saws have longer throats for making deeper cuts, but have been generally superseded by the powered scroll saw.

Rarely used nowadays, the wooden bow saw cuts fairly thick timber. The frame is normally beech, although any close-grained timber is suitable. Blade length is from 200–300 mm (approximately 8–12 in), tensioned with a tourniquet across the opposite ends of the frame. The bow saw has largely been replaced by the powered band saw.

Piercing saw

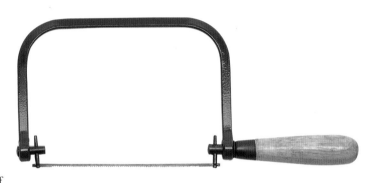

Coping saw

# Japanese saws

Japanese saws are popular as they are beautifully sharp from new and cut a very fine kerf. Unlike most Western saws, they cut on the pull stroke rather than on the push stroke, so blades are under tension and are much thinner as a result. The cutting technique takes some getting used to, but many woodworkers prefer the action of Japanese saws with their razor-sharp teeth. They cut rapidly and efficiently, enabling you to saw to a line easily.

Some tools, such as *dozuki* saws, have steel backs to provide rigidity, while *ryoba* and *kataba* saws for ripping and crosscutting, have thin blades that pass right through the timber. Blades are replaceable on many Japanese saws. Traditional handles are wrapped in bamboo, although plastic versions are also available. You can sharpen teeth with special feather files, although the harder steel means they remain sharp longer than Western saws.

It is possible to replace the blade on many Japanese saws, while retaining the original handle. To change it you gently tap the back of the blade on the bench top. This loosens the blade which is then removed. Insert a new one and tap the end of the handle on the bench to retighten.

Dozuki saw – traditional tenon saw

Ryoba saw with two rows of teeth

Dozuki-me saw with fine teeth

Flush-cutting saw

ABOVE Much quieter than a powered saw, the hand mitre saw is simple to use and accurate. Some models enable compound mitres to be sawn, with the blade tilted over as well as set at an angle.

# Special saws

Certain saws are suitable for unique situations in the workshop and may only get occasional use. The flush-cutting saw has a thin, flexible blade and is used for sawing wooden plugs off level with surrounding timber. Teeth are set on one side only, so will not damage the surface. A veneer saw's blade has curved teeth for making straight cuts. Used against a straightedge, very fine cuts are produced. Compass and keyhole saws have long, pointed blades and are used for cutting tight circles in solid timber and sheet materials. You must insert a pilot hole in the material before inserting the tip of the blade.

# Mitre saws

Essentially a frame saw suspended in a jig, a mitre saw is used for cutting accurate angles in timber. It is the ideal tool for making picture frames, enabling you to cut precise mitres and to crosscut small components exactly to length. You can swing the saw round to 45 degrees left or right, and can usually index the saw at these positions – and at 90 degrees – for fast adjustment. For other angles, a protractor scale provides a guide for locking the saw in place. Position the timber for cutting against a rear fence, held in a clamp if necessary. Stops enable the blade to cut to a predetermined depth.

## JARGON BUSTER

**Crosscutting** Sawing across the grain.
**Hardpoint saw** A saw on which the teeth have been heat-treated so the tips remain sharp for longer, but which cannot be re-sharpened.
**Kerf** Width of cut produced by the blade teeth.
**ppi** points per inch (25 mm).
**Ripsawing** Cutting parallel to the grain.
**Set** Saw teeth are alternately bent slightly to one side of the blade, then the other. The resulting cut (kerf) is wider than the blade itself.
**Taper-ground** The blade on some handsaws reduces in thickness from bottom to top, so reducing friction as it cuts.
**tpi** teeth per inch (25 mm)

## TIP

• If the lighting is not perfect in your workshop, use a portable lamp on the bench to illuminate the saw. If you cannot see properly, there is little chance of cutting accurately to your line. A bench light can throw an invisible scribe line into high relief if caught at the right angle.

### Ripsaw teeth

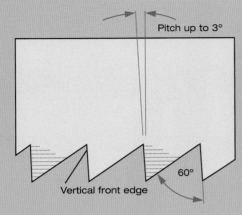

Pitch up to 3°

Vertical front edge

60°

### Crosscut saw teeth

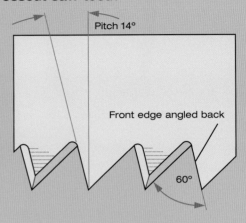

Pitch 14°

Front edge angled back

60°

### Japanese saw teeth

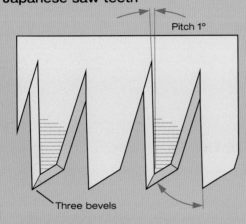

Pitch 1°

Three bevels

### Teeth per inch and points per inch

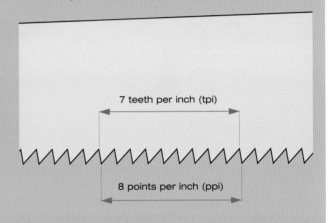

7 teeth per inch (tpi)

8 points per inch (ppi)

## SAW TEETH

Teeth on a crosscut saw act like small knives, severing the wood fibres, whereas the ripsaw teeth act like tiny chisels, paring material away. A crosscut saw is almost essential for cutting damp softwoods, but the ripsaw is more useful with dry hardwoods. Many cabinet-makers reset their fine-tooth panel saws with a rip-tooth configuration. Japanese saws cut on the pull stroke and have razor-sharp teeth that can be sharpened using special files.

How coarsely or finely a saw cuts is determined by the number of teeth per inch (25 mm) along the blade. The number is expressed either as tpi (teeth per inch) or ppi (points per inch). With tpi, the number of teeth is measured along their base, but with ppi, just the tips are counted. For the same blade there is always one ppi more than the tpi, so 8 ppi is the same grade as 7 tpi.

Crosscut saws and ripsaws have their teeth sharpened in different ways. The leading edge of a crosscut tooth slopes away from the vertical, so the tooth is filed at an angle to its face. A rip tooth's leading edge is vertical and is filed at 90 degrees to its face.

The shape of each tooth is known as the pitch, with a leading and trailing edge. Even on the smallest saws teeth are set, or slightly bent, alternately on each side. This provides clearance as the saw cuts without binding in the timber. This cut is known as the kerf.

The teeth on a hardpoint saw are hardened by an electronic process but the teeth are not resharpenable. They are often needle-sharp when new, so take great care when handling these saws.

# How to saw accurately

**1** Before cutting timber with a back saw, scribe the line accurately with a marking knife. Reinforce the scribed line, cutting quite deeply into the timber. With a sharp chisel, pare out a small fillet of waste to create a narrow channel, which will enable you to position the saw blade in this V-groove and get a clean start in the wood. This also creates a clean scribed shoulder to the cut, where there is a risk the saw would tear or fail to cut the fibres cleanly. This is particularly useful in soft-grained or fibrous timbers.

**2** A handy piece of equipment when using a back saw is the bench hook (see page 88). Easily made from workshop offcuts, this hooks over the edge of the bench and allows you to hold the timber firmly while sawing. It is important that timber much longer than the width of the bench hook is supported at the far end. If not, it will not sit squarely on the bench hook, resulting in inaccurate sawing. Sometimes when sawing to a line it is better to use the bench vice to grip the timber, so you can use the saw vertically. This way you can position yourself to control the saw accurately and move your arm efficiently. If this is not possible, cramp the timber to the bench top. Trestles are lower and more comfortable when cutting up sheet material.

**3** When crosscutting timber with a handsaw, place your thumb against the blade. This way you can position the teeth exactly on the waste side of the scribed line. Pull the saw back gently a couple of times to start the cut then start the sawing action. Always try to keep your eye directly above the line. Try to use as much of the blade as possible when sawing. Not only is this more efficient but it means the teeth around the centre of the saw will stay sharp for longer.

**Further information**

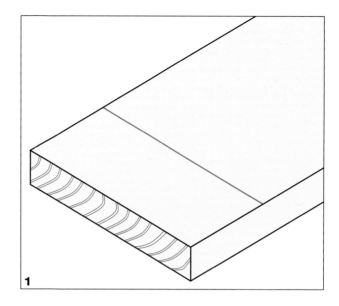

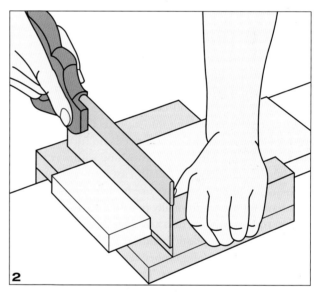

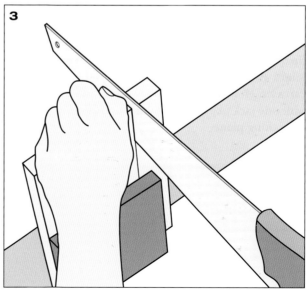

# Specialist planes

There are a number of specialist planes for more specific woodworking tasks. Most are smaller than bench planes, and can be trickier to set up and use precisely.

A block plane is used for trimming end grain as well as working with the grain. It is perfect for adding small chamfers or planing narrow edges and is normally held in one hand. The cutting angle is low and some versions have an adjustable mouth, increasing the tool's versatility. Unlike larger bench planes, a block plane – and some other specialized planes – has its blade set at a low angle in the body of the tool. With the bevel now sitting upwards, this angle (between 12 and 15 degrees), combined with a honing angle of 30 degrees, creates an overall angle of about 45 degrees, the same as a bench plane. The benefit of this is that it enables you to change the overall cutting angle by simply grinding and honing the blade to a different bevel. This is especially useful when planing timbers with wild, irregular grain.

Shoulder planes are narrower and have a blade the full width of the body, enabling them to cut into the corner of a joint, such as a rebate. Used on its side, this tool will trim the shoulder of a tenon neatly. Many woodworkers find that one relatively narrow shoulder plane is sufficient for most kinds of work.

The side rebate plane is a tool that you will rarely need. It is handy for enlarging fractionally – say, a groove to accept the edge of a panel – and on that one occasion it will be virtually impossible to do the job with anything else.

Block plane

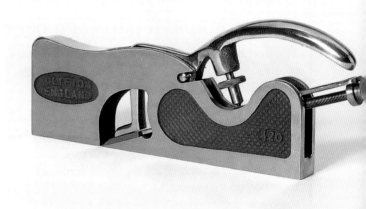

Shoulder plane

---

## JARGON BUSTER

**Face edge** The second surface to be worked when preparing timber. The face edge and face side are always at 90 degrees to each other. Both are used as reference faces for marking tools.

**Face side** When preparing timber, always the first face planed. It must be dead flat and straight.

**Honing** After grinding, edge tools are honed (sharpened) on an abrasive stone to produce a cutting edge.

**Iron** Another name for a plane blade or cutter.

**Winding sticks** A pair of identical hardwood strips with parallel edges. Placed at opposite ends of a board, they are used to check for twist by sighting along one strip and aligning it with the other. Coloured edges make this easier.

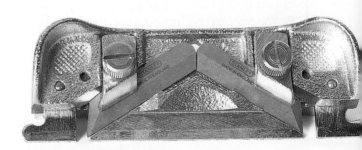

Side rebate plane

# Wooden planes

Although much less common, some woodworkers prefer wooden planes, which can be easier to fettle and set up than their steel counterparts. They are also lighter to use. It is possible to buy old wooden planes relatively cheaply at auctions and specialist stores.

Japanese planes are also popular. Pulled towards rather than pushed away from the body, these simple tools can be delightful to use once you have mastered the unusual technique. The plane bodies are usually oak, with thick blades that you adjust for cutting depth by tapping gently with a special hammer. Various sizes and patterns are available, including planes to cut chamfers.

Wood smoothing plane

# Moulding planes

Moulding planes were important tools for the furniture- and cabinet-maker before the advent of the spindle moulder and portable router. Although no longer made and rarely used, moulding planes cut profiles that are hard to do with any other hand tool. You can still buy them relatively cheaply second-hand.

Japanese plane

Moulding plane

# Adjusting a bench plane

Once a bench plane has been set up to work correctly, you can test it on a piece of timber. A correctly set up plane will have a slightly curved blade. The purpose of this is to create a narrow, ribbon-like shaving about 16 mm (⅝ in) in width, which emerges from the centre of the throat of the plane and is easily controllable. You can cut a wider shaving using a flatter, less curved blade, but this requires much more energy to work and gives you much less control. A curved blade creates a shaving with a centre thickness of about 0.25 mm (¹⁄₁₀₀ in), which tapers out to nothing at the edges.

# Plane blades

Plane blades (also called cutters or irons) are usually made from high-quality carbon or tool steel. They come in two distinct patterns: block and shoulder planes have the bevel facing up with the blade set at a low angle, a lever cap securing the blade to the plane body; conventional bench planes have a high, 45-degree cutting angle, but with the blade bevel facing down. A back iron is fitted to the rear of the blade, which controls the path of the shaving through the mouth of the plane and prevents tears and splits in that shaving. It is important that the back iron is carefully fitted to the blade to enable the plane to function properly.

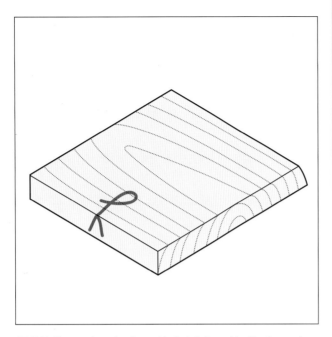

ABOVE Always plane the face side first, followed by the face edge.

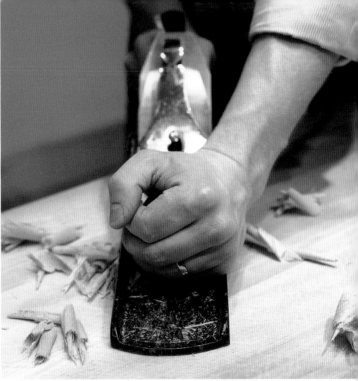

ABOVE Preparing big panels by hand can be rewarding. Prepare the jointer plane with a sharp blade and lubricate the sole of the tool with wax.

## How to plane

Quite often a hand plane is used to remove the machine marks left by a planer. The surface must be planed evenly and with good control of the plane. Always try to plane the timber in the direction it wishes to be planed: this will often be determined by the grain direction of the piece. You can get some idea of which way the grain is running by looking at the edge of the board. When using a plane, bear in mind that you are pressing down on the timber as well as moving the tool forwards. Therefore the trunk of your body can exert considerable power downward if the plane is kept in close to you.

**1**  Move forward, over the work, by keeping your front foot forward and swaying over the work using your knees, rather than pushing the plane using your forearm and shoulders only.

**2**  In this way you can start and stop a plane shaving and continue down a long board, because the tool is close to the body and kept under control. Such control is not possible if you allow the plane to extend too far forward. In a similar way, a long board can be planed easily in a series of short steps, each time starting and stopping the plane under control.

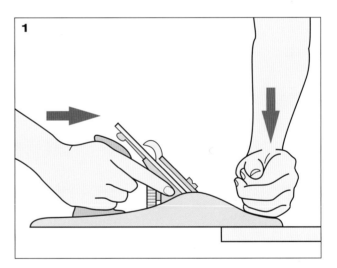

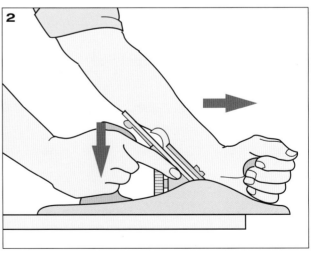

# Planing end grain

Quite often, you will need to plane a sawn surface back to an exact dimension across the grain using either a bench plane or small block plane. If using a bench plane, hold the timber vertically in a vice with the end grain facing up. You can treat larger components, such as carcase sides, in this way, because they give enough support to the larger and heavier bench plane. Bench planes have a certain amount of weight and mass, which are valuable in driving the plane through the cut. It is often necessary to plane from both sides towards the centre. If this is not possible, use a chisel to cut a small 45-degree bevel to help breakout at the far end of the board.

For smaller components use a block plane. Used with one hand, this tool is designed for cutting end grain with a low cutting angle. Some block planes have an adjustable mouth, which should be closed up so that it is no more than about 0.5 mm (¹⁄₆₄ in) away from the end of the blade. Unlike bench planes, block planes are honed with the edge straight across, rather than slightly rounded. This means the shaving is the full width of the blade. With a sharp, well set up block plane it should be possible to produce fine shavings on end grain.

**Further information**
Buying tools  pages 72–73
Essential toolkit  pages 74–75
Fettling tools  pages 76–78
The sharpening process  pages 79–81
Power planers  page 131
Planers and thicknessers  pages 156–159

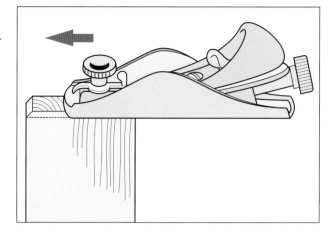

ABOVE There are several ways to plane end grain so that you do not split the wood. Cutting a small chamfer on the rear edge first with a chisel will prevent this. Alternatively, plane in towards the centre from each side.

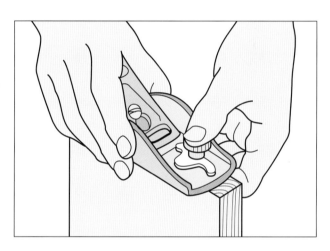

ABOVE A block plane should be really sharp for end grain work. Grip the tool to apply sufficient downward pressure at the front of the sole. Cramping a piece of wood at the back of the work piece will also prevent splitting.

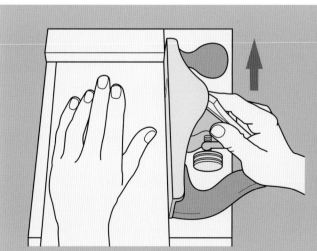

## HOW TO USE A SHOOTING BOARD

A shooting board makes it more straightforward to plane small components. Made in the workshop from MDF or plywood, you cramp it to the bench top. Run a bench plane down the length of the shooting board on its side, with the timber supported at right angles to the plane and held against a stop at one end of the shooting board. In this way, you can trim small components or long edges of thin boards extremely accurately and with great control.

# Chisels

Chisels are made in a variety of patterns and sizes, but they all have one thing in common: to work effectively their cutting edges must be razor sharp. This means that less effort is required to make them cut and they are safer to use because there is less chance of them slipping. There are several styles to choose from. Tools may be sold individually or in sets of common sizes.

ABOVE Both hands should always be behind the cutting edge when using a chisel.

As much as three-quarters of the work you do with chisels will be done with tools ranging between 6 and 19 mm (¼ and ¾ in) in width. There are likely to be times when you will need wider tools – sometimes paring chisels – but these occasions will be rare. If buying chisels for the first time, obtain a good-quality set of small bevel-edge tools. These will become some of the most important hand tools in your workshop. Get the feel of using and sharpening these before investing in larger, more expensive chisels.

Narrow bevel-edge chisel

## Chisel choice

Sets of chisels usually contain popular blade widths of 6, 12, 19 and 25 mm (¼, ½, ¾ and 1 in), although tools can also be bought individually. Many craftsmen rely on an assortment of small chisels less than 12 mm (½ in) wide. Unless they work regularly on large projects they will have perhaps only three other larger chisels of different widths, up to 30 mm (1¼ in). Choose a range of chisels that fits, and becomes an extension of, your hands. A handle should balance the weight of the blade – a small one for a narrow chisel and a larger one for a wider tool. Handle comfort can be as important as the hardness of the steel that forms the cutting edge. Traditionally chisel handles are boxwood, although beech and ash are also common. Plastics such as polypropylene are popular, arguably less comfortable than hardwood, yet more durable.

The most useful chisels for workshop use are those with a bevel edge. A light bevel is ground along both long edges of the chisel, making these tools ideal for cutting joints and getting into corners. Because there

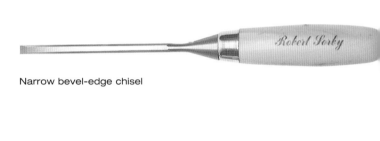

Wide bevel-edge chisel

Narrow firmer chisel

Mortise chisel

is less steel, however, these chisels are not as strong as other chisel patterns and should not be used for chopping mortises.

Heavier, firmer chisels are more useful for general carpentry work than for furniture-making or joinery. Their rectangular-section blades make them stronger than bevel-edged tools, although they are more limited in how they can be used. Mortise chisels have heavier blades still, designed to lever out the waste timber when chopping a joint. Available in several styles, all of them are designed to be used with a mallet. A registered-pattern mortise chisel has a steel hoop and leather washer between blade and handle to absorb shock.

Chisels with polypropylene and splitproof plastic handles

# Specialist chisels

There are several less common chisels that will be useful in certain situations. The first is a matched pair of lef-t and right-handed skew-ground chisels. These are essential tools for cleaning out the corners of lapped dovetails, most commonly found on the front of drawers. You can clear those few corner fibres away with a bench knife, but a skew-ground chisel is a much more efficient tool. It is possible to grind a couple of old chisels to the required angles, instead of buying brand new tools.

Bevel-edge paring chisels are useful for fine, delicate work and should never be struck with a mallet or hammer. Their bevel-edged blades are longer than most chisels, enabling them to be used for cutting housing joints. Useful sizes are 16 mm (⅝ in) and 30 mm (1¼ in) blades. A cranked paring chisel is very useful for cleaning out the inside of an assembled carcase, its handle raised above the work when used with the blade flat on the work. Without the help of this tool, it is almost impossible to slice off neatly those tiny knobs of half-dried glue that squeeze out from a joint.

Right-handed skew-ground chisel

Left-handed skew-ground chisel

Cranked paring chisel

---

**JARGON BUSTER**

**Honing** After grinding, edge tools are honed (sharpened) on an abrasive stone to produce a cutting edge.

**Paring** Removing a thin shaving from timber with a sharp chisel, either from the surface or from end grain.

---

**TIP**

• Long edges of new chisels can be sharp, cutting into your fingers when used for paring. Run a fine sharpening stone along the edges to soften them.

**A Japanese laminated chisel blade**

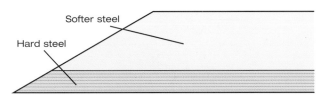

Softer steel

Hard steel

# Japanese chisels

Unlike a European chisel, the blade of a Japanese chisel is laminated. A thin layer of hard steel (the cutting edge) is laminated to a heavier layer of softer steel. If used properly, Japanese chisels retain their edges several times longer than European equivalents. They are honed in the same way as Western tools, though usually with just one bevel, rather than two.

Larger Japanese chisels benefit from the oriental practice of hollow grinding. This enables the user to get the back of the chisel perfectly flat and mirror polished. As the hollow is gradually revealed along the edge through repeated honing, a special hammer is used to restore the cutting edge. Most Japanese chisels have a steel hoop on the handle, so they can be struck with a small metal hammer. Handles are usually made from polished oak and beautifully finished. Although there are benefits to be gained from buying Japanese chisels in larger sizes, many craftsmen prefer European chisels in the smaller, more delicate sizes. European chisels are lighter, easier and quicker to sharpen than Japanese versions.

# How to use chisels

When using a chisel, the sharpness of the edge is paramount. Never let the edge become blunt – as soon as you feel the need to exert undue pressure when paring, it is time to hone the edge. When a chisel is in constant use, it is not unusual to need to hone an edge once every half hour or so. Always keep both hands behind the cutting edge. Never be tempted to hold a work piece in one hand while chiselling with the other. Instead, always grip timber in the vice or to the bench top using a cramp.

# Paring to gauge lines

When paring back to a gauge line, always pare away a shaving that is not too thick. This is because a chisel blade is in fact only a sharpened steel wedge. If the shaving you are attempting to remove is too thick, instead of allowing the chisel to pare at right angles to the surface it will drive the tool back, possibly inside the gauged line.

As you approach the gauge line, pare three-quarters of the way down the end grain. Then turn the timber over and pare down from the other side. In this way you will approach the gauge lines with the end grain becoming flatter at right angles to the face side. When you come to the final shaving, click the chisel into the gauge line (you should feel the sharp edge of the blade engage with the line) and make the final cut three-quarters of the depth. Turn the piece over and complete the cut to give you an exact 90-degree surface to the face side.

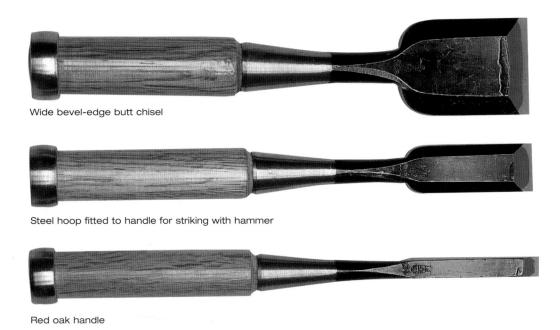

Wide bevel-edge butt chisel

Steel hoop fitted to handle for striking with hammer

Red oak handle

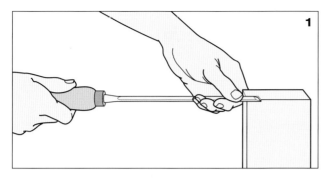

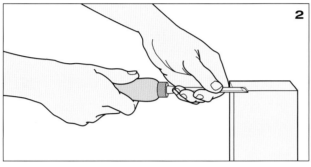

## How to pare horizontally

Cramp the work piece vertically in the vice for horizontal paring, about 152–203 mm (6–8 in) above the bench top. At this height it is possible for the timber not to vibrate too much and yet enable you to get into the correct stance.

**1** Stand with legs apart and your chest and shoulders at right angles to the face of the timber. The line from the chisel blade through your wrist to your elbow should be straight, and almost parallel to the bench top: you may need to spread your feet further apart. In this stance, power is given to the cut by tucking your elbow tight into your chest. Lean on your knees and upper body instead of applying power with the arm and shoulder.

**2** Greater control and flexibility can be provided by using a paring chisel. The length of the tool enables you to exert much finer control over the cuts.

## How to pare vertically

Hold the chisel close to your body with elbows tucked in, so you can exert the power from your upper body rather than hands and forearms. Rest your forearm on the timber and grip the chisel with an upward pressure. Use your other hand to hold the chisel handle and exert downward pressure. This way, you hold the tool in tension, giving greater power and control. You can drive the blade through end grain and yet control the cut, preventing the chisel from skating away from you and digging into the bench. It is a good idea to use a cutting board to protect the bench top just in case.

**1** With a narrow chisel of about 6 mm (¼ in) it is possible to pare relatively soft timber (such as mahogany or walnut) the full width of the blade. With a wider blade it is difficult to retain control of the tool, so start with a narrow chisel first.

**2** Work up to using the widest chisel available, as its width will give you greater accuracy and flatness.

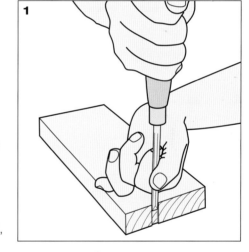

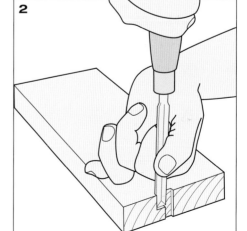

### Further information

# Drills

A simple method of making a hole in a piece of wood is to use a hand drill or brace and bit. Although now replaced for many tasks by cordless tools, hand drills offer greater control, especially when using small-diameter bits. A swing brace enables large-diameter holes to be bored. One big advantage is that no power supply is required for these tools.

ABOVE Always hold timber in the vice or cramp it to the bench when drilling.

## Hand drills

Made from steel or cast aluminium, a hand drill consists of a gear wheel that you rotate using a side handle. Around the perimeter of the wheel are small teeth, which engage with either a single or double pinion, enabling the chuck to revolve. The keyless chuck consists of three jaws, which grip round-shank drill bits. Capacity is usually 8 mm ($\frac{5}{16}$ in). Handles are either lacquered hardwood or plastic.

Hand drill or wheel brace

## Swing braces

Still used occasionally by carpenters, the traditonal swing, or ratchet, brace enables you to drill large-diameter holes. You can swing the handle round partially, which can be useful in a confined space. A cam ring allows you to swing the chuck in either a clockwise or anti-clockwise direction with opposite ratchet action. Chuck capacity is about 13 mm ($\frac{1}{2}$ in) and the four jaws enable both square- and round-shanked bits to be gripped. Special screwdriver bits provide enormous torque when driving or removing large screws.

Swing brace

## Bradawls

The most basic way to start a hole, a bradawl (or awl) forces the wood fibres apart rather than removing any waste. This provides a lead-in hole for a screw or the location for a drill bit. The tip is like a tiny screwdriver blade and is twisted into the grain when making the hole.

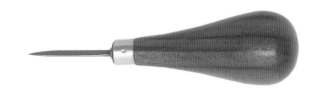

Bradawl

# Drill bits

Some bits are designed specifically for hand tools, others for power and pillar drills. Some, such as twist bits and lip-and-spur bits, can be used either way. Lip-and-spur bits are the best choice for use in hand drills, as they cut very clean holes. They locate easily in the timber with a central brad point, and can be used in either hand or power drills.

Engineer's twist bits (also called HSS bits) are designed for drilling metal, although they work fairly well in timber. Larger sizes will benefit from having the hole position marked with a centre punch before drilling. You can buy sets of twist drills in metric or imperial sizes, typically ranging from 1–13 mm (1/32–1/2 in), although larger bits are available.

Auger and Jennings pattern bits are used in swing braces. Often the end of the shank has a square taper, enabling it to be gripped securely in the chuck of the brace. These bits have a centre thread, which draws it into the timber as you operate the tool. Side spurs cut the outer diameter of the hole, while the spiral on the shank clears the wood waste.

Expansion bits are used with a swing brace and enable you to bore non-standard diameter holes. A single spur cutter is moved outwards from the shank and locked with a screw once adjusted. Holes up to 76 mm (3 in) in diameter are possible.

Use steel countersink bits when you need to recess heads of woodscrews flush with a surface. After boring the clearance hole for the screw, insert the countersink bit in the tool and give a few turns. The most common angle is 90 degrees, matching the underside of the screw head, although 60-degree versions are available. Styles include fluted (rose pattern) and snail countersinks, which reduce chatter. Loose countersinks are hollow and can be fitted to existing twist bits, which slide up the centre. They are locked in place with a small hex screw.

Twist bit

Lip-and-spur bit

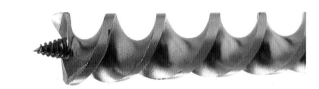

Combination auger bit

Jennings pattern bit

Irwin pattern bit

## Further information

Buying tools  pages 72–73
Essential toolkit  pages 74–75
Cordless tools  pages 120–123
Power drills  pages 126–127
Pillar drills  pages 160–161

## How to drill

**1** With the timber held in a vice, make sure that the drill and twist bit are at the correct angle before drilling. Placing a small try square alongside can act as a guide when drilling at 90 degrees. Position yourself so that you are looking directly down over your work.

**2** Turn the handle, ensuring that, when starting to cut, the centre of the drill bit remains in the correct point on the timber. You can easily make a simple depth stop by wrapping masking tape around the bit.

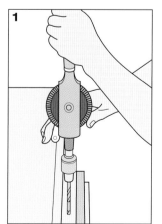
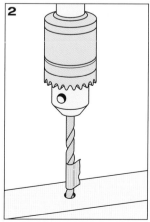

# Screwdrivers

Despite the increased popularity of cordless tools, the traditional screwdriver has a valuable role in the workshop. For assembly work, a cabinet screwdriver offers greater control than a powered version, which is important when working with delicate surfaces. A good-quality set of screwdrivers will usually include the popular slotted and cross-headed patterns.

## Screwdriver types

Most screwdrivers used for woodwork fall into two categories: slotted and cross-headed, relating to the types of screw used. Slotted screws are more traditional but still widely used, while cross-headed screws are better suited for use with power tools.

The hardened steel blade on a slotted screwdriver has a flattened head. The tip may be flared or have parallel edges. A flared tip is stronger and enables you to use extra torque. To recess a screw, use a screwdriver with a parallel blade, as a flared tip is likely to bind in the screw hole. The most traditional tools in this family are cabinet screwdrivers, which have turned, oval hardwood handles, usually beech. These are available in several sizes to fit screws from No. 6 up to No. 14, with blade lengths from about 75–250 mm (approximately 3–10 in).

A cross-headed screwdriver has a cross projection at the tip of the blade, which fits into a matching recess on the screw head. Although this design was intended to reduce slippage that can occur with ordinary slotted screws, it can be easy to damage a screw head if the wrong size screwdriver is used, particularly when driving screws with a mains or cordless drill/driver. The most popular cross-headed pattern has extra projections between the cross members on the tip, which increase the grip and further reduce slippage.

New screw patterns are constantly being introduced, some of which are used as security fixings for cabinet fittings or in machinery.

Screwdriver blades are usually circular in section, although heavier tools may be square. This allows you to clamp on an adjustable spanner or wrench, so

ABOVE You will need several screwdrivers, as blade tips vary in width to suit different screw sizes.

BELOW The three most common screwdriver blade patterns (from left to right): Phillips, Pozidriv and traditional slotted.

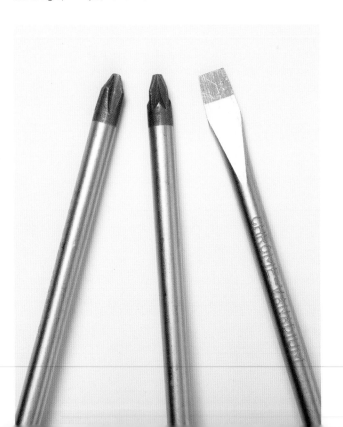

providing greater torque when driving or removing stubborn screws. Some screwdrivers have a short hexagonal section below the handle for the same reason. Blades are generally chrome vanadium steel and may have a hardened tip. Textured tips help to grip the screw better, while magnetic tips on smaller tools are useful for positioning tiny screws that may otherwise get dropped.

With the exception of cabinet screwdrivers, most handles tend to be moulded plastic. Glossy PVC handles can be unpleasant to hold and can slip, while those with a soft, textured grip are more comfortable to use over an extended period. A variety of handle shapes and styles mean it is easy to find a set of screwdrivers that fit your hand perfectly.

Cordless drill driver

# Spiral screwdrivers

Once a favourite tool of joiners and shop fitters, the spiral, or pump-action, screwdriver drives screws home. Interchangeable bits are inserted into a small chuck at the end of a spiral-shaped steel shank. Operated by pumping the handle, a cam ring is used to change the bit rotation from clockwise to anti-clockwise. Although largely replaced by cordless tools, spiral screwdrivers are still produced.

Screwdriver with PVC handle

Screwdriver with soft-grip, plastic handle

---

### JARGON BUSTER

**HSS**  High-speed steel
**Torque**  The twisting force when driving a screw. Measured in Nm with power tools.

---

Screw extractor

Cabinet screwdriver

**Further information**
Buying tools  pages 72–73
Essential toolkit  pages 74–75
Cordless tools  pages 120–123
Screws and nails  pages 236–237

Interchangeable bits for spiral screwdriver

Spiral- or pump-action screwdriver

# Hammers

Even the most highly skilled fine furniture-maker uses a hammer. These simple tools are not just for driving in nails and pins when making jigs or mock-ups, but for assembling joints and carcases, and general maintenance work around the workshop. Hammers used by carpenters and roofers can be sophisticated, using materials such as titanium and fibreglass.

ABOVE Grip a hammer near the end of its handle. This gives better control, enabling you to swing the tool efficiently.

## Hammers

Most woodworkers have several hammers for different tasks. They are classed by weight rather than size. Handles on more traditional tools are usually ash or hickory, wedged into a socket on the steel head. Claw-hammer handles can be hardwood, steel or fibreglass with soft grips.

The claw hammer is probably the heaviest tool you will need. Used for driving large nails, the claw extracts bent nails easily with little damage. A weight of 450 or 550 gm (16 or 20 oz) is recommended. The cross pein hammer is suitable for smaller nails and general woodwork. One end of the head has a narrow wedge, which you use to start tapping a nail or pin while you hold it in place. Once established in the wood, use the other striking face to drive the nail home. A good weight for workshop use is about 280 gm (10 oz). The smallest of the hammer family is the pin hammer, typically weighing 100 gm (3½ oz).

Nylon or rubber-faced hammers are frequently used in pre-assembly work, as they do not mark the surface. These soft-faced hammers are often replaced in the final glue-up with a steel-faced hammer because the ringing sound will change as the joint is knocked home, so giving a skilled craftsman greater control.

Claw hammer with graphite core and soft-grip handle

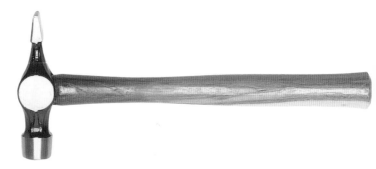

Traditional cross pein hammer

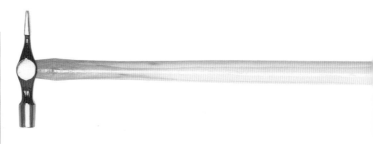

Pin hammer

**TIP**

• Keep the striking face of a hammer clean by rubbing it on abrasive paper. This will prevent it slipping off the nail and damaging a surface when in use.

## Mallets

Always use a mallet when striking a chisel – there is less chance of damaging the handle and the larger face means it is safer to use than a hammer. Usually made from a close-grained hardwood such as beech, making your own mallet is a useful workshop exercise.

Traditional beech mallet

## Nail punches

When using panel pins or small nails on decorative woodwork, you usually punch the heads below the timber surface to conceal the fixing, and add a suitable filler to the holes. Steel nail punches come in several sizes to match the nail heads. Always use a punch slightly smaller than the nail head.

BELOW Whenever using a chisel and mallet, the work piece should be held securely. Either cramp it to the bench top or grip it in the vice.

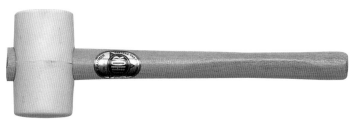

Nylon (or rubber) faced mallet

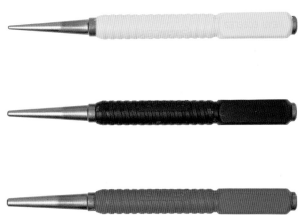

Nail punches

### JARGON BUSTER

**Pein** A wedge-shaped end of the head on some hammers, used to start off nails.

**Ringing sound** The sound produced as timber components, particularly joints, are hammered together. The sound becomes solid, rather than hollow, as the surfaces mate together.

**Further information**
Buying tools pages 72–73
Essential toolkit pages 74–75
Screws and nails pages 236–237

# Cramps

There will be plenty of situations in the workshop for which a cramp is essential. The most obvious time is to apply pressure when gluing two or more pieces of wood together. You may need to hold timber temporarily on the bench top while sawing or routing. Or you might want to hold materials accurately when screwing them together.

ABOVE For some tasks you will need to use practically every cramp in the workshop. Buy them as and when you can afford them.

## G-cramps

Made from malleable cast iron, G-cramps (also called C-cramps) are available in several sizes and depths, and can be used to apply enormous pressure. Invariably you do not need so much pressure, however. A well-made joint simply needs a small amount of glue and a little bit of pressure. You do need consistent pressure all along the joint, which may mean using a number of cramps for one small assembly job. Capacities vary from a tiny 25 mm (1 in) up to about 254 mm (10 in). Deep-throat cramps enable you to apply pressure further in from the edge of a board. Edge cramps are usually based on a small G-cramp and are handy when gluing lipping to panel edges. There are usually three screw adjusters, so off-centre cramping is also possible.

## F-cramps

Useful general-purpose tools, these are sometimes known as speed cramps, as they are fast to adjust. In complex gluing operations where time is of the essence, these tools can be invaluable: simply tighten the sliding shoe against the work by rotating a threaded handle. These cramps may have metal or reinforced-plastic

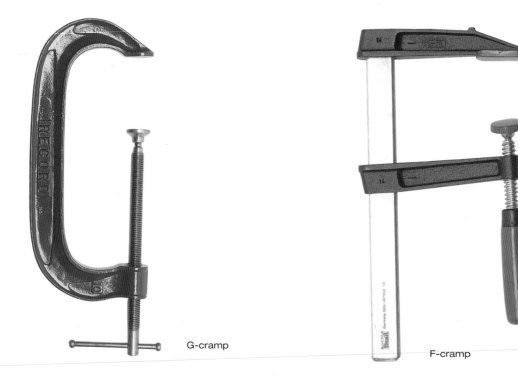

G-cramp

F-cramp

shoes, with large capacities restricted only by the length of the steel bar. Bars are usually serrated along the back edge to enable the shoe to lock as you tighten up the adjuster handle. Typical maximum cramping capacity is around 790 mm (approximately 31 in).

# Cam cramps

Although wooden cam cramps are not capable of applying high pressure, they are lightweight and easy to use. Fixed and sliding heads are made from hardwood such as maple and faced with cork to prevent marking surfaces. Attached to a rectangular steel bar, these cramps can be made in the workshop. They are popular with musical-instrument makers, where too much pressure could easily damage delicate timber parts.

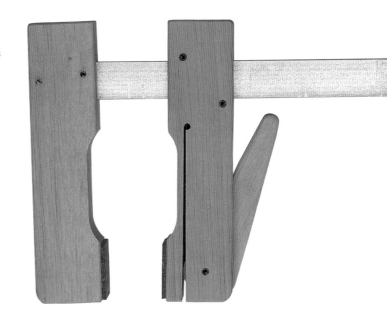

Cam cramp with cork-faced jaws

# Solo cramps

Ideal for rapid cramping, you can lock and position steel solo cramps on your work with one hand. They are useful when cramping work to a portable bench and take up little space in a toolbox.

# Quick-action cramps

Designed for use in one hand, these cramps are fairly lightweight, with narrow steel bars and plastic shoes. Squeezing a trigger draws the shoes together. This clamp may be reversed to act as a spreader – useful in taking dry joints apart, such as when making drawers.

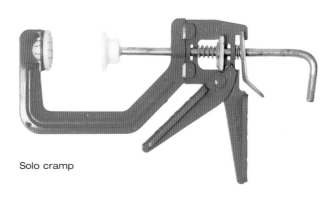

Solo cramp

# Spring cramps

From tiny model-makers' cramps up to heavy-duty versions with powerful action, spring cramps may be made of steel or plastic. These are handy for gluing small components and only need one hand to operate. Larger ones tend to be stronger and are great for holding jigs in place, or guide battens when routing or sawing. Variations of spring cramps use a ratchet action.

Spring cramp with ratchet action

# Sash and bar cramps

A favourite with joiners when gluing heavy items such as doors and windows, a sash or bar cramp can exert considerable pressure. Ideal for gluing boards edge to edge to make wide panels, bar lengths up to 1,650 mm (65 in) are standard. At one end of the steel bar a shoe is adjusted with a threaded tommy bar. The other shoe

### TIPS

• When gluing up boards with sash cramps, keep glue off the bars by laying newspaper across them before positioning the boards.
• Protect timber from the jaws of sash cramps by adding wooden pads or spacers to the shoes. These can stay in place for each cramping job.

slides along the bar and is locked in position with a steel pin. This is inserted in a suitable hole, of which there are a number evenly spaced along the bar. Lighter sash cramps have a small rectangular section bar, while heavy-duty versions consist of a bigger T-section bar. Lightweight sash cramps use extruded aluminium bars, rather than steel.

It is possible to buy just the steel shoes and make your own cramps quite easily, planing lengths of suitable hardwood to the correct dimensions, and boring holes at equal intervals along the length for inserting the steel pins.

## Pipe cramps

Popular in the United States, these cramps make use of regular steel plumbing pipes, ½ and ¾ in (no metric equivalent) in diameter. These are cut to length and a thread cut at one end, onto which a fixed shoe is attached. This incorporates an adjuster handle. A sliding shoe or tailstock fits over the other end like a sash cramp, except this is locked in place by a clutch mechanism, rather than a steel pin. The advantage of this system is that you need to buy fewer sets of cramping heads, as pipes are interchangeable to suit the cramping distance required. Pipes can also be joined with couplers.

## Band cramps

It is sometimes necessary to cramp up irregular shapes – when assembling chairs for example. Sash cramps are not always the best solution, and you may require a more flexible system. Band cramps use a flexible fabric that runs through a tensioning mechanism. The band is loosely arranged around the object, and a knob used to tighten it fully. This cramping method is ideal for gluing up picture frames, too.

## Mitre cramps

These are substantial steel cramps used for holding two pieces of timber together at 90 degrees, while gluing and pinning the joint. Used mostly for picture framing, the mitres are sawn at 45 degrees. Some cramps incorporate a slot for a tenon saw, so that you can saw the mitre in place before assembly.

Quick-action cramp

T-bar sash cramp

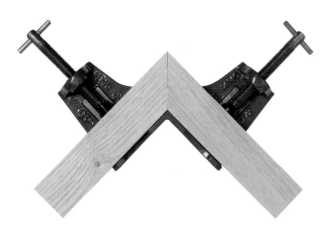

Mitre cramp

**Further information**
Buying tools  pages 72–73
Essential toolkit  pages 74–75
Joints  pages 190–219
Glues  pages 234–235

# Spokeshaves and scrapers

A spokeshave is, essentially, a narrow plane, but is used for cutting convex or concave curves. It is more difficult to use than a plane, and practising on narrow softwood offcuts will help you master the necessary skills. You will probably need a pair of spokeshaves, as convex and concave curves require separate tools. The difference is the sole.

ABOVE Spokeshaves produce shavings just like a bench plane, except they are used for shaping convex and concave edges, rather than flat surfaces.

## Spokeshaves

Most spokeshaves are cast metal, although you can still buy traditional tools with hardwood bodies. There are basically two patterns: flat-sole spokeshaves for cutting convex curves and curved-sole tools for concave shapes. Both are identical apart from the sole, and the sharpening technique is the same as for block planes.

The blade is held in place by a cap iron, tightened with a thumbscrew. The simplest spokeshaves have no adjuster – you slacken off the cap iron and slide the blade up or down to judge the depth of cut. Once set correctly, these basic tools can be very satisfying to use. More sophisticated spokeshaves have twin-screw adjusters, which enable you to align and set the blade precisely. More specialized spokeshaves for chair-making have half-round and radial faces. These are used for shaping chair legs and rails, as well as seats.

Flat-sole spokeshave

Specialized convex spokeshave

**Standard spokeshaves**

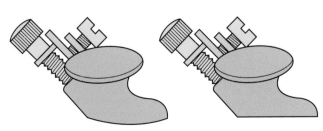

Curved-sole for concave surfaces

Flat-sole for convex surfaces

Specialized concave spokeshave

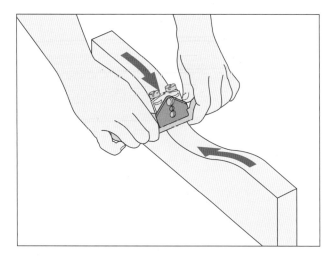

ABOVE Gripped in both hands, the spokeshave cuts on the push stroke. Develop a light rocking action but work with the grain direction.

## How to use a spokeshave

Both types of spokeshave are held and used in the same way. With the blade set to make a shallow cut, grip the handles with your thumbs sitting on their rear edges. Push the tool away from you, making a series of short strokes. If a clean shaving is not produced, adjust the blade setting or alter the angle at which the sole meets the wood. Often you will need to do both.

A flat-sole spokeshave is used for shaping convex curves. A curved sole is slightly more versatile and is used for shaping concave curves, although can also be used on shallow convex curves if necessary.

Because of their size, spokeshave blades are more awkward to grip when sharpening than plane irons. To make this easier, cut a slot in a suitable scrap of hardwood and insert the blade, so extending the grip.

Scraper plane

## Scraper planes

A scraper plane resembles a steel bench plane, except for the blade which you sharpen like a cabinet scraper. A handled scraper looks rather like a large spokeshave. Both tools relieve the pressure and heat on the thumbs common with conventional cabinet scrapers. Each has a flat sole and cutting depth is adjusted with a thumbscrew that exerts pressure on the blade. This is an excellent tool for finishing wide, flat surfaces without creating the burning sensation on your thumbs that occurs when using a normal cabinet scraper.

## Cabinet scrapers

The cabinet scraper is probably the simplest woodworking tool to use, and sharpened and used effectively it will produce a fine surface which needs no further cleaning up. Straight and curved scrapers enable a wide range of surfaces to be prepared.

Made from a piece of thin, tempered steel, a cabinet scraper may be rectangular or have curved edges. A correctly sharpened tool produces a shaving, rather than dust. After preparing the steel with a file and oilstone, create a small burr along its cutting edge using a burnisher.

BELOW A sharp cabinet scraper can clean up irregular or wild grain effectively that could easily be ruined by a conventional bench plane.

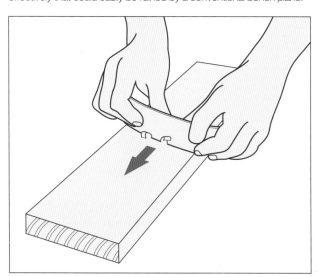

### How to use a cabinet scraper

To use the scraper, grip it in both hands and place it on the timber, then push it across the surface with your thumbs exerting pressure on the middle of the blade. You can adjust the cut by changing the angle and amount of curve on the blade.

# How to sharpen a cabinet scraper

**1**  With the scraper held in a vice, draw a flat file along the long edge to get it square. Repeat on the opposite edge. Remove the scraper from the vice.

**2**  Hold each face of the blade flat on an oilstone and slide it across the surface to remove the burr. Change the blade position frequently to prevent a groove appearing.

**3**  Hold the scraper flat on the bench top and draw the burnisher firmly along the edge several times. Keep the burnisher flat as well.

**4**  Return the scraper to the vice. Holding the burnisher at about 85 degrees, draw it firmly along the edge of the blade to form a burr. Lean the burnisher towards you for two or three strokes, then away from you to create two separate cutting edges. Repeat the process along the opposite edge.

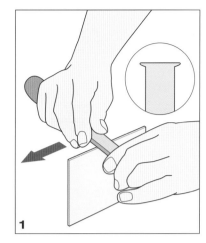

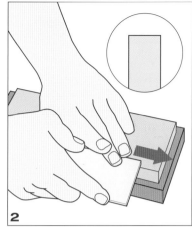

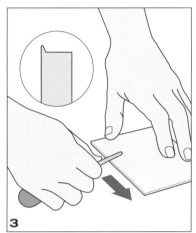

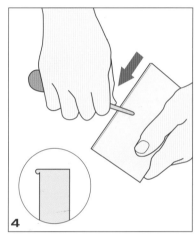

## JARGON BUSTER

**Burnisher**  A straight, hardened steel blade set into a handle for raising the burr on a scraper. It may be oval or circular in section.
**Sole**  The machined face of a spokeshave or plane, which comes into contact with the timber. A spokeshave will have either a flat or curved sole.

Burnisher with hardened steel blade

Straight cabinet scraper

## Further information

Curved cabinet scraper

# Rasps and files

Abrasive tools are useful for shaping both hard and softwoods. Rasps and files come in a variety of sizes and patterns, for rough shaping and fine cutting. Rasps will cut wood and have fairly coarse teeth. Files have rows of finer teeth for wood, metal or plastics. Unlike planes and chisels, the advantage of rasps and files is that you can use them in any direction on wood, irrespective of grain, without the risk of fibres tearing or splintering.

ABOVE A rasp is an efficient way of rapidly shaping timber. Always make sure the tool is fitted with a suitable handle first.

## Rasps

Rasps will smooth out heavy, uneven surfaces quickly, and are powerful tools. Tools with hand-cut teeth are more expensive than machine-cut versions, but the results are better. Teeth are cut with a more random pattern, which mean fewer marks evident on the finished timber, which also tends to be smoother. The most popular type of rasp has a flat side and a half-round side, useful for shaping concave work.

The surform is a more advanced type of rasp with teeth punched from hardened steel plate. Holes in the teeth mean they are less likely to clog up than traditional rasps. Inexpensive and undoubtedly useful, surforms can be used on all sorts of materials, including plastics and non-ferrous metals. They are available in a variety of shapes and sizes, including straight and curved patterns. Blades are replaceable and require no adjustment.

Microplanes are a more recent development, with very efficient blades with razor-sharp teeth. These are interchangeable and make finer cuts than surforms,

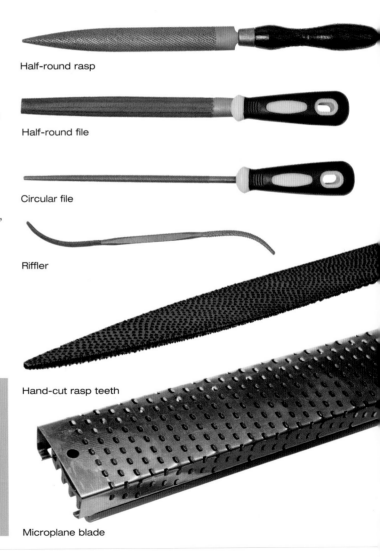

Half-round rasp

Half-round file

Circular file

Riffler

Hand-cut rasp teeth

Microplane blade

### CLEANING RASPS AND FILES

When used on some of the more oily or sappy timbers, such as teak or Scots pine, rasps, rifflers and files have a tendency to clog up with sawdust. A wire brush will help here, or for the more stubborn blockages, a blowtorch. For cleaning files, use a piece of file card.

which tend to be rather coarse. Blades are relatively narrow and more delicate, so more care is needed when using them to prevent them flexing. Various blade patterns are available, from flat to V-groove to half-round.

## Files

A rasp will leave a fairly rough surface, which can be made smoother using a file. A file is less aggressive and will smooth most of the marks made by the rasp. You should regard it as an intermediate step before applying abrasive paper. Teeth extend across the face of a file, unlike a rasp, which has individual teeth. Teeth patterns most suitable for woodworking are single-cut and double-cut. On a single-cut file, teeth extend diagonally across its face, producing a fine surface when cutting using a light touch. On a double-cut file teeth are still diagonal but run in both directions. This pattern cuts faster and produces a rougher surface.

Files are also graded according to the coarseness of cut: coarsest of all is the bastard cut; second cut gives a smoother finish; and smooth cut is the finest of all. You will need files for the odd metalworking task as well as for smoothing wood. Occasionally tool edges need softening or drill-bit shanks become burred. A rectangular single-cut mill file is ideal in these situations, and is a good all-rounder.

Files are often sold as blades without handles. It is important to fit handles to the tangs, however, as this makes these tools safer to use and will give you greater control when working with them. You can make or buy handles to fit.

Needle files are much smaller than conventional files, typically 152 mm (6 in) in length. Good-quality needle files can be used for precise cutting and cleaning up intricate edges that would be impossible to finish with other tools.

## Rifflers

Unlike straight rasps and files, rifflers are S-shaped, with curved faces at either end. Those with coarse teeth have more of a ripping action, and although they can remove heavy bumps, you will still need to finish with finer rasps and files before you can do any work with abrasive paper.

Surform with convex blade

Surform with flat blade

### TIP

• Keep files used for metal away from wood, and vice versa. If not, there is a risk of metal particles becoming embedded in the grain.

### JARGON BUSTER

**Bastard cut**  File with coarse teeth for an aggressive cut.
**Double-cut**  Teeth criss-cross in both directions across the file.
**Second cut**  File with medium teeth.
**Single-cut**  Teeth slope in one direction across the file.
**Smooth cut**  File with fine teeth for the smoothest cut.
**Tang**  The tapered end of a file or rasp, designed to be driven into a handle.

### Further information
Buying tools  pages 72–73
Essential toolkit  pages 74–75
Power sanders  pages 128–130

# 6

# Power tools

Power tools can eliminate much of the drudgery of woodworking – such as sawing up sheet materials and thick boards or planing timber – leaving more time for developing those finer hand-tool skills. With advances in electronics and engineering, both mains-powered and cordless tools are becoming increasingly sophisticated. Ergonomics play a major role, with comfort, vibration and noise levels just as important as safety considerations. Increased competition between brands means that power tools are generally very good value, but do not be tempted to invest in real budget items at the expense of quality and accuracy. The more costly, professional, tools generally offer greater precision, reliability and a longer working life.

# Cordless tools

When cordless tools first arrived on the woodworking scene, they struggled to match the performance of their mains-powered cousins. With developments in battery technology, however, many cordless tools are now just as powerful and are very sophisticated. As well as being safer, with no mains cables trailing, they are also convenient and can be used where there is no power supply.

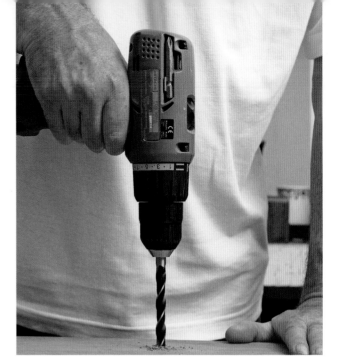

## Battery technology

When cordless technology first became popular, 7.2-volt (v) tools were commonplace, with 9.6 v the reserve of professional units. Voltages then began to creep upwards, with 12-, 14.4- and 15.6-v tools becoming increasingly common. Site workers considered the greater power, performance and run time provided outweighed the corresponding increase in weight. Many manufacturers now regard 18 v as standard for professional equipment, with 24 and 36 v available if you need it.

Batteries consist of several 1.2-v cells linked together, so ratings are multiples of this number (9.6 v, 12 v, 14.4 v and so on). Capacity is measured in amp hours (Ah), which helps determine how long the battery provides power to a tool before it needs recharging. Many nickel batteries will not reach optimum performance until they have been through several charge/discharge cycles. Some batteries have digital displays to show remaining capacity, as well as indicating temperature. Cordless tools are usually sold with at least two batteries.

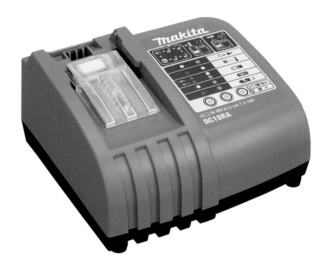

TOP Cordless tools are safer to use than mains-powered equipment, both in the workshop and outdoors.

ABOVE A good battery charger is essential for cordless tools.

## Battery types

Nickel metal hydride (NiMH) batteries are more environmentally friendly than cheaper nickel cadmium (NiCd) power packs and have higher amp-hour ratings (up to 3.5 Ah). NiCd batteries (up to 2.4 Ah) require less sophisticated chargers and will work at much lower temperatures. The downside is they contain cadmium, a toxic metal, and must be recycled.

Historically, cordless NiCd tools suffered from 'memory effect'. Unless the battery was fully discharged, then recharged, capacity would diminish and remaining battery life would be reduced. Simply, it means the battery will not deliver its full capacity. After a long storage period, NiCd batteries tend to discharge themselves and must be recharged before use. Newer lithium ion (Li-ion) batteries are lighter, have no memory effect and suffer far less from negative discharge. It is not necessary to fully recharge a Li-ion battery each time. By comparison, a 28-v Li-ion battery can give up to twice the run time of a more conventional 18-v power pack.

# Chargers

You need a mains supply for the battery charger, although you can power some from a car. Typical recharge time is one hour, and some professional fast chargers take just 15 minutes. More sophisticated diagnostic chargers analyse battery condition and history, and charge accordingly. Most units switch from a fast charge rate to a trickle charge, so you can leave the battery safely in the charge. Some units charge both NiCd and NiMH batteries.

9.6-v drill/driver (NiCd battery)

# Cordless drill/drivers

A drill/driver has a clutch or torque control for driving screws. With 16 or more settings, this allows you to drive a screw flush with the surface of the timber and prevents the screw head becoming stripped. A 9.6-v drill is fine for light maintenance work. A 12-v tool is a good choice for general woodwork, with enough power to drive long screws. An 18-v tool creates more torque for drilling large-diameter holes. Bigger drills are more tiring to hold and more awkward to use in a confined space.

Most drill/drivers have two or three variable speeds, selected by a lever or button on top of the motor housing. Select a low speed with high torque for driving screws or boring large holes. A high-speed range creates lower torque for drilling smaller holes. Use the forward/reverse selector above the trigger to change the spindle direction when driving in screws or removing them.

Keyless chucks are standard, with capacity normally 13 mm (½ in). Single-sleeve chucks have an automatic spindle lock and are tightened with one hand, while double-sleeve chucks need both hands.

Combination drills have a hammer-action mode for drilling masonry, plus a standard rotary drilling action. These tools usually have a detachable side handle for greater control of the drill. There may also be an adjustable-depth rod fitted into this handle for limiting drilling depth.

18-v combination drill (NiMH battery)

# Cordless impact drivers

Designed specifically for driving screws, an impact driver delivers considerable torque (typically 85 Nm) in a tool that is more compact than a standard cordless drill. Typical no-load speed is from 0 to 2800 rpm. Impact drivers range from 9.6 to 18 v and the most powerful tools will drive screws up to M16 in diameter. The ¼ in hex pattern chuck means standard drill bits will not fit, although adaptors are available.

12-v impact driver (Li-ion battery)

# Cordless jigsaws

Excellent for cutting sheet materials to size, cordless jigsaws are powered by batteries between 12 and 24 v. Most tools have a fast blade change system, with cutting capacity around 60 mm (2⅜ in) at 90 degrees. You can tilt the base plate to 45 degrees for bevel cutting. Usually variable speed machines, the stroke rate can be up to 3,000 spm.

18-v jigsaw (NiCd battery)

# Cordless planers

Useful for applying quick chamfers to finished joinery or furniture, cordless planers are handy tools when woodworking away from the workshop. Most come equipped with a pair of reversible carbide knives in the cutter block. Standard planing width is 82 mm (3¼ in), while rebating depth is adjustable up to about 15 mm (⅝ in). Powered typically by batteries up to 18 v, the no-load speed can be up to 13,000 rpm.

14.4-v planer (NiMH battery)

# Cordless circular saws

Handy for cutting timber to size at the sawmill, most cordless saws are powered by batteries up to 24 v. As with a mains-powered saw, you can tilt the base plate to 45 degrees. Blade diameters vary from 140–165 mm (5½–6½ in), giving a cutting capacity of 40–54 mm (1⅝–2⅛ in) at 90 degrees. Thin-kerf blades reduce battery consumption, as there is less metal to pass through the timber. Speed is around 4,000 rpm.

18-v circular saw (NiCd battery)

---

## JARGON BUSTER

**Ah (Amp hour)** Measurement of battery capacity. The higher the Ah rating, the longer the tool will run.

**Kerf** Width of cut produced by the teeth on a saw blade.

**Li-ion** Lithium-ion

**NiCd** Nickel cadmium

**NiMH** Nickel metal hydride

**rpm** revolutions per minute

**spm** strokes per minute

**Stroke length** The distance a jigsaw or reciprocating saw blade moves in and out.

**Torque** Twisting force, measured in Nm.

**v** volts

# Cordless reciprocating saws

Cordless versions of the reciprocating, or sabre, saw make recycling timber or house-renovation work safer, with no power cable to worry about. Batteries are generally 18 v, with one or two variable speeds to around 3,000 spm. Maximum depth of cut can be 90 mm (3½ in) in timber.

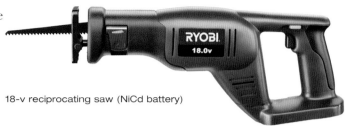

18-v reciprocating saw (NiCd battery)

# Cordless sanders

Most cordless sanders have a delta-shaped base and use hook-and-loop abrasive sheets. Reasonably compact, they can be particularly useful for sanding and finishing in tight corners on completed cabinets and furniture. Batteries rated at 18 v are typical.

# Cordless screwdrivers

Compact, pistol-grip screwdrivers are suitable for fitting hinges and other cabinet hardware. Handles may swivel or be hinged for comfort. Batteries are usually 2.4, 3.6 or 4.8 v, with charge times of up to six hours. You use a direction button to select forward or reverse, with torque collars on the more sophisticated tools. Bits slot into ¼ in hex-pattern chucks, with adaptors for drill bits. Screwdriver bits are sometimes stored on the body of the tool.

18-v corner sander (NiCd battery)

## SCREWDRIVER BITS

Ends of screwdriver bits are hexagonal in section and fit into appropriate chucks. You can insert them into the chuck of an impact driver, but usually require a bit holder for use with a drill/driver. A quick-release holder makes it easy to change from one bit to another rapidly. A variety of screwdriver bits are available, including slotted, cross-headed, torx and hex, in a wide range of sizes. Drill bits with hex fittings are also increasingly available.

**Further information**

14.4-v combination hammer drill/driver

# Power saws

Portable saws are extremely useful both inside and outside the workshop, especially for the woodworker with little in the way of machinery. In a cramped space it may be necessary to cut up sheet materials outdoors. A circular saw is the easiest way for making straight cuts, while a jigsaw is almost essential for curved cutting. Most saws will cut material at least 51 mm (2 in) thick.

ABOVE With a sharp blade fitted to a jigsaw you can make accurate curved cuts in both hardwoods and softwoods.

## Circular saws

Use a circular saw to rip timber to width, cut boards to length and reduce sheet materials to size. A side fence slots into the cast-alloy or steel base plate and is clamped at a chosen ripping width. You can tilt the base plate to 45 degrees for bevel cutting, locked with a lever or thumbscrew. Blade depth is adjustable by raising or lowering the base plate, which usually pivots on the motor housing.

Motors are rated from about 500 watts (w) on basic saws to more than 2,000 w on big, professional tools. Speed is fixed at around 5,000 rpm on smaller saws, down to 3,000 rpm or less on the biggest machines. Most saws have a lock-off button for safety, to prevent accidental start-up. You have to depress this before you can activate the on/off trigger.

### Circular-saw blades

Saw blades are normally TCT and suitable for both man-made boards and solid timber. A combination blade is designed for both ripping and crosscutting, with between 24 and 40 teeth – a good choice for general woodwork.

Most saws incorporate a spindle lock system for blade changing. Use a wrench to release a retaining nut on the blade, while the lock button prevents the spindle from turning. Blade diameters vary from 165–355 mm (6½–14 in), giving a cutting capacity of some 51–127 mm (2–5 in) at 90 degrees. A riving knife behind the blade prevents timber binding on the blade during a cut although, increasingly, circular saws are available without this function. This enables you to cut grooves, as the blade will not have to pass right

through the material. For maximum cutting efficiency you should adjust blade depth so that a full tooth protrudes below the timber thickness.

## Jigsaws

Fitted with a narrow blade, a jigsaw is designed to cut curves to fairly tight radii, if necessary. Although you can use this tool for sawing straight lines as well, the resulting cut will need tidying up unless you are merely converting rough timber. There are two common jigsaw body styles: top (enclosed) handle and body grip. Some manufacturers produce identical models with either body option.

Motors are rated from about 350 w on budget tools up to about 750 w on heavier saws. Most jigsaws are variable speed, either controlled by finger pressure on the on/off trigger, or a built-in dial. Typical range is from 800 to 3,000 spm. A lock-on button means you do not have to keep the trigger squeezed while cutting.

Most jigsaws are now equipped with a fast blade change system. You simply move a spring-loaded lever across to insert the blade. Basic tools may use a either hex key to tighten a locking screw, a screwdriver

**TIP**

• For straight cuts, a batten cramped to the board as a guide is a simple but effective sawing aid.

through the top handle or a locking mechanism built into the handle itself. On most jigsaws the blade moves with an orbital action, which is more efficient than a straight up-and-down movement. It minimizes blade wear and clears sawdust away quickly. Also known as pendulum action, you can normally adjust the amount of orbit by a lever on the side of the tool.

A roller supports the back of the blade when cutting, and professional tools have guides to prevent lateral movement. Cutting capacity at 90 degrees is around 60 mm on basic saws up to 135 mm (2⅜–5¼ in) on professional tools. The stroke length is about 25 mm (1 in). Some jigsaws have a built-in blower device to keep the cutting line free of sawdust. An outlet under the tool allows you to connect a vacuum extractor.

You can tilt the base plate of steel or cast alloy either way for making bevel cuts up to 45 degrees, locked with a lever or hex key. On some jigsaws you can fit a plastic shoe over this to prevent scratching delicate surfaces when cutting. On some models you can insert a plastic anti-splinter shoe in the base plate to prevent laminated surfaces from chipping.

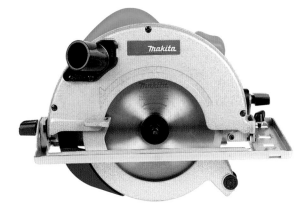

Circular saw

Body grip jigsaw

## Jigsaw blades

Jigsaw blades are available in two types. Most tools are fitted with bayonet blades, while a couple of brands use a universal pattern, tightened with a hex key. They come in a wide range of teeth pattern to suit different materials. Lengths vary from 51–102 mm (2–4 in). Reverse teeth blades are designed for cutting laminate-faced worktops without causing the surface to splinter. You can use TCT blades to cut ceramic tiles, and can also cut mild steel, alloys and non-ferrous metals with the correct blades.

# Reciprocating saws

Most likely to be used for construction and house-renovation work than in the workshop, the reciprocating, or sabre, saw is a specialized cutting tool for timber, sheet materials, metals, plasterboard and plastic. Ideal when sawing up recycled timber, it will cut through embedded nails when fitted with the correct blade. Unlike a jigsaw, you hold a reciprocating with both hands. Its advantage over other power tools is cutting capacity. Fitted with a long, straight blade, it is possible to cut up to 305 mm (12 in) in timber. Rather like a giant jigsaw, there is no fence for guiding straight cuts, although curved cuts are easy to make. The motor is about 1,000 w, with variable speed from 0 to 3,000 spm.

### JARGON BUSTER

**PTFE (Polytetrafluoroethylene)** A material used in industrial applications where sticking must be avoided; also used as coating on cookware.

**rpm** revolutions per minute

**spm** strokes per minute

**Stroke length** The distance a jigsaw or reciprocating saw blade moves in and out.

**TCT (tungsten-carbide tipped)** Circular saw-blade teeth and router bits are usually tipped, remaining sharp longer than high-speed steel (HSS) versions. Better for man-made materials.

**Further information**

# Power drills

The traditional mains-powered electric drill is a good standby for the workshop and general maintenance work. Its real advantage is that it will never run out of power, unlike a cordless drill. For heavy masonry drilling a power drill with hammer action can be unbeatable in terms of power and performance. Mounted in a vertical stand the tool becomes a small-scale pillar drill, capable of boring holes with greater precision.

Electronic impact drill

## Motors

Motors range from 250 w on compact drills up to 1,200 w on heavy-duty impact or percussion tools. A more powerful motor is an advantage for masonry drilling, but the increased weight can make the tool more tiring to hold when drilling timber continuously. Drills may have one or two speeds, the gears selected by a lever or button on top of the motor housing. Two-speed ranges are typically from 0 to 1,000 and 3,000 rpm. For boring large-diameter holes select a low speed with high torque. A high speed creates lower torque when drilling smaller holes. Variable speed is a useful feature, with an adjuster dial built into the power trigger or casing. Squeezing the trigger gently enables you to start drilling a hole slowly while checking for accuracy. A lock-on button keeps the tool running without having to maintain pressure on the trigger. A forward/reverse selector above the trigger is used to change spindle direction when driving in screws or removing them. Unlike cordless drills there is no torque collar, so you cannot adjust screw depth.

## Chucks

Most chucks are keyless, with capacities from 10–16 mm (⅜–⅝ in), although 13 mm (½ in) is most common. Single-sleeve chucks have an automatic spindle lock and are tightened with one hand, while double-sleeve chucks need both hands. Some drills are still fitted with keyed chucks. When inserting a drill bit, always tighten with the key located in at least two of the three holes provided. The key is usually stored on the cable to prevent it becoming lost.

## Special features

Bigger tools usually have a detachable side handle for greater control of the drill. An adjustable-depth rod may be fitted into this handle for limiting drilling depth. Impact drills have a hammer-action mode for drilling masonry, plus standard rotary drilling action. A lever or button enables you to select the correct mode. Typical impact rate can be as much as 58,000 bpm. Only carbide-tipped masonry bits should be used in this mode.

---

### JARGON BUSTER

**bpm** blows per minute. The measurement for impact drilling.
**Chuck** Fitted to the end of the spindle, three self-centring jaws close on the bit when inserted. May be keyless or tightened with a key.
**rpm** revolutions per minute
**SDS (Special Direct System)** A tool-free clamping system.
**w** watts

Mains drill mounted in stand

Ergonomics are important with power drills, where vibration can be a major problem. Handles on many tools feature a soft, rubberized grip to improve comfort and help reduce vibration being transmitted through the user's arm. Lightweight plastic housings, reduced noise levels and improved balance, all reduce fatigue.

## Drill stand

Most electric drills have a 43 mm (1⅞ in) collar, so it is possible to mount the tool in a stand for vertical drilling. Not only does this leave both hands free to guide the work, but holes will be more accurate than when drilling freehand. Screw a piece of MDF or plywood to the stand to prevent drilling into the base accidentally. This will also prevent the work piece from breaking out underneath and makes it easy to attach a fence, which is almost essential for accurate repeat drilling. Cramp or bolt the drill stand to a bench top for added stability.

## SDS hammer drills

Designed for drilling into hard masonry and concrete, an SDS hammer drill uses specialist bits that lock quickly, but securely, into a special chuck. You cannot use these chucks with conventional drill bits. SDS bits have a standard shank that is fitted into a quick-release chuck. Most SDS drills can also be fitted with conventional keyless chucks for using normal drill bits.

### TIPS

• For safety, always plug into an RCD (residual current device) when using any power tool. This will shut off the power instantly in an emergency and prevent electrocution.
• Do not use auger bits (with centre thread) when using a drill stand. The drill will lift the work piece up off the table with potentially disastrous consequences.

### Further information
The work environment  pages 66–67
Health and safety  pages 68–69
Drills  pages 104–105
Cordless tools  pages 120–123
Pillar drills  pages 160–161

# Power sanders

It is not unusual to have several power sanders in the workshop for different tasks. Some are designed to remove stock rapidly, or old finishes using coarse abrasives. Others are built for fine-finishing a surface. You can fit various grades of abrasive, although patterns and sizes are not always standard. Most sanders are fitted with a dust bag or collector box, but it is still wise to wear a dust mask whenever using them.

ABOVE A powered sander is often used when a woodworking project is nearing completion.

## Orbital sanders

An orbital sander's vertical electric motor drives an off-centre shaft, rotating in an eccentric, or oscillating, orbit. The platen is mounted to the tool's housing and vibration is reduced by a counterweight for balance. A rigid rubber, or polyurethane, backing pad is glued to the platen for attaching the abrasive paper. Speeds vary from 6,000 to about 22,000 opm, with motors ranging between 150 and 350 w. A lock-on button near the trigger enables you to leave the tool switched on for continuous sanding. Roughing sanders have an orbit diameter of up to 5 mm (³⁄₁₆ in) – ideal for fast stock removal. With a smaller orbit diameter from 1.5–3 mm (¹⁄₁₆–³⁄₃₂ in), finishing sanders will give a better finish to the timber.

A disadvantage of some orbital sanders is that small swirls can appear across the surface of the timber. These will show up under a clear finish such as varnish, and must be removed by final sanding by hand.

There are two standard sizes of orbital sander, each relating to the size of the abrasive paper required to fit the rectangular platen plate. Half-sheet sanders need paper measuring 280 x 115 mm (11 x 4½ in), while third-sheet sanders need paper measuring 230 x 93 mm (9 x 3⅝ in). A full sheet of abrasive paper measures 280 x 230 mm (11 x 9 in). The machine pads are smaller than the abrasive paper sizes, and allow for tucking the ends of non-hook-and-loop paper under a pair of steel retaining clamps. Many sanders offer both clamps plus the hook-and-loop system.

The action of a rotating fan sucks dust up through holes in the platen and directs it through to an outlet connected either to a dust bag or a vacuum extractor hose. Some orbital power sanders incorporate dust collector boxes with reusable filters. There must be corresponding holes in the abrasive paper for the extraction to work.

### JARGON BUSTER

**opm** orbits per minute
**Orbital** The action of a sanding pad moving around a central point without spinning.
**Platen** The cast-alloy or plastic base plate flexibly mounted to an orbital sander.
**Stock** Prepared timber, planed all round and ready to be worked.
**Tracking** The lateral movement of the belt across the rollers on a belt sander.
**w** watts

### TIPS

• Unbacked abrasive paper is cheaper if you buy it by the roll and cut it to suit your sander. It comes in various widths and lengths.
• When the abrasive on a belt sander begins to clog, hold a rubber cleaner against the surface as it rotates. This unclogs the abrasive, prolonging its life.

# Random orbit sanders

A random orbit sander has a free-running, circular pad positioned off-centre on the motor's drive shaft. It means that the disc moves eccentrically, while also rotating, creating a random motion. This results in fewer swirls as newer rotations cancel out previous scratches. Common disc diameters are 115, 125 or 150 mm (4½, 5 or 6 in). Motors range from 250–600 w, with speeds from 4,500–13,500 opm. Electronic variable speed is common on bigger random orbital sanders. This makes it a good choice for sanding veneered work, with little risk of sanding through if you reduce the speed. Some professional sanders have dual random orbit and more aggressive orbital oscillating action, selected via a lever on the base. All sanding discs are of the hook-and-loop variety, and punched for dust extraction. Fitted with a polishing bonnet, you can use a random orbit tool waxing or buffing finishes.

Orbital sander

Random orbit sander

# Belt sanders

The most aggressive electric sander of them all, the belt sander is the tool for rapid stock removal or preparing recycled timber. A continuous abrasive belt rotates around a pair of rollers, one of which is driven by the motor. This may be mounted in-line or transversely above the belt, ranging from 180 w on budget tools up to 1,200 w on professional sanders. More sophisticated sanders may have variable speed, selected via a thumbwheel. Speeds vary from 250–450 m (800–1,500 ft) per minute.

Paper removal is easy by opening a side lever to release tension on one of the rollers. A new belt is tensioned automatically when the lever is closed again. Some sanders have automatic belt tracking over the rollers, others are adjusted manually with a side knob. Rollers are often slightly cambered to aid central tracking.

Belt widths are 76 and 104 mm (3 and 4 in), the wider machines generally being heavier to use. Some belt sanders can be inverted on the bench top for stationary sanding. It is important when sanding not to keep the tool static, otherwise you will quickly sand a hollow in the timber.

Belt sander

# Palm sanders

A smaller version of an orbital tool, the palm sander is compact and designed for use with one hand. Usually with a ¼-sheet pad size – 114 x 104 mm (4½ x 4 in) – paper may be hook-and-loop or clamped in place. Orbit diameter is similar to a finishing sander at about 1.5 mm (¹⁄₁₆ in). Motors are small at around 200 w, with a single speed of 14,000 opm.

Palm sander

# Detail sanders

With a triangular or delta-shaped sanding pad, a detail sander is ideal for reaching into the corners of assembled cabinets and drawers. Tips tend to wear more quickly than the rest of the sheet, but you can usually rotate the backing easily. Hook-and-loop abrasives mean you can also simply re-attach the paper in a different position. You can fit some detail sanders with narrow pads, rasps, scrapers, cutting tools, polishing pads and even saw blades for cutting thin material. Although unguarded, the oscillating action makes the exposed saw teeth safe in use. With motors at about 200 w, variable speeds up to 21,000 opm are common.

Multi-sander

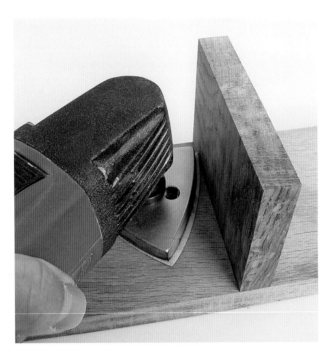

# Multi-sanders

Popular with hobbyists, multi-sanders have larger abrasive pads than detail sanders. Backing pads are interchangeable, so you can use them to sand virtually any surface, whether it is flat, concave or convex. You can substitute an iron-shaped pad for a disc or fit shaped attachments at the front for sanding profiles. Abrasive paper is attached with the hook-and-loop system. Motors are about 150 w, with typical speeds between 11,000 and 24,000 opm.

# Hook-and-loop abrasives

Although more convenient, hook-and-loop abrasives are more expensive to buy than unbacked paper. The advantage is that it is much faster to change from one grade of paper to another, with no cutting or clamps to worry about. Abrasives are normally pre-punched for orbital and random orbital sanders.

LEFT Ideal for sanding in confined spaces, a detail sander has a triangular backing pad which can be swivelled as the tip wears.

BELOW Hook-and-loop abrasive sheets may be very easy to change, but often the shape or dust hole format is exclusive to each manufacturer.

**Further information**

# Power planers

Unlike a static, surface-planing machine or jointer, where timber is passed over the cutters, a power planer enables you to take the tool to the work. This makes it ideal for trimming long boards and the edges of doors and panels, and for reducing stock quickly before final-finishing by hand. You can use it vertically as well as horizontally.

Planer fitted with fence

## Tool basics

Motors are rated between 650 and 850 w, with cutter block speeds of up to 20,000 rpm. You must press a lock-off button before you can activate the on/off trigger. You adjust cutting by rotating a knob at the front of the tool. This raises or lowers the front part of the alloy base in relation to the cutter-block knives. Maximum cutting depth varies between about 1.5 and 4 mm (1/32 and 1/8 in) in one pass. Planing width is generally 82 mm (3¼ in), although heavy industrial tools capable of planing up to 312 mm (12¼ in) are available. The carbide knives are normally reversible. Fitting a side fence enables you to cut rebates, typically to a depth of 25 mm (1 in) on professional tools.

Some planers have a detachable dust bag or collection box. These fill rapidly, so for extended working it is better to connect a vacuum extractor. Other tools have a chip deflector that you can set to eject from either the left or right side.

Most planers have a hinged shoe at the end of the base, which flips down at the end of a cut. This makes it safer to place the tool down on a surface before the cutters have reached a standstill.

## Thicknessing stand

It is possible to fit some planers into an aluminium stand, available as an extra. Mounted upside down the tool becomes a small jointer. You pass timber over the knives just like a surface planer machine, with the fence fixed at 90 degrees or tilted. Mounted the right way up, the tool becomes a small thicknesser. Depth adjustment is possible by raising or lowering the planer. Unlike a thicknessing machine there is no power feed, so you must feed timber through the jig manually. Always use a pushstick to do this.

### TIPS

• It is better to take several shallow cuts rather than make one deep cut.
• Most planers have a hinged shoe at the end of the base, which flips down at the end of a cut. This makes it safer to place the tool down before the cutters have reached a standstill.

### JARGON BUSTER

**Cutter block** A cylindrical steel or aluminium block into which cutting blades are inserted.
**Knives** The removable cutters or blades on a planer or spindle moulder; usually two on a power planer, although some tools have just one spiral.
**Pushstick** A wooden safety device. Prevents fingers getting too close to the moving blade.
**rpm** revolutions per minute
**Stock** Prepared timber, planed all round and ready to be worked.
**w** watts

**Further information**
The work environment  pages 66–67
Health and safety  pages 68–69
Planes  pages 94–99
Cordless tools  pages 120–123
Planers and thicknessers  pages 156–159

# Biscuit jointers

The biscuit jointer excels at making simple butt joints in both sheet materials and solid timber, but relies on edges being planed straight and square. A rotating blade plunges into the material, producing a curved slot – horizontally, vertically or at angles up to 90 degrees, set by adjusting the front fence. You make a second slot in the matching component, glue a biscuit between them and cramp together. Most jointers have a horizontal motor and body rather like an angle grinder. Less common are tools with a pivoting body, where the cutter is vertical, making it easier to cut grooves along the edges of boards with a side fence.

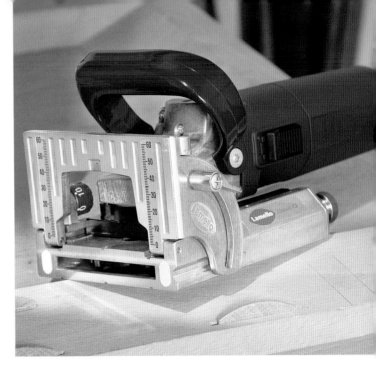

ABOVE The biscuit jointer is a fast, efficient way of jointing timber and sheet materials. Hinged and temporary joints are also possible.

## Tool basics

The motor is rated between about 500 and 700 w, with an on/off trigger at the side, underneath or on top of the body. A second handle is mounted at the front of the tool. Cutter diameter is 100 mm (approximately 4 in), usually with six TCT teeth, rotating at a speed of about 10,000 rpm. Concealed inside an alloy casing, the teeth are only exposed when you push the body of the tool forwards into the work piece. This plunge action is spring loaded, so the cutter withdraws immediately you release pressure at the end of the cut.

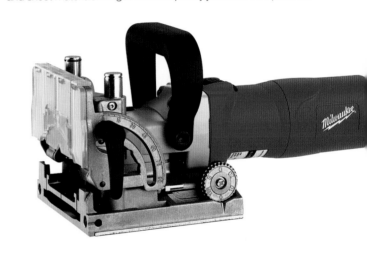

Horizontal motor biscuit jointer

Most machines have several preset depth settings that correspond with common biscuit sizes. You simply rotate the dial to match the biscuit and the cutter slot depth is set automatically. The front fence can be quite sophisticated, with reference marks to line up the tool with pencil marks on the timber. You can tilt the fence for making cuts at any angle between 0 and 90 degrees, with indexing at 45 degrees. This makes mitred edges just as straightforward to joint as square edges. To suit the material thickness you are jointing, you can raise or lower the fence relative to the cutter. It is important to locate the slot centrally in the edge of thin boards. Most jointers are supplied with a dust bag, although it is possible to connect an extractor hose instead.

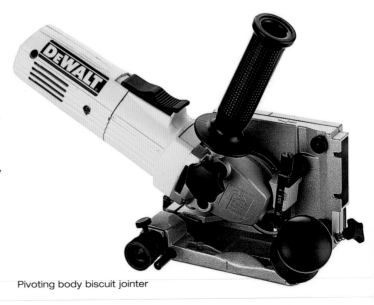

Pivoting body biscuit jointer

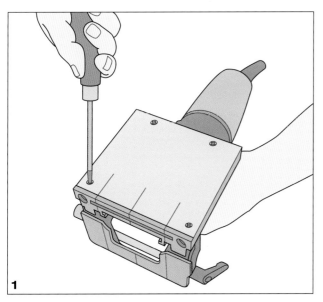

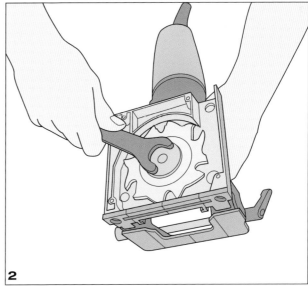

## How to change a blade

**1** Remove the base plate of the tool to access the cutter. You may need a screwdriver or the tool may have a thumbscrew, which is faster to release.

**2** Remove the blade. You normally do this using a wrench supplied with the tool in conjunction with a spindle lock button.

### Further information
The work environment  pages 66–67
Health and safety  pages 68–69
Biscuit joints  pages 200–201

## BISCUIT ASSORTMENT

There are three popular sizes of hardwood biscuit available to suit different thicknesses of material. The bigger S6 and smaller H9 biscuits are less common.

| Biscuit | Dimensions |
|---|---|
| No. 0 | 47 x 15 x 4 mm (1⅞ x ⅝ x ⅛ in) |
| No. 10 | 53 x 19 x 4 mm (2³⁄₃₂ x ¾ x ¼ in) |
| No. 20 | 56 x 23 x 4 mm (2⁷⁄₃₂ x ¾ x ⅛ in) |
| S6 | 85 x 30 x 4 mm (3⅜ x 1¼ x ⅛ in) |
| H9 | 38 x 12 x 3 mm (1½ x 1⁵⁄₃₂ x ³⁄₃₂ in) |

Specialist plastic biscuits can be inserted where the joint must be free from glue. These have barbs to ensure a tight fit in the slot. Aluminium biscuits are hooked, allowing you to take a joint apart – for example on a screen or radiator cabinet. Curved brass hinges match the curve of the cutter and can be used as decorative fittings on boxes.

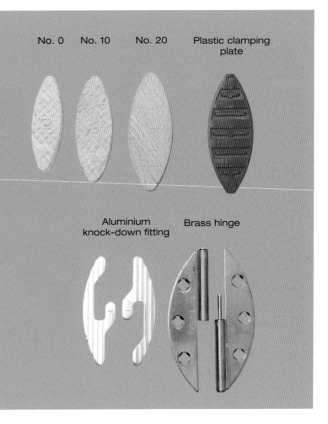

No. 0    No. 10    No. 20    Plastic clamping plate

Aluminium knock-down fitting    Brass hinge

# Routers

The fact that an electric router can accept so many different-shaped cutters makes it the most versatile and indispensable power tool in the workshop. Its invention has revolutionized woodworking, making it possible for even a relatively unskilled person to cut mouldings, shape components, rout housings and other joints, and carry out various other tasks that required a host of hand tools in the past.

ABOVE A versatile power tool, the plunge router can be used freehand above the work or mounted upside down in a table.

The router is, in effect, a small machining centre used for a wide range of cutting and shaping tasks, both in solid timber and sheet materials. You can use it freehand – guided with a side fence for straight cuts – or with bearing-guided cutters for curved work. Unlike other power tools, the router is only restricted by the creativity and imagination of the user. Both proprietary and workshop-built jigs increase its potential enormously.

## Tool basics

A plunge router consists of a powerful motor suspended above two steel columns. These are attached to a base plate and allow the motor to move up and down on springs. A collet at the base of the motor accepts interchangeable cutters, also called router bits (see pages 137–138). The cutter rotates at high speed and can be lowered into the timber by pressing down on the motor against the springs in the columns. Alternatively, it can be set at a fixed position and entered into the wood sideways. Handles on each side help you guide the tool.

Many workshops have at least two routers, so that one machine can be left set up for a particular job. A small router with ¼ in collet is an ideal first purchase, enabling you to develop routing skills while controlling the tool easily. A heavy-duty router with ½ in collet is more powerful and capable of making bigger cuts. It can produce large mouldings – for example, a raised and fielded panel for a door. Less manageable than a small machine, developments such as soft-start electronics make these routers easier to control than early models. Mid-range routers fall between these two categories.

Lightweight ¼ in router

Heavy duty ½ in router

## Motors, speeds and switches

The motor on a small, ¼ in router may only be around 750 w. On a big, heavy-duty machine it may be 2,000 w. Most routers are equipped with electronic variable speed, controlled by a dial. Speed range is typically from 8,000 to 30,000 rpm. Select low speeds for large-diameter cutters, and high for small bits. Many routers have sophisticated electronics, offering soft start and maintaining a constant speed under load. Some bigger machines have electronic braking. On/off switches vary: some routers have a simple up/down slider button, while others may have a double-action trigger built into one of the handles. This is a safety feature, so the router can only be activated when you are gripping the handle correctly. Although accidental start-up is less likely, this type of switch is more awkward to use when the router is inverted in a table.

Plunge base without motor

## Collets and cutter change

The collet tapers slightly and is secured with a nut. When you insert the shank of the cutter, you use a wrench in conjunction with a spindle-lock mechanism to tighten the nut. Usually a push button at the base of the motor housing, this prevents the motor spindle from rotating. Older routers may use a pair of wrenches for tightening instead. Collet sizes are ¼ in and ½ in, with 6 mm, 8 mm, ⅜ in, 10 mm and 12 mm less common. Cutter shanks match these sizes. Bigger routers usually come with two or three interchangeable collets.

Although metric and Imperial sizes appear to be almost identical, never attempt to mix the two when it comes to router cutters. A ¼ in collet is actually bigger than a 6 mm collet. The same applies to ½ in and 12 mm collets. If a cutter shank will not slide easily into a particular collet, do not force it. Conversely, if too loose the cutter cannot be tightened properly and is unsafe.

It is important to keep collets and shanks clean. Remove the locking nut and collet occasionally and check for corrosion. Remove debris carefully with a fine brass brush designed for the task. Cutter shanks can be sprayed with a rust inhibitor and dry lubricant.

Fixed base with motor fitted

**TIP**

• Clean resin build-up on cutters by soaking in white spirit, then rubbing them carefully with a fine brush.

½ in collet    ¼ in collet    Collet with locking nut

Basic steel fence for small router

Cast alloy fence with fine adjuster

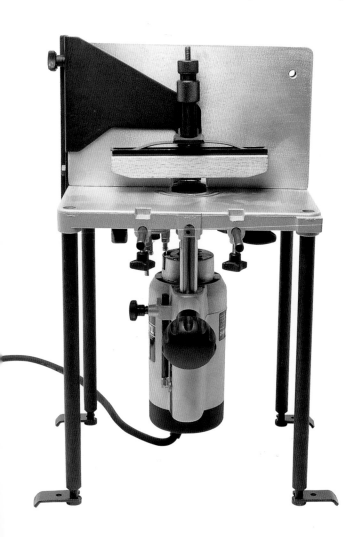

Router inverted in stand

## Router bases

Most routers have a spring-loaded or plunge base, so that you can plunge the cutter downwards into the work. You can lock this, either with a lever or by twisting one of the side handles. On completing the cut, you raise the cutter again. Most bases are cast alloy and may have a thin plastic plate to aid movement across the work and also to prevent scratching of delicate surfaces. Bases may be circular, D-shaped or have two parallel edges. Threaded holes enable you to bolt the base into a table or screw it to various jigs. A cutout in the centre enables the cutter to pass through when plunging.

Fixed bases are found on some professional routers, giving greater precision when setting cutting depth. With handles closer to the timber the centre of gravity is lower, making the machine easier to control. A disadvantage for some routing procedures is that you must tilt the machine to start the cut and lift it off again afterwards. Some heavy-duty routers come with interchangeable plunge and fixed bases. You simply withdraw the motor unit from one collar and lock into the second one. With this option you could leave the fixed base permanently mounted upside down in a table, removing the router quickly for overhead routing work.

## Depth adjustments

To determine cutting depth, plunge routers have a locking system for the plunge mechanism. In its simplest form, you lock an adjustable metal rod in place. As you plunge the router down, the end of the rod hits a fixed stop on the base plate. Many routers have a rotating depth turret, with three or more adjustable stops. It is possible to set two or three exact cutting depths by rotating this to the desired position. More sophisticated routers have a built-in fine adjuster as well. Once you have set the cutter depth, this can be fine-tuned if necessary by rotating a knob or dial.

## Plunge capacity

This is the maximum depth the motor unit (and cutter) will plunge. This may be around 51 mm (2 in) on a small router, up to 80 mm (3⅛ in) on a bigger machine. When plunging to a predetermined depth, you can lock this setting either with a lever or by twisting one of the handles.

## Fences

A guide fence made from cast alloy or pressed steel enables you to cut parallel to a straight edge. It is attached to a pair of steel rods that pass through the base, which is locked in position at the required distance. A fine-adjuster wheel built into the fence simplifies precise setting for width.

## Router tables

Mounted upside down in a table, the router becomes a small-scale spindle moulder and can provide greater accuracy than using the tool freehand. The cutter protrudes above the table and you feed timber across the top, either against a fence or attached to a template. Some stands rely on the fence guide rods to position the router correctly. On other stands you may simply bolt the router in place or clamp it with brackets. Some tables have a channel for a sliding mitre fence, enabling you to carry out tenons and other end-grain routing tasks. You normally remove the fence when routing with a template, so the complete top of the table can be used. There is usually a dust outlet at the back of the fence to connect an extractor.

When using a router upside down in a table the power switch must be accessible. Some machines require a clamp around the power trigger to keep it locked on while making a cut. The safest option is to plug the router into a separate NVR switch, which you can mount below the table. In this way the machine can be left switched on, but still operated independently. Always use safety guards provided with the table, and a pushstick for feeding timber past the cutter.

## Dust extraction and safety

Routers eject a lot of waste material as they cut and will soon cover a workshop in chips, as well as the operator. Some tools have clear plastic shields that clip into place on the base to restrict chip ejection. They also incorporate dust outlets for connecting to a vacuum extractor hose. Other routers have a swivel outlet built into the top of one of the plunge columns. When routing MDF in particular, wear a dust mask or respirator. Eye protection should always be worn as well as ear defenders.

## Laminate trimmers

Although designed primarily for trimming plastic laminate flush with the edge of a board, laminate trimmers make handy small-scale routers for edging work. Easy to control for cutting inlay grooves, adding profiles or forming housings for hinges, you grip the tool in just one hand. Although these tools do not have a fence, an adjustable L-shaped guide with roller runs against the edge of the timber below the cutter. This makes it easy to follow a convex or concave curve without having to use a bearing-guided cutter. With

6 mm, 8 mm or ¼ in collets, laminate trimmers will accept standard router bits, although overall cutter diameter is limited. Some models have spindle locking, while others need two wrenches for locking the bit in the collet. Some trimmers have a tilting base for angled cutting. Motors are comparatively small at around 350–600 w, with variable speed options up to about 35,000 rpm.

## Router cutters

Router cutters, or bits, come in a huge range of shapes and sizes: straight bits for dimensioning timber and cutting joints such as housings, rebates and tenons,

Laminate trimmer with fence for edge banding

Laminate trimmer fitted with bearing-guided cutter and dust extraction hose

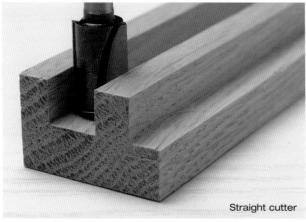

Straight cutter

Bearing-guided chamfer cutter

Dovetail cutter

V-groove cutter

Bearing-guided Roman ogee cutter

Bearing-guided rounding-over cutter

and shaped profile cutters to create decorative mouldings, usually along the edges of timber.

Bearing-guided bits enable the cutter to follow a curved or straight edge consistently. A roller bearing may be located above or below the profile edge, and is usually secured with a hex key. There is no need to use the guide fence for straight cutting, as long as you cut the edge dead straight to begin with.

Cutting edges are usually either HSS or TCT. While the former are sharper and give a better finish on softwoods, the latter hold their edge far longer but are less sharp. Although more expensive than HSS, always use TCT bits on man-made boards, which tend to be quite abrasive.

Router cutters vary enormously in price. For occasional work a cheap boxed set of assorted bits may be fine. The quality is not likely to be as high as more expensive cutters, which will be better made and stay sharp for longer. Because of the cost, it is usual to buy these cutters individually as and when you need them. Large-diameter profile cutters, above approximately 51 mm (2 in) should only be used with the router mounted in a table. TCT bits can be honed lightly with a small hand-held diamond stone, but it's best to send them to a saw doctor for professional sharpening.

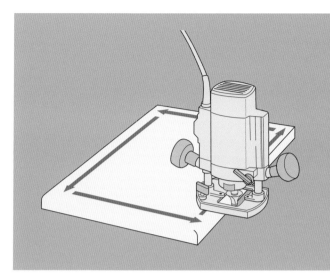

## DIRECTION OF CUT

The router cutter rotates clockwise when viewed from above. It is important when routing outer or inner edges to move the tool in the correct direction. Fed the wrong way, a router can wrench forward and become difficult to control. In theory, the router should move anti-clockwise around the outside of a panel, and clockwise for internal edges. Depending on the timber, however, this may lead to tearout in the grain. Reversing the cutting direction will improve the quality of the cut, but will demand careful control of the router.

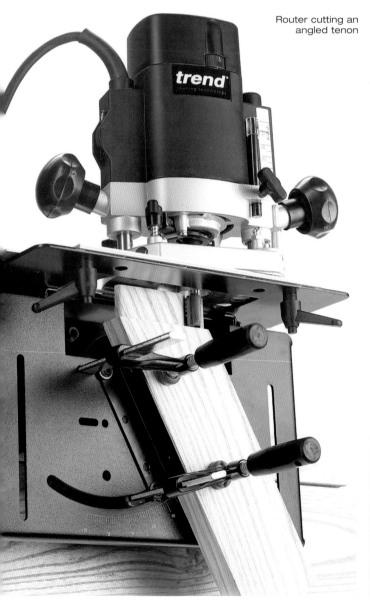

Router cutting an angled tenon

# Router tools and jigs

There are more accessories and jigs available to extend the capability of the router than for any other power tool. Most are primarily templates for producing various joints in both solid timber and sheet materials. A joint that may take considerable time and skill to cut with hand tools can be produced in a few minutes with an appropriate jig and router.

## Mortise and tenon jigs

This jig enables you to rout the end of a work piece to create a tenon and matching mortise. You machine both mortise and tenon with the same jig by using interchangeable plates in conjunction with a guide bush on the router. Clamp the timber vertically, either at 90 degrees to the cutter or at an angle. Compound angles are also possible. This tool is ideal for furniture-making.

### JARGON BUSTER

**Collet** Split, tapered sleeve that grips the cutter shank. Retained by a locking nut on the end of the motor spindle.

**Guide bush** A steel collar screwed to the router base, enabling the tool to follow a template. The cutter passes through the middle.

**HSS** High-speed steel

**Jig** A proprietary or workshop-built device that enables a power tool or machine to cut or shape a timber component accurately and safely.

**TCT** Tungsten-carbide tipped

**Tearout** Wood fibres tend to lift and break when planing timber in the wrong direction, or against the grain.

ABOVE A dovetail template enables precise and consistent dovetails to be machined with a router.

BELOW More elaborate jigs can be used to make sloping, sliding and bevelled dovetails, finger joints and mortise-and-tenon joints.

# Dovetail jigs

Most dovetail jigs consist of a horizontal rail system that you clamp over the end of a board held in the vice. On this you place the dovetail template, which consists of a series of fixed or adjustable fingers. With a guide bush fitted to the router base, you guide the tool between these fingers, usually at equal intervals across the end grain. You can set appropriate dovetail and matching straight cutters to cut at a precise depth to cut the tails and pins.

Some basic jigs will only produce lapped dovetail joints, while more sophisticated versions will cut through and sliding dovetails, multiple mortise and tenon and finger joints. You can vary the spacings on more expensive jigs, to give more of a hand-cut look to the finished joint. Maximum panel width can be up to 610 mm (24 in), while basic jigs may only accommodate boards up to 305 mm (12 in) wide. Timber thickness is restricted on most jigs to a minimum of 13 mm (½ in) and a maximum of 25 mm (1 in).

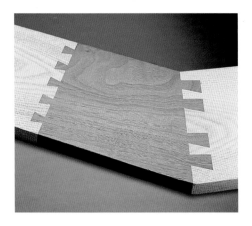

**Further information**

The work environment  pages 66–67
Health and safety  pages 68–69
Essential toolkit  pages 74–75
Workcentres  page 141
Combination machines  pages 166–167
Machine safety  page 169
Joints  pages 190–219

## WOODRAT

The unique Woodrat is a comprehensive machining centre. Fitted with a suitable router, it can cut an infinite variety of joints. It will rout tenons, mortises and dovetails as well as cut profiles, dowelling and carry out pin routing. Unlike a router table, where the tool is inverted, here the router remains upright, so it is easy to see precisely where the bit cuts. Ideally fixed to the wall, horizontal aluminium beams support a mounting plate for the router. You clamp the work piece in place easily, either vertically or horizontally. Instead of following a fixed template, the router can remain stationary or be fed across the timber. A manually-operated power feed moves the timber sideways beneath the rotating cutter when the router is stationary.

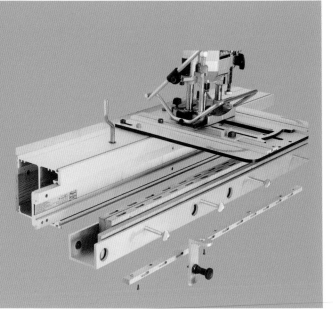

# Workcentres

With a workcentre you can fit various power tools in a table leaving both hands free to guide the timber over or under a sawblade or router cutter. This offers greater accuracy and control, especially when working with large sheet materials or lengths of timber. A cost-effective but inferior alternative to dedicated woodworking machines, tools can be removed for hand-held use.

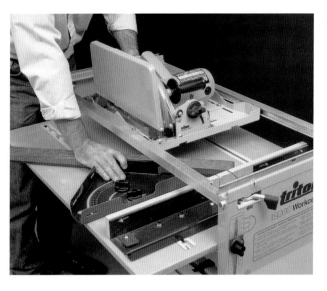

ABOVE A workcentre is ideal if you do not have the space or budget for separate machines.

## Using a workcentre

Although circular saws and routers are most commonly fitted to workcentres, you can also mount jigsaws, faceplate sanders and planers with the correct accessories. You normally fit the power tool to a universal mounting plate, which accepts most routers and circular saws. For best results the bigger diameter the saw blade, the better. You can then position this plate quickly in the workcentre, with the tool either above or below the timber to be machined.

## Sawing on a workcentre

When you mount a saw upside down, the workcentre becomes a table saw. An adjustable fence enables you to rip timber and sheet materials. A sliding-mitre fence makes crosscutting and angled sawing possible, while you can tilt the saw blade over to cut compound mitres. With the saw fixed above the timber in overhead mode, you can use it for crosscutting and grooving, simply by sliding the tool along parallel guide rails. The timber sits on a lower table that you can raise or lower for height, making tenons and housings possible. An adjustable stop enables you to machine timber at angles between 45 and 90 degrees.

## Routing on a workcentre

Mounted upside down, a router becomes a small spindle moulder. With the fence in place you can cut grooves, housings, tenons and rebates with a straight cutter. Insert a profile cutter and you can mould edges. For routing several identical components, either tape or cramp them together. For template routing, remove the fence and use bearing-guided cutters. A router can also be mounted above the workcentre for overhead machining work. The tool can either be used in a stationary position with the timber travelling underneath, or it can slide in the cradle. This is useful for producing housings and grooves.

## Safety

Always use the crown guard and riving knife when using the workcentre as a table saw. Use a pushstick when ripping timber or panels. Before switching on a saw when positioned for overhead cutting, make sure that the blade will not come into any part of the workcentre. Fit an NVR switch to the machine if it does not already have one. Not only is this safer, but it makes switching a power tool on and off far easier.

### TIP
• When machining several components to the same dimensions, always cut one or two spares. Then you will not have to set up the machine again for a replacement if one gets damaged.

**Further information**
The work environment  pages 66–67
Health and safety  pages 68–69
Combination machines  pages 166–167
Machine safety  page 169

# 7

# Machines

Although a woodworker may own several portable power tools, stationary workshop machines are unrivalled when it comes to timber preparation and accuracy. Rather than the material supporting the tool, the machine supports the timber, leaving both hands free to guide the work. With capacities that can handle bigger timber sizes, heavy build quality often includes cast-iron tables for stability and accuracy, and large fences to guide the timber or sheet material. Most domestic workshops will have a 230-volt (v), single-phase power supply, although many bigger machines are available in 415-v, three-phase options.

# Table saws

The powerhouse in many cabinet-making and joinery workshops, the table saw is one of the most useful woodworking machines. It enables you to make precision cuts, either ripping timber to width along the grain or crosscutting to length. Accurate mitre cuts are easy to make with a sliding fence or carriage, while you can also achieve compound by tilting the blade. Large-dimension or panel saws are designed to handle full-size sheet materials, creating a very clean cut. A table saw produces a cleaner cut than a band saw and, fitted with the right TCT blade, can produce a cut almost as smooth as that made by a plane.

Table saw fitted with an extension table

## Machine basics

A table saw is mounted on a steel cabinet, which houses the motor. An adjustable rip fence is mounted on the fixed table to the right of the blade. The sliding table on the left allows you to carry out precise crosscutting. The blade is mounted on a rise-and-fall arbor for adjusting the height of the blade above the table. For bevel cutting, the arbor enables you to tilt the blade up to 45 degrees in relation to the table.

## Motor and controls

Budget table saws may be equipped with brush motors. They are less powerful and noisier than induction motors, which are built to run for longer periods. Induction motors are generally fitted to heavier, more professional machines. These are often available as three-phase or single-phase. Motor rating is from about 1,000–2,000 w on small machines, while heavier saws may be 3,000 w or more. Activated by a simple on/off button or switch with a large, easy-to-reach emergency stop button. Separate power isolator switches are normal on professional saws. On a cabinet saw, the motor is supported on cast-iron trunnions.

## Table

A heavy, cast-iron table provides greater rigidity and less vibration than one made from steel or extruded aluminium. On some machines a groove in the table accepts a basic mitre fence for accurate crosscutting. The mitre angle required is read off the protractor scale and the fence locked with a thumbscrew. A removable insert surrounds the blade and gives support to the material being sawn. You remove this from the table to provide access for changing the blade. On some machines the insert is hardwood, so can be replaced easily as it wears.

## Ripsawing timber

The rip fence must lock firmly to the front bar for accurate ripsawing. You adjust the cutting width by releasing and sliding the fence across. A fine adjuster built into the handle enables you to tweak the width setting if necessary. You should be able to reduce the effective length of the fence by sliding it back from the saw blade when cutting solid timber. On sheet materials, slide the fence past the blade to support the edge of the material.

## Crosscutting timber

A simple sliding mitre fence should fit snugly into its slot in the table. Too much play will cause inaccurate cuts. For more precise crosscutting and mitres, some saws are fitted with sliding tables, which can be locked in place for ripsawing. A holdfast ensures that timber is secure and will not move while passing through the blade. A hinged stop is normally fitted to the crosscutting fence, which has a graduated scale. You simply slide the stop along the rail to the measurement required and hold the timber against it while cutting. Indexing pins for the rail at 90 degrees (and often 45 degrees) enable you to make accurate repeat cuts without having to check the angle each time.

## Blade

Blade diameters range from 203 mm (8 in) on small hobby machines up to 406 mm (16 in) on industrial saws. A 254 mm (10 in) table saw is capable of a cutting depth of about 76 mm (3 in) at 90 degrees, so it can do most of the work required in a small workshop with great accuracy. Tilted to 45 degrees, depth of cut is reduced, however.

BELOW A table saw is the easiest way to cut boards accurately. A roller stand or extension table at the rear supports the material.

### JARGON BUSTER

**Crosscutting** Sawing across the direction of the grain.
**Crown guard** Adjustable steel or plastic safety cover above the saw blade.
**Kerf** Width of cut produced by the blade teeth.
**Kickback** When a work piece is ejected from a machine towards the operator by a rotating cutter or blade.
**Ripsawing (ripping)** Cutting parallel to the grain of the timber.
**Riving knife** A curved steel plate fixed behind the blade to prevent timber closing up and pinching as it passes through. Slightly less than kerf width but wider than blade thickness.
**Set** Saw teeth are alternately bent slightly to one side of the blade, then the other. The resulting cut (kerf) is wider than the blade itself.
**TCT** Tungsten-carbide tipped
**Trunnion** A casting on which the band saw table is mounted, enabling it to tilt. Usually incorporates a protractor scale to set the angle accurately.

Most table saws are fitted with TCT blades, which should only be re-sharpened by a saw doctor. Patterns vary from simple positive-hook teeth to trapezoidal, triple-chip designs for cutting plywood. The number of teeth per blade varies from a few as 16 for coarse ripping up to 100 or more for extremely fine finishing cuts in veneered boards. For general-purpose ripping and crosscutting in timber and sheet materials, a medium blade with about 48 teeth is suitable.

Behind the blade, a riving knife prevents timber from closing up and binding as it passes through the saw. An adjustable crown guard is fitted to this guard or to a pillar bolted at one corner of the table. If you remove the crown guard, never use the machine without making a jig of some sort to enclose the teeth. Hand wheels on the front of the machine enable you to raise and lower the blade and to tilt it from 90 to 45 degrees. For clean cutting you should adjust the blade so that teeth are protruding just above the timber.

## Sliding carriage

Many mid-size and bigger table saws can be fitted with a sliding carriage, bolted on as an extra. The table may be extruded aluminium or cast iron and will support bigger panels and longer lengths of timber than a smaller sliding table. A sliding carriage will add considerably to the footprint of the machine, however.

ABOVE The left blade is a thin kerf, ripsaw blade with 42 teeth. On the right is a fine-finish blade with 96 teeth, used for cutting melamine boards.

## Scoring blades

A large panel saw is generally fitted with a scoring blade, about 102 mm (4 in) in diameter. Located in front of the main saw blade, it provides a cleaner cut on sheet materials that would normally chip underneath, such as veneered or melamine-faced boards. The blade is raised so that the teeth pre-cut the material just above the table surface, in line with the main blade behind. On some table saws it may be necessary to reduce the size of the main saw blade in order to accommodate a scoring blade as well.

A sliding carriage for precision crosscutting of sheet materials

# Bench-top saws

If space in the workshop is really tight, you can mount a compact, portable saw on the bench top and store it out of the way when not needed. Instead of cast iron, the table is cast aluminium, while the body is heavy-duty moulded plastic, making the machine light enough to be used outdoors or even loaded into a car.

Blade diameter is generally 254 mm (10 in), making the saw capable of cutting 76 mm (3 in) timber. Motors are rated from about 1,600 w upwards. Although primarily a ripsaw, small-scale crosscutting and mitre cutting are also possible.

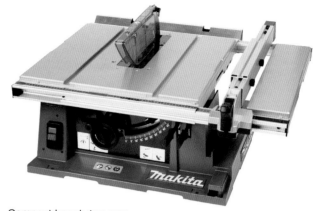

Compact bench-top saw

# Site saws

A basic saw bench, the site, or contractor's, saw is mainly used for ripping timber with the grain. The table is normally galvanized steel to prevent rust and steel legs make it reasonably portable. Some even come with a built-in folding stand and wheels.

# Hybrid saws

With much sturdier build quality than a site saw, a hybrid saw is mounted on legs so is less enclosed than a normal cabinet saw and more compact. An optional mobile base makes it easy to move around in a small workshop. A moving, cast-iron table is built in, although sliding carriages are optional. This table normally has slots either side of the blade for a mitre fence. A substantial rip fence is standard, often with a fine adjuster. Auxiliary side tables may be steel, rather than cast iron.

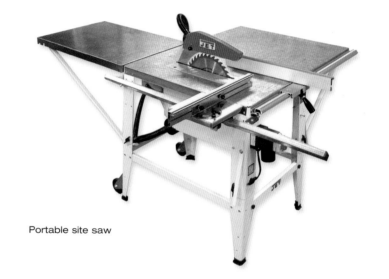

Portable site saw

**Further information**
Workshop layout  pages 60–61
The workbench  pages 64–65
Saws  pages 88–93
Power saws  pages 124–125
Standalone versus combination machines
  page 168
Machine safety  page 169

Hybrid saw

# Radial arm saws

The radial arm saw is designed for accurate crosscutting, mitre and bevel sawing. Both the saw head and motor are suspended on a rigid horizontal arm above the table. Raising or lowering the arm adjusts the depth of cut. A familiar machine in the joinery workshop, the radial arm saw cuts joints such as tenons, rebates and housings precisely. Unlike the table saw, timber is stationary while being sawn, held against a rear fence. The machine is normally positioned against a wall, so it is usual to build long, narrow tables either side to support the timber being sawn. They may even include rollers to help slide heavy boards into position.

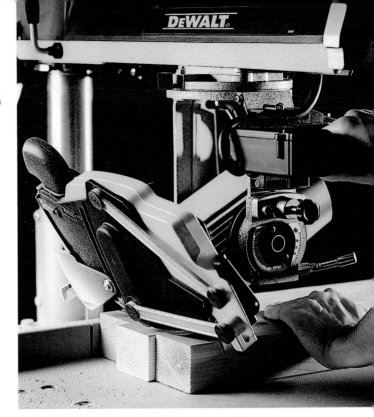

ABOVE Compound mitre cuts are precise with a radial arm saw. You can tilt the blade as well as pivot it at almost any angle.

---

**JARGON BUSTER**

**Crosscutting** Sawing across the direction of the grain.

**Kickback** When a work piece is ejected from a machine towards the operator by a rotating cutter or blade.

**Pushstick** A wooden or plastic safety device used to push narrow or small components past the blade on a saw. Prevents fingers getting too close to the moving blade.

**Ripsawing (ripping)** Cutting parallel to the grain of the timber.

**Riving knife** A curved steel plate fixed behind the saw blade to prevent timber closing up and pinching as it passes through the blade. Slightly less than kerf width but wider than blade thickness.

**rpm** revolutions per minute

**TCT** Tungsten carbide tipped

**w** watts

---

## Machine basics

The machine is normally mounted on a sturdy stand, but can also be bolted to a purpose-built unit. You should fit a sacrificial board (such as MDF) to the table: the saw blade cuts into the surface about 2 mm ($\frac{1}{16}$ in) when it makes a crosscut or mitre cut, and the more angles and bevel cuts you make, the more this board starts to disintegrate and needs replacing.

To make a cut you simply grip the handle and pull the blade across the table. A spring ensures the saw head returns when the cut is completed. A lower guard encloses the blade until you begin to pull the saw head outwards, when it opens up to expose enough of the rotating blade to suit the depth of timber being cut. It then retracts automatically at the end of the cut. An adjustable guard is located in front of the blade below the handle. To adjust blade height, you rotate a cranked handle or knob at the rear, which raises the arm via a rack-and-pinion action. The blade parks automatically behind the fence at the end of a crosscut pass.

Induction motors fitted to radial arm saws are fairly quiet and rated between approximately 1,500 and 2,000 w. The blade rotates at about 3,000 rpm. The on/off switch is located conveniently at the front of the arm.

Blade diameter is between about 254 and 350 mm (10 and 13¾ in). Cutting depth is around 68 mm (2$\frac{11}{16}$ in) at 90 degrees on smaller saws, up to 110 mm (4⅜ in) on industrial machines.

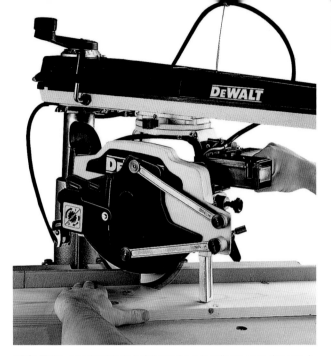

ABOVE The rotating blade is fully enclosed until you start the cut. A replaceable sacrificial board is necessary to support the timber.

## Crosscutting and ripping timber

Crosscutting capacity is determined by the length of the arm. It varies from about 380 mm (15 in) on a small saw up to 610 mm (24 in) on bigger machines. For repeat cutting, clamp an offcut to the fence to act as a length stop. You can rotate the saw head through 90 degrees for ripping timber or panels to width, although this is less satisfactory than using a table saw. In this mode the saw blade is parallel to the rear fence, which guides the timber as you saw. You adjust the width by sliding the head along the arm and locking in position. Most radial arm saws will cut panels at least 610 mm (24 in) wide, or half a standard-size sheet.

A riving knife is lowered behind the blade when ripping. When you revert to crosscut mode, the knife is raised and stored inside the blade guard. To prevent timber being thrown back if the blade jams, anti-kickback pawls are provided. Fitted on an adjustable arm in front of the blade, lower them to make contact with the work piece, and raise them clear of the timber when crosscutting. Always use a pushstick when ripping material.

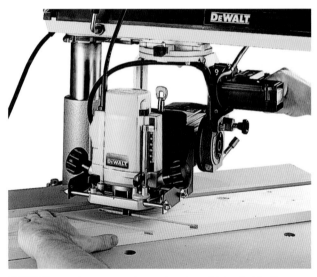

ABOVE To create an accurate overhead machining facility, fit a router into a cradle, which moves along the arm or is stationary.

BELOW You can add a drum sander attachment, ideal for finishing curved work, by rotating the motor vertically and locking in position.

## Mitre and bevel cuts

Indexing at 90 degrees and 45 degrees makes it straightforward to saw at these common angles by swinging the arm around and locking with a clamping lever. A protractor scale at the rear of the machine enables you to lock the arm at any angle to the right or left of the centre (90 degree) position. For bevel cuts, you tilt the saw head over and lock in place. Again, indexing at 90 degrees and 45 degrees is normal.

### Further information
Workshop layout  pages 60–61
Table saws  pages 144–147
Mitre saws  pages 150–151
Machine safety  page 169

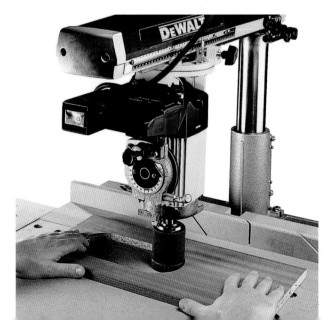

# Mitre saws

Sometimes referred to as a chop saw because of its fast, pivoting saw action, this portable machine excels at making accurate mitre, bevel and crosscuts. Although timber sizes are limited on some machines, the introduction of the sliding mitre saw has considerably increased cutting capacities. On this machine trenching cuts are possible, the saw head sliding horizontally in a similar way to the radial arm saw.

Sliding mitre saw

## Machine basics

On a sliding mitre saw the head moves horizontally on steel rails, enabling you to saw wide material. The blade pivots downwards when making a normal cut and can be locked along the rails at any point. Depth of cut is adjustable so you can set the blade to make uniform trenching cuts across the timber.

The base of the machine is usually constructed from cast alloy, making it relatively lightweight but sturdy. A curved front apron includes a useful protractor scale for mitre cutting. You release either a front handle or lever to enable the saw head to swing round to a chosen angle. Common mitre angles (0 and 45 degrees left and right) are indexed, so cutting accuracy is virtually guaranteed. On some machines it is possible to swivel the head round to as much as 57 degrees.

For bevel cutting, a knob or lever at the rear enables you to tilt the saw head over to any angle up to 45 degrees, again with a protractor scale for guidance. Combining the mitre and tilt angles creates a compound cut. The mitre saw is the ideal machine for cutting coving or cornice mouldings for cabinets, which must be mitred at a precise angle.

Some professional mitre saws with 305 mm (12 in) blades have a cutting capacity of up to 115 mm (4½ in) with the blade set at 90 degrees. Tilted to 45 degrees, you can saw timber up to 64 mm (2½ in) thick. Blade diameters vary from 190–305 mm (7½–12 in). Motors are rated up to 1,800 w, with typical speeds of 3,500 rpm on bigger machines. Soft-start and electronic braking are common on professional mitre saws.

## Accessories

You can use most mitre saws on the bench top, although it is a good idea to mount a bigger machine on its own stand. Work supports either side of the saw make manhandling and cutting long, heavy boards to length much easier. Universal stands are available for mitre saws – ideal when using the machine away from the workshop. Adjustable laser guides are fitted to many mitre saws, also available as attachments. They enable you to line up a beam with a pencil line on the timber. The beam indicates exactly where the blade will actually cut, removing some of the guesswork from using a mitre saw.

---

### JARGON BUSTER

**Holdfast** A metal arm inserted in a collar in the bench top for holding timber flat. May have a threaded screw adjuster or be simply tapped in place with a hammer.

**rpm** revolutions per minute

**TCT** Tungsten-carbide tipped

**Trenching** A housing cut across the grain to a set depth. A number of cuts are made with the saw blade, moving the work piece each time until the required width is reached.

# Compact mitre saws

A compact mitre saw is ideal for picture framing or other small-scale cutting, and can be stored easily when not required. Unlike a sliding mitre saw, the saw head only pivots downwards to make the cut. This limits cutting capacity in terms of width, but not depth, of cut. A dust bag is usually provided on smaller machines, increasing their versatility as portable saws.

Commonly, steel rods are incorporated into the base and pulled outwards to act as work-piece supports. A holdfast is often provided to clamp the timber against the base while cutting. You normally slide the two-piece rear fence sideways when tilting the blade over to make 45-degree cuts. Motors are rated from about 800 w, with speeds up to 6,000 rpm. Blade diameters vary from 190–305 mm (7½–12 in). A general purpose TCT saw blade will have around 40 teeth.

Compact mitre saw

# Flipover saws

Designed to be portable, these unique machines enable you to alternate between a mitre saw and a table saw. The saw head and motor are built into a folding stand and, to change from one cutting mode to the other you simply raise and flip over the cutting head in its frame. As a table saw, the saw head is locked in place with the blade protruding through the cast-alloy table. Flipped over, you operate the machine in the same way as a compact mitre saw. The switch remains easily accessible for both modes. Motor rating is up to 2,000 w, with speeds of around 3,000 rpm. Blade diameter is typically 254 mm (10 in) giving a 70 mm (2¾ in) depth of cut.

Flipover saw

ABOVE A flipover saw provides the best of both worlds: it can be used as a compound mitre saw, or changed to a table saw.

**Further information**
Workshop layout  pages 60–61
The workbench  pages 64–65
Radial arm saws  pages 148–149
Machine safety  page 169

# Band saws

The band saw is one of the most versatile machines in the workshop; it is also one of the most misused. Ideal for making timber smaller, you can use it to rip and crosscut. Unlike the table saw, it will cut curves as well as perform deep ripping or re-sawing tasks. It is one of the safest stationary saws, and one of the quietest. Compact band saws are suitable for the bench, with bigger saws floorstanding.

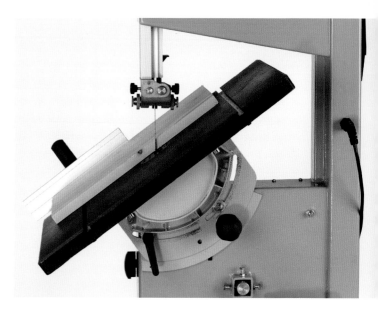

ABOVE The table is mounted on a trunnion and can be tilted for bevel cutting. Keep the blade guard as low as possible when sawing.

## Machine basics

As substantial tension is applied to the blade, a band-saw frame should be completely rigid and is usually made from heavy-gauge steel. The narrow, continuous blade is tensioned by a device that compensates for slight variations in blade length, and must be fitted and tensioned correctly for best performance. If you allow the blade to become blunt, you will need more effort to push the timber through the saw. It then becomes more difficult to cut to a line and there is a greater chance of the blade breaking. Fitted with a suitable blade, a band saw can also be used to cut non-ferrous metals and plastics.

## Table

The table on a band saw may be cast iron or alloy. You can move a rip fence across this and lock in position for straight cutting. Most tables also have a slot in

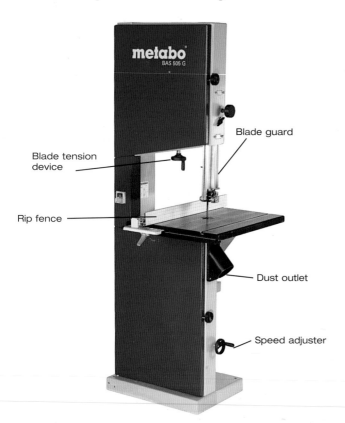

- Blade tension device
- Blade guard
- Rip fence
- Dust outlet
- Speed adjuster

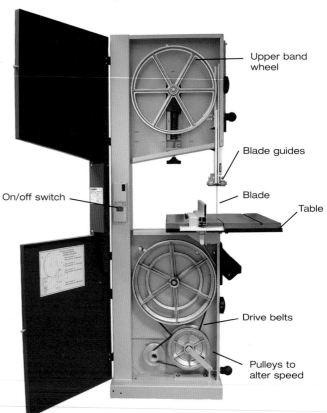

- Upper band wheel
- On/off switch
- Blade guides
- Blade
- Table
- Drive belts
- Pulleys to alter speed

which you can slide a mitre fence. Used for crosscutting, you can lock it at various angles for mitre sawing via a protractor scale. For bevel cuts, you can tilt the table by releasing a lever underneath.

## Band wheels

Some small hobby band saws may have three band wheels, although most machines have two larger diameter ones. Three wheels increase throat capacity and therefore the cutting width, but there is a greater tendency for the blade to snap. Rubber or cork tyres on the band wheels are usually cambered, and provide grip for the blade.

## Blade guides

You raise or lower the upper guide mechanism according to the depth of timber being cut. It incorporates a blade guard and should be lowered to just above the work piece. You then position guide blocks either side of the blade to keep it running in line. A thrust wheel behind the blade rotates to take up the pressure when sawing.

## Motor and controls

Fitted at the back of the machine, the motor powers the lower band wheel, usually via a drive belt. Band saws may be single, two-speed or variable. There is a simple push button to activate the saw and a separate stop button.

## Cutting capacities

Important dimensions on a band saw include the height under the guides when fully raised. In theory, this is the maximum thickness, or width, of timber that you can saw. Most small band saws should really be restricted to cutting timber of no more than about 102–152 mm (4–6 in). Bigger, more powerful machines may have a depth capacity of up to 406 mm (16 in), although 254 mm (10 in) is more common. The other critical dimension is the throat capacity. This is the distance from the blade to the pillar of the band saw. A throat of about 380 mm (15 in) is usually adequate for most cutting operations in a small workshop.

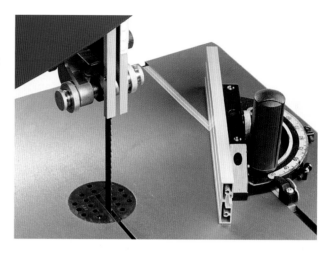

ABOVE Blade guides are fitted above and below the table. For smooth running adjust side and rear rollers or blocks correctly.

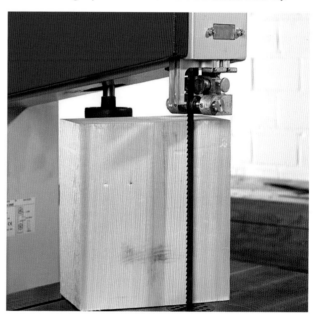

ABOVE Deep cutting is possible on all but the smallest band saws, but the blade must be sharp. This is vital for woodturning blanks.

BELOW Accurate curved cuts are easy to make, although check blade tension first. For tight radii you will need to fit a narrow blade.

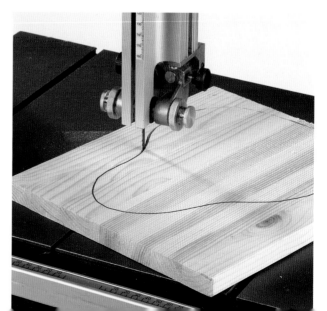

---

### JARGON BUSTER

**Gullet** The valley between two teeth points.
**tpi** teeth per inch (25 mm)
**Trunnion** A casting on which the band-saw table is mounted, enabling it to tilt; usually has a protractor scale to set the angle accurately.

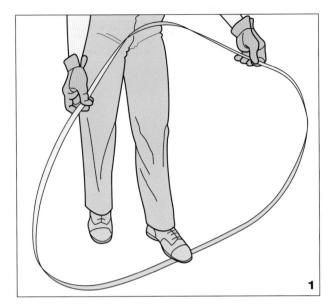

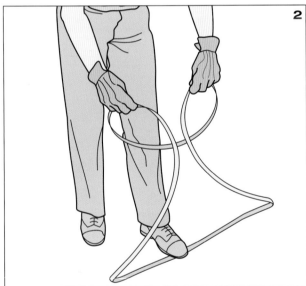

## How to fold a band saw blade

**1** Wearing suitable gloves, grip the blade with both hands palms outwards. Hold it down with one foot, blade teeth facing outwards.

**2** Form a loop in the blade by turning your hands in towards each other.

**3** Form three coils in the blade by crossing it over and allowing it to fall to the floor.

## Blades

Some band saws will accept blades as narrow as 3 mm (⅛ in), for cutting radii as tight as 10 mm (⅜ in). Big machines may take blades as wide as 38 mm (1½ in), ideal for re-sawing deep, heavy timber. For general sawing, a width of 12 mm (½ in) is a good choice, capable of cutting radii of 64 mm (2½ in).

Blades are available in two types: normal and skip tooth. Regular or triangular tooth pattern is common above 10 tpi, where less wood is removed. A skip tooth has a wide, shallow gullet with plenty of space for waste to accumulate, more suitable for cutting dry hardwood. Bimetal steel blades have teeth hardened by heat, producing harder tips and longer life. The rear of the blade is untreated and so more flexible. Standard steel teeth can be re-sharpened many more times than bimetal versions, although the time involved makes this uneconomical on small blades. Owing to their hardness, bimetal teeth cannot be reset.

## Adjusting the band saw

Place the blade over the band wheels and tension using a knob at the back of the machine. The blade should run approximately central on the band wheel. Known as tracking, adjust this by turning the knob at the rear of the top band wheel. Check by rotating the band wheel by hand with the door open. Once the blade is tracking correctly, adjust the guides above and below the table. They should support the blade but not rub against it. Paper thickness is sufficient clearance. Check these adjustments each time a blade is replaced.

**Further information**

# Scroll saws

Also known as a fretsaw, the scroll saw is one of the safest powered saws for the workshop. Fitted with a very fine vertical blade, it gives an exceptionally clean, curved cut in relatively thin wood and sheet materials. Often used by toy and model makers, it is possible to cut tight radii, and cuts need no further finishing.

ABOVE An incredibly fine blade makes a scroll saw the ideal machine for cutting jigsaw puzzles. It is safe and very quiet to use.

## Machine basics

The blade of a scroll saw is supported either on a pair of parallel, horizontal arms or on a 'C'-shaped frame machine, which pivots at the back. On a parallel-arm machine, each arm pivots independently, so the blade remains vertical, ensuring a true perpendicular cut. The cutting action of a C-frame machine is to rock slightly, so the blade is not constantly vertical. Stroke length is quite short at about 20 mm (¾ in).

The table is cast iron or alloy, and is tilted for making bevel cuts. Cutting depth capacity is about 65 mm (2⁹⁄₁₆ in) on more powerful machines, while hobby scroll saws may only cope comfortably with material about 20 mm (¾ in) thick. Throat size can be up to 610 mm (24 in) on big saws.

A plastic tube connected to the bellows unit acts as a dust blower. An adjustable holdfast keeps thin timber from lifting and chattering as it is cut. Either bolt a scroll saw to the bench or mount it on a floor stand.

## Motor and controls

Motor rating is between about 70 and 120 w, providing sufficient power. Better-quality machines offer variable speed, selected by a rotary switch. Slow speeds (400 spm) are suitable for cutting hard materials like brass and plastics, while a faster speed up to 1,700 spm is better for timber. The on/off switch is usually below the table. It is quiet and produces little vibration.

## Blades

A scroll saw will use either plain- or pin-end HSS blades, all of which are 125 mm (5 in) long. Some machines have adaptors so you can fit both types. Spiral-teeth blades enable you to cut without rotating the timber. A coarse blade will have about 10 tpi, while a very fine blade may have as many as 30 tpi. Blade tensioning is via a control knob or lever at the rear of the saw. Once tensioned, this does not need to be altered each time you change a blade. Most machines have a quick-release lever for rapid blade change.

Scroll saw equipped with blade quick-release lever

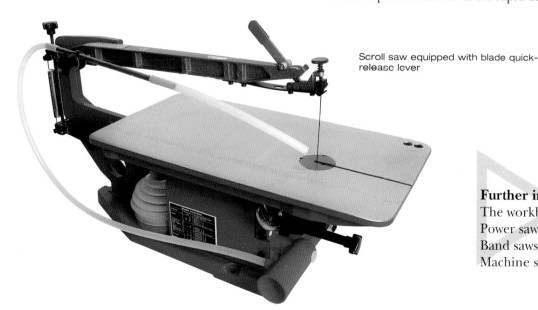

### Further information
The workbench  pages 64–65
Power saws  pages 124–125
Band saws  pages 152–154
Machine safety  page 169

# Planers and thicknessers

A woodworking machine that saves most time and effort is the planer. You can prepare rough-sawn timber rapidly and precisely. In drying, timber cups and twists after it is sawn into planks. To deal with this, a jointer needs a long table both in front of and behind the cutter block. This will take out irregularities, and leave a dead flat, straight surface.

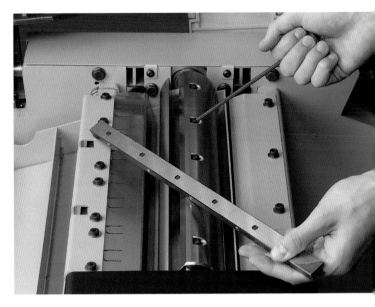

ABOVE The cutter block has at least two planer knives. Most are fairly easy to replace, but sharpening and balancing can be an art.

A jointer is used to prepare the face side and edge, while a thicknesser machines timber to a specific width and thickness. You can choose to have a separate jointer (surfacer) and thicknesser, or a combination planer-thicknesser. On a combi planer, you feed timber across the top of the tables in one direction when surfacing. For thicknessing you feed it under the cutters in the opposite direction.

## Planer-thicknesser

On some combination planer-thicknessers you need to open up both hinged tables for access to the thicknessing bed. On others you may have to remove the outfeed table, or in some cases both tables remain in place. Overall length of both tables should be as long as possible. On a compact machine, this will be between 1,000 mm and 1,220 mm (39¾ and 48 in). Drive rollers are engaged when thicknessing – these move the timber forward through the machine – and disengaged for surface planing.

Because the rollers and cutter block are driven simultaneously, the motor needs to be powerful. It may be 1,500 w on a small planer-thicknesser, up to 3,000 w on a bigger single-phase machine. The cutter block rotates at about 6,000 rpm, with feed speed between 3.5 and 8 m per minute (11½ and 26 ft).

## Cutter block and knives

Knives or cutters are usually HSS and can be removed for re-sharpening. Disposable carbide knives are fitted to some machines. Faster to replace, these cannot be re-sharpened, but will retain their edge for longer.

## Planing capacities

Typically, a small planer-thicknesser has a surfacing width capacity of 254 mm (10 in), while maximum depth when thicknessing is 152 mm (6 in). You use a rotary handle knob to adjust depth, which is read off a scale alongside the thicknessing bed.

## Extraction

An extraction system is essential with a planer or thicknesser. Without one, chips will rapidly accumulate around the cutter block, resulting in dents to the surface of the timber. A combination planer-thicknesser usually shares one dust hood for both operations.

**Surface planing**

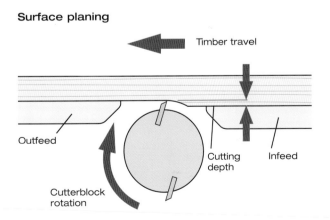

Timber travel

Outfeed

Cutting depth

Infeed

Cutterblock rotation

# Jointer

Cast-iron tables are common on a jointer, designed for surfacing narrow boards and components. Typical cutter width is 152 mm (6 in). You adjust the infeed table using a knob for depth of cut. Industrial machines have an adjustable outfeed table as well, which you set in line with the top of the rotating cutters. There is no built-in thicknessing facility. The fence may be extruded aluminium or cast iron, and you can tilt it to 45 degrees.

# One machine or two?

If you tend to use prepared softwoods or hardwoods, you may get away with just a jointer for squaring up edges. A thicknesser is needed for reducing wide boards to a desired thickness, but used on its own it will not necessarily get them straight.

The major benefit of the combi planer-thicknesser is its size. In a small workshop, why have two machines when one will do the work of both? Most have one motor for surfacing and thicknessing, so work out cheaper than buying two separate machines. There are disadvantages. It can be frustrating on many compact planer-thicknessers to swap from one mode to another. When changing from surface planing to thicknessing you may need to remove the fence first. Often the outfeed table has to be taken off or swung out of the way. If building a project, it can be frustrating to find you are short of a rail or stile, meaning you have to repeat the whole surfacing/thicknessing procedure.

Surface jointer

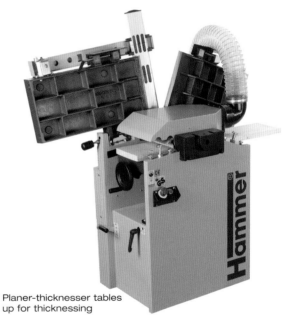

Planer-thicknesser tables up for thicknessing

Planer-thicknesser tables down for surfacing

## PLANING THIN TIMBER

For surface planing thin or short material, make a simple push block from MDF or ply to hold the timber down firmly on the tables. Without this, the timber could lift – or even break up – as it passes over the cutters, endangering your fingers.

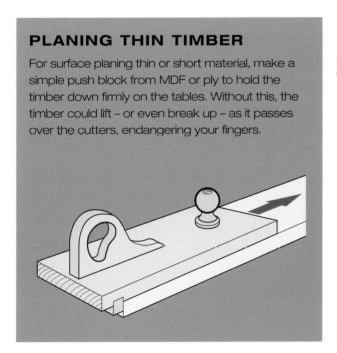

Bench-top thicknesser

**Thicknesser mechanism**

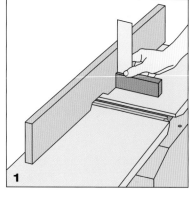

Counterblock rotation

Infeed roller

Outfeed roller

Pressure bar

Timber travel

On heavier, industrial planer-thicknessers the cast-iron tables either remain static for thicknessing or flip up easily. Fences tend to be longer and more rigid, too.

# Thicknesser

You can use most small thicknessers on the bench top. Infeed and outfeed tables are hinged, and usually incorporate rollers to aid the movement of timber through the machine. You adjust the rise and fall of the bed by rotating a cranked handle on top. Most have two knives and motor rating is between about 1,500 w and 2,000 w. Typical planing width is from 254–330 mm (10–13 in) and depth capacity is about 152 mm (6 in).

## How to plane timber

Whether planing timber by hand or machine, the sequence is the same. Begin by sighting down the board to check for twisting and bowing. If the board is bowed, plane the concave face first, so there are points of contact at each end with the tables. If reasonably straight, choose a suitable face side and edge.

## Planing the face side and edge

**1** Check the fence is at precisely 90 degrees to the surfacing tables. Adjust the bridge guard to conceal as much of the cutter block as possible. A wide board should pass underneath.

**2** Plane concave face first. Work with the grain to prevent the wood tearing. Keep both hands behind the guard.

**3** Transfer hand pressure from infeed to outfeed table as the timber passes over the machine. Lift your left hand, moving it to the front of the board, but do not pass directly across the cutters. Draw a pencil face mark on the timber.

**4** Close up the guard to suit the board thickness so there is little gap. Hold the previously planed face side against the fence and pass the timber across the cutters. Keep firm pressure down on the table and into the fence. Mark the face edge next to the face side mark.

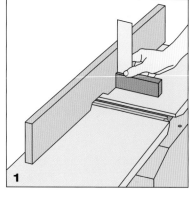

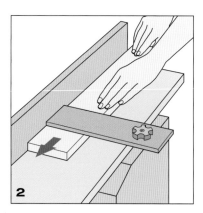

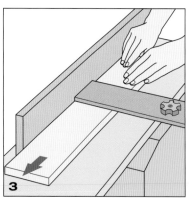

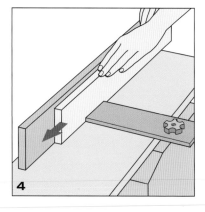

## Planing to width and thickness

**1** Cut off excessive width on a table saw or band saw. Measure the timber width and adjust the height of the cutters to about 1 mm (1/32 in) less for the first pass. Place the timber face-edge down on the thicknessing bed and feed into the machine. Repeat this process until you have reached the required width. With narrow boards, place two or three side by side and feed in together for stability.

**2** Reset the thicknessing bed to suit the timber thickness. It is better to make several light passes rather than a single heavy cut.

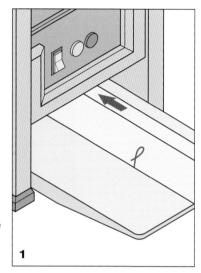
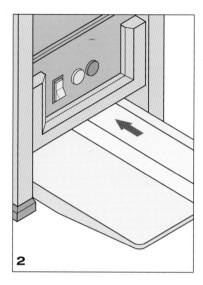

# Face marks

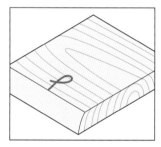

Face side marked with loop

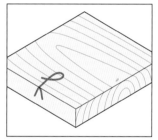

Plane and mark face edge with V

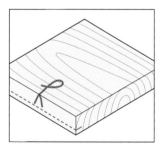

Gauge required width

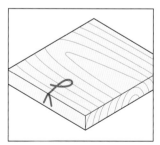

Plane timber to width

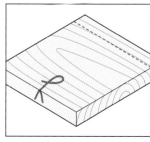

Gauge required thickness

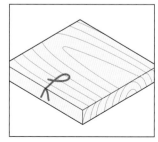

Plane timber to thickness

---

## JARGON BUSTER

**Cutter block** A cylindrical steel or aluminium block into which straight or shaped cutting blades are locked. Found on stationary surface planers and spindle moulders, but also power tools such as portable planers.

**Feed speed** The rate at which timber passes through a thicknesser automatically. The slower the speed the better the finish to the timber.

**HSS** High-speed steel

**Infeed** The front table on a machine that supports timber before and during a cut.

**Knives** The removable cutters on a planer or spindle moulder. There may be two, three or four per block.

**Outfeed** The rear table on a machine that supports timber after a cut.

**rpm** revolutions per minute

**TCT** Tungsten-carbide tipped

---

### Further information

# Pillar drills

The pillar drill is a heavy-duty stationary machine designed for precision hole boring, at 90 degrees or angles. Also known as a drill press, it is extremely versatile and can be used as a sanding machine fitted with a sanding drum or flap wheel. You can fit some machines with mortising attachments, although these are not as efficient as dedicated bench mortisers. You can also use them for drilling metals and plastics. Floor-standing or pedestal drills free up bench space and offer a greater timber capacity.

ABOVE When using a pillar drill, secure the timber to the table with a cramp if possible. Always use the chuck guard provided.

## Machine basics

The drill head is mounted on the top of a steel column, or pillar. At the front is the spindle and chuck, while the motor is bolted vertically at the back. The motor drives the spindle via a pulley-and-belt system. This column is attached to a heavy, cast-iron base, which you should bolt to a stand or bench top for stability. Throat distance is measured from the column to the middle of the table. Chuck travel (maximum plunge distance) varies from about 51–85 mm (2–3⅜ in).

The table is normally cast iron and can be tilted for angled drilling. You adjust its working height using a cranked handle with rack-and-pinion action. Slots in the table enable you to bolt a machine vice or jigs in place. A hole in the centre allows a drill bit to pass through the work piece without hitting the table.

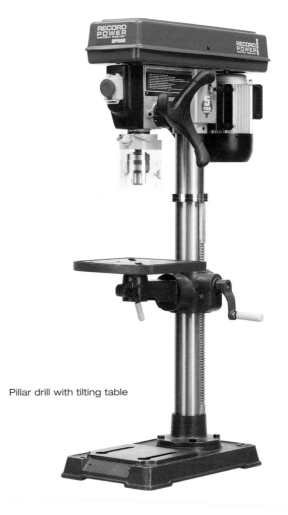

Pillar drill with tilting table

### TIPS

• Unless the timber is particularly big, always cramp the work piece to the table before drilling. A sacrificial board (MDF or plywood) fitted over the table makes this easier and the underside of holes will be cleaner.
• Do not be tempted to use a bit with a centre thread in a pillar drill. The action of the screw thread will draw the bit downwards too rapidly.

To operate the machine, you insert a drill bit in the self-centering three-jaw chuck, with maximum bit diameter 16 mm (⅝ in) on large machines. The chuck may either by keyless or tightened with a key. Switch the machine on and rotate the side feed lever to lower the drill head and bit towards your work piece. After drilling, a spring-loaded lever returns the head automatically. An adjustable stop means you can set the depth of a blind hole exactly. A clear-hinged guard prevents swarf from flying off towards the operator. When using a sander attachment, you can lock the chuck depth so that both hands are free.

## Motor and speeds

Induction motors vary between about 180 and 550 w, operated by a simple NVR switch. Most machines offer at least five speeds, selected by adjusting the belts inside a hinged top casing. Speeds typically range from about 250–2,750 rpm. Slower speeds are best for large-diameter bits and metals, while high speeds suit small-diameter bits drilling into timber.

Drive belts and pulleys to change speed

ABOVE Sanding attachments for a pillar drill, from left: contour, rotary flap and foam drum sander (with replaceable sleeve).

### DRILL BITS

**Flat, or spaded, bits** are good for drilling large-diameter holes, and are relatively cheap. Make sure the point of the bit is engaged with the timber before starting the machine.

**Forstner bits** are unlike most other types of boring bits in that they are guided by their rims and not by the centre point or spiral. Holes bored with Forstner bits are clean and accurate, and have flat bottoms. Only a Forstner bit can bore half a hole on the edge of a board or overlapping holes. They are completely unaffected by grain or knots in the timber.

**Hole cutters** have bimetal teeth for cutting into thin metals. The threaded arbor is interchangeable and used for several different blade sizes.

**Lip-and-spur bits** (also called dowel bits) are most widely used by woodworkers. The central brad point locates easily in timber and does not deflect when the power is activated. Two wing points scribe the circumference of the hole.

**Sawtooth bits**, with teeth around the rim as well as a cutting edge, are better in end-grain work.

**Twist bits** are designed for drilling metal, but work reasonably well in wood. For accuracy, mark the hole position with a centre punch before drilling.

### JARGON BUSTER

**Morse taper** The chuck spindle is slightly tapered to fit securely in the head of the machine.
**NVR (no volt release)** A type of safety switch.
**rpm** revolutions per minute
**w** watts

### Further information

# Mortisers

The bench-top or floor-standing mortiser is designed specifically for cutting mortises accurately in timber. A hollow chisel feeds down into the wood, making a square hole. Inside this chisel, a rotating auger bit cuts and removes the waste material, which is ejected through a hole in the side of the chisel. Bigger mortisers have a sliding table, enabling you to move the timber sideways for increasing the width of the mortise.

Bench-top mortiser

## Machine basics

You can mount a mortiser's cast-iron base to a stand or place it on the bench top. Fitting a piece of MDF or softwood to the base prevents the chisel from hitting the metal. A steel column supports the mortising head, which contains the motor and spindle. Motor rating on small machines is from about 350 w upwards, operating at a single speed.

Timber is held against the fence and clamped with a holdfast to prevent it lifting when the chisel is withdrawn. A sliding table has a hand wheel or lever to operate its lateral travel. On some mortisers the table also moves from front to back. A side lever operates the plunge mechanism, which returns automatically at the end of a cut. Chisel stroke is typically 75–102 mm (3–4 in) on a small machine. A depth stop enables you to chop blind or stopped mortises.

### Chisels and bits

Chisels are available in both metric and imperial patterns, from 6–20 mm and ¼–1 in sizes. You can buy a replacement chisel alone or with matching auger bit. Two types of auger bit are available. The English pattern – preferred by traditional cabinet-makers – has no centre point at the end. It has two cutting spurs and spirals for chip clearance. Cutting rapidly and easier to sharpen, the Japanese pattern has a point at the tip plus a single cutting spur and spiral. Chisels and bits should be kept sharp and fed into the work piece slowly to prevent steel overheating. The slot in the chisel should be at the side, so chips are ejected properly.

## JARGON BUSTER

**Face side**  When preparing timber this is always the first face to be planed. It must be perfectly flat and straight.
**Holdfast**  A metal arm inserted in a collar in the bench top for holding timber flat. May have a threaded screw adjuster or be simply tapped in place with a hammer.
**Mortise**  A rectangular hole in a piece of timber to accept a tenon. It may extend right through the wood, or can be stopped so the tenon is not visible on the outside face.
**w**  watts

Hollow chisel and auger bit

# How to chop a through mortise

It is important to insert the auger bit and chisel correctly. There should be slight clearance, so the bit can rotate without touching the inside bevel at the bottom of the chisel. Use the machine's key to lock both tools. You can cut a through mortise either completely from one face, or from both sides. The latter prevents breakout underneath and is done simply by turning the work piece over once you have cut through just over half the timber thickness.

**1** Insert the auger bit and shank of the chisel into the machine. Tighten so there is a gap of about 2 mm (³⁄₃₂ in) between the shoulder of the chisel and the bottom of the bit holder. The slot should be at one side, not at the front.

**2** Lower the chisel so it is just above the table. Adjust until square with the rear fence. Check this with a try square. Slacken off the chisel and raise it until its shoulder is tight against the bit holder. Re-check with the square.

**3** Place the work piece on the table and set the chisel depth to just over half the timber thickness. Place the face side against the fence and line up the chisel to the pencil mark at one end of the mortise. Cramp and feed the chisel down slowly, with a smooth action. Withdraw the chisel

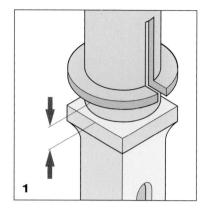

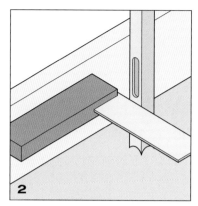

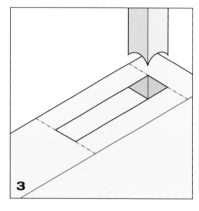

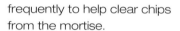

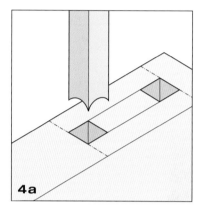

frequently to help clear chips from the mortise.

**4** Move the timber to align the chisel at the opposite end of the mortise (a). When both ends are chopped, make a series of cuts across the middle (b). Turn the wood upside down and tap out waste. Clear the table of chips, reposition the timber and repeat until the mortise is completed.

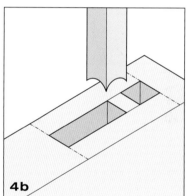

## SHARPENING HOLLOW CHISELS

Chisels should be sharpened with a special fluted reamer (rather like a countersink bit) mounted in a drill and rotated by hand. Interchangeable pilot pins locate inside the chisel and fit different diameter tools. A few turns removes a small amount of metal from the inside bevel of the chisel. You should remove the resulting burr with a light touch of the chisel on a fine diamond or waterstone. Sharpen the cutting spur of the auger bit with a flat needle file.

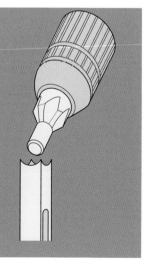

### Further information

# Sanders

There are several workshop machines for fast shaping and finish sanding work. Some are fitted with abrasive discs, others with belts or drums. Most useful in a small workshop is the combination sander, which consists of a small disc and a belt, and can be used horizontally or vertically. You can use a stationary drum sander to reduce hardwoods with difficult grain to a specific thickness.

Bench-top disc sander

## Disc sander

One of the simplest machines to use, the disc sander is a safe, fast way to clean up end grain and shaped convex curves. A self-adhesive or hook-and-loop-backed abrasive sheet attaches to an aluminium or steel flat disc. Mounted vertically, this is driven directly by a motor positioned at the rear. The work piece sits on a horizontal table in front, and moves against the disc as it rotates. A groove enables you to use a sliding mitre fence, which is handy for sanding mitres and bevels. You can tilt most tables for compound bevel sanding, although it is always best to check for accuracy with a square when resetting this at 90 degrees. Disc diameter is about 305 mm (12 in) on a compact, standalone machine. With a motor rated at 500 w or more, the disc rotates at some 1,400 rpm. Abrasive disc grades range from 60 to 180 grit. It is essential to use a dust extractor and advisable to wear a face mask when using any type of sanding machine, particularly when working with irritable hardwoods. A dust outlet enables a flexible extractor hose to be connected.

## Bobbin sander

Also known as an oscillating sander, a bobbin sander will shape concave curves as well as convex curves, with the edge of the timber remaining at 90 degrees to the face. The motor is housed inside a cabinet, while the spindle protrudes through the upper worktable. A sanding drum fits over the end of the spindle, which reciprocates up and down. This action means that more of the abrasive sheet is used, clogging is reduced and there is less chance of burning the work piece. Some machines will allow you to tilt the table up to 45 degrees.

The abrasive sleeve is a push fit over the bobbin and grades range from 60 to 150 grit. Spirally-wound sleeves are best as there is no bump where the paper joins. Bobbin diameters range from 6 mm up to 100 mm (¼–4 in) and can be up to 230 mm (9 in) in length. Stroke length is typically between 25 and 38 mm (1 and 1½ in).

Bobbin sander

## JARGON BUSTER

**Grit** Abrasive sheets are graded by particle size. Each number relates to the number of particles passing through a mesh per unit area. The lower the number, the coarser the grit.

**rpm** revolutions per minute

**w** watts

# Drum sander

Used for thicknessing panels to precise dimensions, a drum sander consists of a wide abrasive belt fitted around a horizontal metal drum. This is adjusted for height above a table, which feeds the timber through the machine on an abrasive conveyor belt. A motor at the end of the drum powers both sanding and feed belts. You can adjust feed speed up to about 3 m per minute (approximately 10 ft per minute). The drum is machined and balanced for minimal vibration. Sanding width capacity is about 254 mm (10 in) on small machines. This means you can sand panels up to twice this width simply by turning the timber around and feeding it through in two passes. Sanding belts are loaded spirally around the drum and held in place with spring clips. Grades range from 60 to 240 grit, capable of a fine finish on difficult timbers.

Drum sander

# Combination sander

Comprising a small-diameter disc and an abrasive belt, you can mount a combination sander on the bench or on a stand. The horizontal motor drives both disc and belt and varies from 250 w up to around 1,100 w or more.

On most machines, you can raise the belt to a vertical position, where it is necessary to use the table to support the timber. You can do shaping work with a coarse belt, and use the disc sander to round off corners and sand end grain true and flush. A fence across the belt prevents the timber from being thrown forward as you sand it.

Belt widths are commonly either 102 or 152 mm (4 or 6 in). Ideal for sanding small components, you may also use the belt for grinding edge tools with care. A small table in front of the disc normally incorporates a sliding mitre table, with protractor scale for sanding angled timber. Disc diameter may be from 125–305 mm (5–12 in).

Combination
sander with belt horizontal

## Further information
Workshop layout  pages 60–61
Power sanders  pages 128–130
Machine safety  page 169
Abrasives and sanding  pages 222–224

Combination sander
with belt vertical

# Combination machines

A small workshop may benefit from a machining centre that combines sawing, planing and moulding functions in one unit. Known as a combination machine, combi or universal, operations are usually based around a table saw and typically include a planer, thicknesser and spindle moulder. The table, or bed, is at the same height for each function apart from thicknessing, which has separate beds.

A factor that largely confines these machines to the amateur market is the difficulty for more than one person to work on one combination machine at a time. For this reason, most commercial workshops tend to buy standalone machines, of which there is a greater choice. Budget combination machines are fitted with one motor. By electronic switching or moving drive belts, the power is directed to the saw, planer or spindle moulder. More professional combination machines may have a separate motor for each function, although this adds significantly to the cost.

---

### JARGON BUSTER

**Crosscutting** Sawing across the direction of the grain.

**Crown guard** Adjustable steel or plastic safety cover above the saw blade.

**Cutter block** A cylindrical steel or aluminium block into which straight or shaped cutting blades are locked. Found on stationary surface planers and spindle moulders, but also power tools such as portable planers.

**Ripsawing (ripping)** Cutting parallel to the grain of the timber.

**rpm** revolutions per minute

**TCT** Tungsten carbide tipped

**v** volt

---

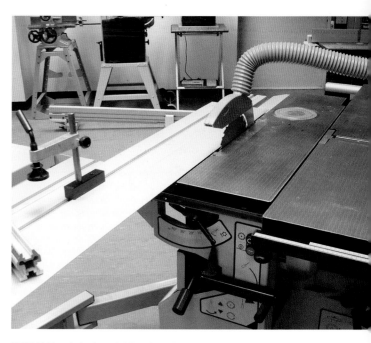

ABOVE Usually in the middle of the floor, a combination machine has a minimum of crosscutting, ripping, planing and thicknessing modes.

## Machine basics

Most combination machines are equipped with induction motors. Those with several motors have a central control panel and are likely to have several stop buttons – an excellent safety feature. On/off switches should be easy to reach and, to comply with European regulations the saw blade and cutter block must reach a standstill within 10 seconds of being switched off. Because of the power required, larger industrial combination machines are generally only available in a three-phase (415 v) option. There is often a choice of single phase (240 v) or three phase for smaller machines.

### Table saw

Operating like a standalone table saw, you can use the combination saw for ripping, crosscutting and mitre sawing. You can usually tilt the blade to 45 degrees for making bevel cuts. Normally a TCT, general-purpose blade is fitted, from about 254–305 mm (10–12 in) in diameter. Depth of cut at 90 degrees can be anything from 85–100 mm (3⅜–3¹⁵⁄₁₆ in). Rise and fall and blade tilt are operated with hand wheels. The rip fence extends the full depth of the table, which is usually cast iron, and slides along a front-mounted rail. Often shared with the planer, you may need to reverse the fence for surface planing.

A sliding carriage may be fitted as standard, or added as an optional extra. Fitted to the side of the machine, this device takes up even more space, but enables you to mitre and crosscut timber precisely to length. Extruded aluminium crosscutting fences are light yet sturdy, and used in conjunction with a sliding table.

## Planer and thicknesser

The cutter block may be fitted with either two or three knives, rotating at a speed of around 4,500 rpm. For thicknessing, the surfacing tables are usually for access to the lower adjustable bed. A guard covers the now exposed cutter block and incorporates a dust hood for connection to an extractor. Timber feed speed is about 6 m per minute (20 ft per minute).

## Spindle moulder

A spindle moulder enables you to add profiles to straight or curved timber or to cut tenons with the wood clamped to a sliding table. Guards are essential and you should never use the machine without them in place. A circular recess or well in the table enables you to raise the spindle above the table. To insert the cutters you must first engage a lock to prevent the spindle rotating. Spindle diameter on European machines is commonly 30 mm (1¼ in), rotating at a speed of around 6,000 rpm. Two-speed spindle moulders run typically at 3,000 and 6,000 rpm.

## Dust extraction

There will be several ports for connecting an extractor hose. Besides one at the rear of the saw, there is likely to be a smaller diameter outlet on the crown guard. The planer and thicknesser usually share a port, while a spindle moulder horseshoe fence will have a separate outlet. A mobile dust extractor will be adequate, although you may wish to install a fixed system for convenience. Standard outlet diameter is 100 mm (3¹⁵⁄₁₆ in).

## Extras

Some combination machines enable you to fit a mortising attachment on the side of the planer. This consists of a horizontal machining bed to which you clamp the timber. Levers or rods enable you to move the timber in towards a rotating cutter, as well as laterally. You insert the mortising cutter in a chuck mounted on the end of the planer cutter block.

**Further information**
The work environment  pages 66–67
Workshop layout  pages 60–61
Standalone versus combination machines
    page 168
Machine safety  page 169

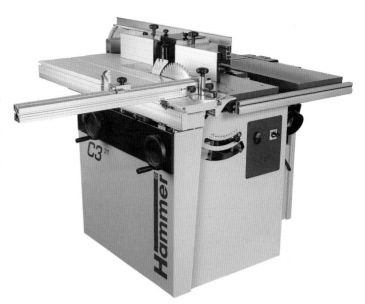

Combi machine in crosscutting mode

ABOVE For planing, the surfacing tables are level with the saw table. For thicknessing, the lower bed rises and falls in operation.

ABOVE A horseshoe fence unit is fitted to the machine for spindle moulding, enclosing the cutter block. It has adjustable hold-downs.

# Standalone versus combination machines

Space is usually at a premium in a small workshop. Add machines and it becomes even tighter, and you need space free behind them for taking off timber that has passed through a saw or planer. Will a combination machine or standalone units suit you best?

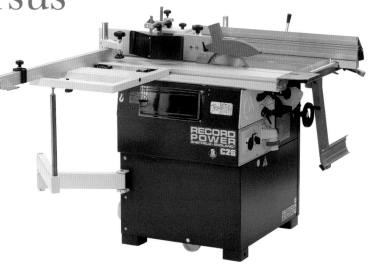

A combination machine includes several operations

## Combination machines

For the small workshop there are several advantages in having a combination machine. A single unit incorporating saw, planer, thicknesser and spindle moulder takes up less space than four separate machines. Cheaper versions are equipped with a single motor so, unlike standalone machines, you are not paying for three or four motors. After all, if working alone you can only use one machine at a time. It must be positioned close to the centre of the workshop, however, to give you access all the way round.

A disadvantage of a combination machine is the inconvenience. This is variable and depends on the design of the particular machine. Imagine wanting to machine-square, mould and dimension a single component. That action will take you from the table saw to the planer, to the thicknesser, possibly back to the saw and finally to the spindle moulder. This ability to change from one operation to another is less efficient on a combination machine than it would be using standalone machines.

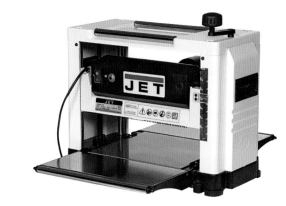

Separate machines may be more costly

## Standalone machines

Despite costing more, there are advantages to this option. Firstly, you do not have to buy every machine at once. You could start with a table saw and add a thicknesser when funds permit. You may consider a spindle moulder a luxury and it might be an unnecessary expense. Depending on the sort of woodwork you intend to do, a band saw may be more useful than a table saw anyway. Standalone machines

obviously have their own motors, which add to their cost, but a real benefit is that fence or depth settings do not have to be moved. When you use a combination machine, you may need to reset fences when changing from one function to another. Unlike a combi machine, most standalone machines can be positioned against the walls, leaving central floorspace free. If sharing, there will be less queuing, too.

**Further information**
Workshop layout  pages 60–61
Combination machines
   pages 166–167

# Machine safety

Most accidents in the workshop can be prevented by taking sensible precautions. Get into the habit of wearing safety goggles when using both machines and power tools. Prolonged exposure to machines such as planers, or power tools such as routers, can damage your hearing, so always wear ear defenders.

ABOVE Ear and eye protection is essential equipment when using most woodworking machines.

## Machinery

- Keep the floor around each machine clear of debris. Store offcuts in bins or on shelves. Have a regular clearout of waste timber and sheet materials and get rid of small pieces.
- Never operate a machine after drinking alcohol or when feeling tired.
- Never use a table saw with the crown guard removed, unless you replace it with a jig that fully covers the blade.
- Do not use any saw with the riving knife removed.
- On a band saw, always keep the guard as low as possible, with no more than 13 mm (½ in) of the blade exposed if possible. Use a pushstick to keep fingers away from the blade.
- With any saw, keep your hands well back from the blade and make sure they are not in line with the cut.
- Never remove the bridge guard on a surface planer. Adjust so that it is no more than 10 mm (⅜ in) above

the work if the timber is passing underneath. For narrow stock, lower the guard completely and slide it until the end is within 10 mm (⅜ in) of the timber.
- If timber jams when feeding through a thicknesser, do not place your hands on the bed. Stop the machine, wind down the thicknessing bed and retrieve the timber with an offcut.
- If buying a second-hand machine, consider replacing the switch with an NVR version.
- Keep a pair of heavy gloves to habd when manhandling large, heavy planks of rough-sawn timber to prevent splinters.
- Always use a pushstick when ripping timber on the table saw.
- Never brush waste material from a machine table with your hand if the blade is still rotating.

## Power tools

- Always unplug a tool when changing a blade or cutter.
- Plug the tool into an RCD. In the event of the cable being cut, this will switch off the power supply in a fraction of a second.
- Do not use power tools outside in wet weather.
- Keep trailing leads across the workshop to a minimum.

**Making a pushstick**

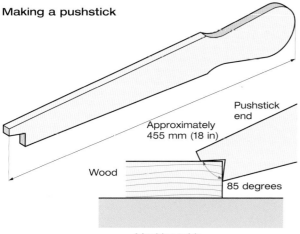

Pushstick end

Approximately 455 mm (18 in)

Wood

85 degrees

Machine table

---

### JARGON BUSTER

**NVR (no volt release)** A type of safety switch.
**Pushstick** A wooden or plastic safety device used to push narrow or small components past the blade on a saw. Prevents fingers getting too close to the moving blade.
**RCD** Residual current device

# 8

# Specialist techniques

Several techniques are unique to specific areas of woodworking, such as chair- or musical-instrument making. Steam bending, laminating and veneering are usually important specialist procedures in the overall construction of a project, rather than entire processes in their own right. Other techniques, such as woodturning and carving, are complete disciplines, although they may also feature as decorative highlights in furniture or joinery work. A woodworker practising these skills may well become a proficient turner or woodcarver, specializing solely in that chosen field.

# Spindle turning

You need relatively small sections of timber for spindle turning. Typical examples are chair legs and stair spindles. Before spending money on raw materials, practise your technique on the cheapest wood you can find, even branches lopped from trees. These have the advantage of being roughly circular in cross-section and 'wet' (unseasoned). Aim to use dry timber eventually, as it is harder to obtain a good finish and will increase your skill level. Short lengths of about 51 mm (2 in) in diameter are good, but make sure you rotate them by hand before starting as they will not be perfectly round. Reclaimed timber is also good for practising, but watch out for hidden nails and avoid pieces with splits or knots. Never use wood that has been treated with preservative, as this will be toxic.

Spindles are rotated by the lathe through a drive centre in the headstock, with the grain running parallel to the axis of the lathe. A second – dead or live – centre supports the other end of the blank in the tailstock. This is a cone that engages in a hole in the wood. (A 'dead' centre does not rotate with the wood so needs lubrication with wax to prevent it burning, whereas a 'live' centre contains ball bearings, so rotates and is much easier to use.)

ABOVE Spindle turning is often necessary when a matching leg or stair spindle is needed in furniture restoration or house renovation.

## SAFETY

- Use a dust extractor whenever possible during turning. Always wear eye and face protection – a powered respirator and visor is best.
- Rotate the wood by hand to make sure it does not catch on the tool rest. If the blank comes off the lathe the likeliest trajectory is at right angles to the faceplate, so when you start the motor it is best to stand to one side.
- Before switching on the lathe, check the tool rest is locked firmly in position on the bed.
- Always switch off the lathe before adjusting the tool rest, measuring or checking diameters with calipers. Do not use a tool too close to the end of the tool rest. Instead, stop the machine and move it along.
- Never wear loose clothing which could get caught up easily when using a lathe.
- Avoid using burrs for turning your first bowls. They are expensive, difficult to work and turning them may be dangerous due to inherent flaws.

## Mounting a spindle blank

To mount the wood you need to find the centre of each end. If the blank is perfectly straight and square in section you can mark diagonals which will meet in the middle, but if the wood is irregular in section use a pair of dividers. Guess the centre and put a point there, then rotate the other point to see if you have judged correctly. Press the point home if you have, and move it if not.

Remove the drive centre from the lathe and force it into the end of the wood with a mallet. Place the blank between the centres (headstock and tailstock) and slide the tailstock until almost engaging in the end grain of the wood. Lock the tailstock in place and wind the live centre up into the blank. Slacken off the live centre slightly so there is not too much pressure on the bearings of the lathe.

If you do not have ideas about what to turn, consider joining a woodturning club or attending a course. You will also get advice about buying tools and equipment.

A lathe should be used at the correct height. When standing upright, your elbow should be in line with the machine's centres.

# How to turn a spindle

**1** Move the tool rest as close to the work as possible and level with, or just below, spindle centre height. The exact position will depend on your height relative to the lathe, but ensure that the work will not snag the tool rest before you switch on the machine. Always start slowly and increase the speed as you feel confident.

**2** Use a 32 mm (1¼ in) roughing gouge to turn the spindle into a cylinder – removing all square edges.

**3** Once you have turned a spindle to a cylinder, you can add decorative shapes such as hollows, beads and fillets using a spindle gouge and parting tool. Mark the positions of beads and hollows along the timber, using a pencil and steel rule. Place the pencil tip against the work piece and switch on the lathe: this will create a continuous line. Cut any square-edged fillets to their finished diameter first, using a parting tool.

**4** Using a spindle gouge, carefully form the hollows between the fillets. Use calipers to check that overall diameters are consistent, making sure you switch off the lathe before doing so and adjusting the tool rest.

**5** Use the skew chisel to form the curved shoulders to the beads, using a rolling action to obtain a smooth curve.

**6** If you do not want the marks made by the lathe centres to be seen in the finished piece, allow extra wood at each end of the blank so that a short length (a spigot) can be left. Turn this with the parting tool while forming the overall shape. When the spindle is finished, use a parting tool to cut through the spigot and separate the wood from the lathe.

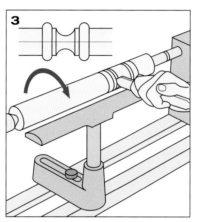

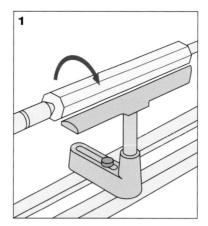

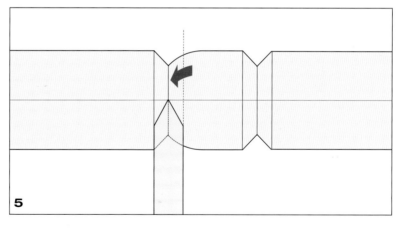

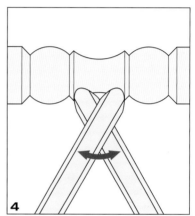

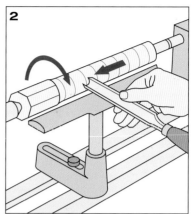

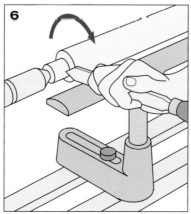

ABOVE Common timbers, such as ash (left), make attractive bowls. More expensive timbers, such as burr elm (right), can be turned to produce something that is really special.

## TIMBERS FOR TURNING

Most species of timber can be turned and your choice depends on various factors as well as suitability for the project. Certain woods, such as yew, are toxic, so you must take great care not to inhale the dust. Others, such as beech and elm, may be carcinogenic. You may even find that you are sensitive to a particular timber or become sensitized by frequent use. Contact dermatitis can develop in this way and can be a serious problem.

Woods that are soft, such as pines and poplar, are rarely used for bowls because they can easily become damaged in use. There is a tradition of using such woods for spindles, however.

Timbers with curly grain or burrs are sought-after by experienced bowl turners but should be avoided by the novice – they are expensive and difficult to use. These woods are also unsuitable for normal spindle work because they are hard to finish and do not have the necessary longitudinal strength required. Whatever woods you turn, use a dust extractor with hose mounted on a stand next to the lathe.

# Faceplate turning

Faceplate turning involves producing bowls, but also includes flat items such as breadboards, where the principles are the same. It entails fixing one face to the lathe with either a faceplate or a chuck. The faceplate holds the timber blank with screws passing through it. Screws should be at least 5 mm (No. 10) in size and project into the blank by at least 13 mm (½ in) when screwed in tightly. Blanks are usually cut from boards with the grain running along them, since this is how most wood is prepared for seasoning. Screws will also grip more securely as they are going into side grain. You can buy ready-cut blanks from woodturning suppliers or can cut your own using a band saw.

A timber blank should always be a larger diameter than the faceplate – its foot, or flat base, at least half the overall diameter of the finished bowl if it is to be used as a working vessel. (However, the foot can be smaller and the vessel walls turned much thinner for decorative pieces.)

## Mounting a faceplate blank

A good size bowl for the beginner is one about 203 mm (8 in) in diameter by 51 mm (2 in) deep. Choose a straight-grained piece of a medium-hard timber such as sycamore. A blank this size will need a 152-mm (6-in) diameter faceplate.

Mount the faceplate on the surface that will become the top of the vessel. This way you can turn the foot easily first. If you have a chuck with expanding jaws, it is straightforward to cut a recess around which the jaws can be tightened. This means you need to decide which will be the top and bottom of the piece before you start. Examine the blank for features you wish either to incorporate or omit from the finished piece.

Mount the blank securely and check the lathe is set to the appropriate speed: the larger the timber the slower the speed. Before activating the lathe, adjust the tool rest so that it is at the correct height for the tool to cut through the centre of the work at the proper cutting angle.

**Further information**
Timbers of the world  pages 30–37
The sharpening process  pages 79–81
The work environment  pages 66–67
Health and safety  pages 68–69
Polish, wax and oil  pages 227–229

# how to turn a bowl

**1** Attach the faceplate to the blank with screws, making a note of how far they penetrate into the wood. Fit the blank on to the lathe.

**2** Draw a circle on the blank the same diameter as the jaws of the chuck. When cut on the outside, the jaws will be able to grip the remaining spigot, which forms the foot.

**3** With a parting tool, cut a slot next to the pencil mark to form a groove about 20 mm ($^{25}/_{32}$ in) wide. This creates the foot of the bowl. Give the foot a dovetail edge using the same tool to enable the combination chuck to grip the blank securely.

**4** Start shaping the outer surface of the bowl with the roughing gouge, working from the centre towards the outside edge. As the bowl takes shape, stop the lathe and adjust the position of the tool rest from time to time.

**5** Use abrasive paper on the outside with the tool rest well out of the way. Start with a coarse grit such as 100, moving it in and out to avoid creating lines on the surface. Only progress to the next grit when you have removed all the rough grain.

**6** Mark the thickness of the bowl's rim by making a cut in the top of the bowl using the corner of the square-ended scraper or the parting tool.

**7** Hollow out with the spindle gouge, working from the rim of the bowl towards the centre.

**8** On reaching the desired wall thickness, make a final pass with a freshly sharpened 10 or 13 mm ($^3/_8$ or $^1/_2$ in) bowl gouge. Finish with abrasive paper and apply an oil finish. Apply at least three coats with paper towel, leaving each to dry. Make sure the lathe is switched off for this procedure.

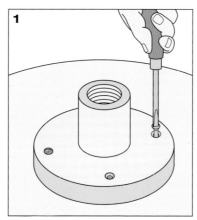

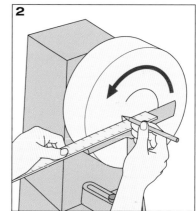

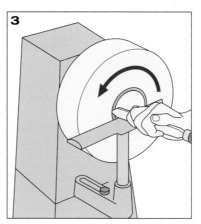

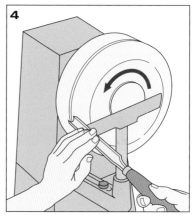

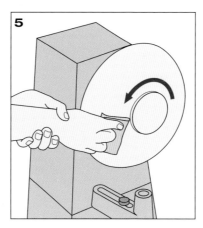

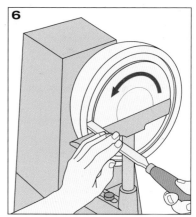

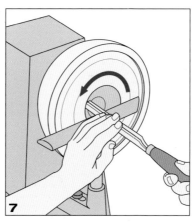

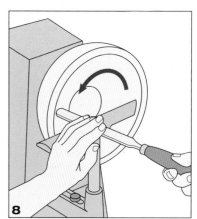

# Veneering

Veneering is one of the oldest woodworking techniques and is also environmentally friendly. As many of the world's most exotic timbers become scarce, it is still possible to use many of these beautiful hardwoods for furniture or cabinet-making without depleting the forests. Veneer is far cheaper than solid timber, and offers greater stability when used with sheet materials.

ABOVE Most veneer suppliers sell entire flitches or single leaves.

BELOW Traditional veneering still relies on the use of animal glue, heated in a pot. An electric iron is used when laying the veneer.

Veneers come in a variety of colours, grains and textures. Box-making is a popular way of using small pieces of veneer with exotic grain, where highly figured burrs, curls, ripples, stripes and bird's-eye effects are not unusual.

## Tools for veneering

### Veneer saw
The veneer saw has a curved blade with fine teeth, about 152 mm (6 in) long and cuts through veneer of any thickness, producing a square edge for tight jointing. Use a veneer saw against a straightedge for greater accuracy.

### Veneer hammer
With a wide, non-ferrous metal blade, the veneer hammer is used to squeeze excess animal glue and air out from beneath the veneer.

### Knives
Several knives with different blades are useful for cutting veneer – a fine scalpel blade for intricate work, a heavier, stiffer blade for general cutting.

### Straightedge
A straightedge is necessary for the accurate cutting of veneers. It should be thick enough that the knife does not run over the edge and into your fingers. Recommended length is 1 m (39 in). A 305 mm (12 in) steel rule is useful for making smaller cuts.

**TIP**

• Store unused veneer away from strong daylight, either rolled up or in a drawer. The colour will deteriorate if exposed for any length of time.

## Cutting mat

Handy for finer work, a self-healing cutting mat allows the knife tip to penetrate without causing damage or dulling the blade. For larger areas cut on a piece of MDF or plywood.

## Glue

Traditionally, animal glue is used in granule (pearl) or sheet form, soaked in water and heated. You can also use modern synthetic glues, such as PVA, successfully.

## Glue pot

A traditional double-walled glue pot is used for heating animal glue. You fill the outer container with water while the inner pot houses the glue. This prevents glue from overheating. Traditional glue pots are heated on electric or gas rings, while modern versions are electrically powered.

## Glue spreader

If using PVA glue over a large area a spreader saves you time and guarantees an even spread. Alternatively, use a sponge paint roller.

## Electric iron

An old iron softens animal glue on veneer and groundwork – ideal for heat-sensitive glue film.

## Veneer trimmer

For removing surplus veneer along panel edges, a trimmer cuts cleanly both across and along the grain.

## Tape

Essential when jointing veneers, gummed paper tape is applied across and along the joint before laying the leaves. Tape prevents the joint from opening up through shrinkage. The best tape is made from a thin paper covered on one side with a water-soluble gum. Once the glued veneer has set, remove the tape by moistening and scraping. Self-adhesive tapes should be avoided unless they are of the low-tack type: they invariably tear the veneer when removed and can leave glue deposits in the pores of the wood that present problems with finishing.

## Vacuum press

A small air pump extracts air from a plastic bag, into which the work piece has been placed.

## Shooting board

Used with a bench plane on its side, this home-made jig helps create a dead straight, square edge on flat veneer. Make a shooting board from MDF or plywood.

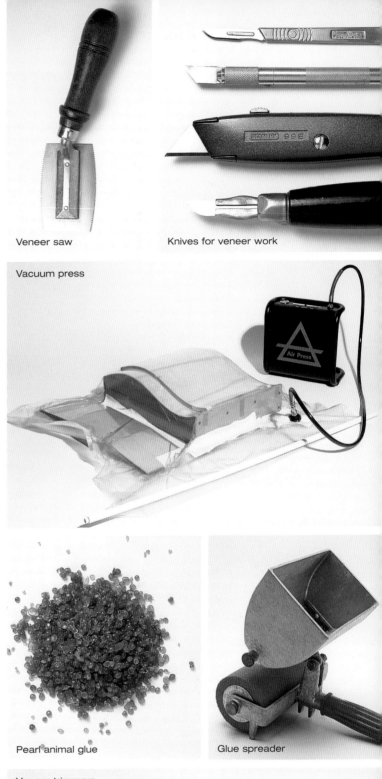

Veneer saw

Knives for veneer work

Vacuum press

Pearl animal glue

Glue spreader

Veneer trimmers

# Using veneer

Veneer leaves are stacked as they are sliced or peeled off the log, so a bundle will match all the way through. You can buy one leaf at a time or a whole flitch. Never be tempted to pull a sheet from lower down a stack, but lift sheets off the top, keeping them in sequence. Common veneers come in lengths up to 3.35 m (11 ft) or more, so are usually rolled when sold. As veneer is brittle, unroll carefully when opening to prevent leaves splitting. Several specialists supply by mail-order.

## Flattening

It is important that veneer is flat before gluing and, although most veneers lie flat naturally, burrs and some highly figured woods are notoriously uneven. To rectify this, first dampen both sides of the veneer with a sponge. Place the veneer between two boards and cramp together or put a weight on top. After a few hours it will be flat and more pliable. Cut, joint if necessary, and lay the veneer straight away to prevent it distorting again.

## Groundwork

Veneer is laid on a backing material known as the groundwork, which must be flat. This may be sheet material or solid timber, such as pine. MDF is most popular as a ground and you may also use chipboard. If using plywood, veneer must run at 90 degrees to the grain of the board to prevent cracks appearing later. On a solid-wood ground, veneer and timber-grain direction should match, so the veneer can move with the timber. Wood should be free of knots and defects, which could show through the veneer. You must veneer groundwork on both sides, otherwise it is likely to distort as glue and veneer dry. You can use a cheaper veneer on the reverse side to the face, but make sure it is of the same thickness.

## Hammer veneering

This is the traditional method of laying veneer, still used by furniture restorers. It requires few tools but considerable skill, and is suitable for knife-cut veneer in relatively simple designs. You brush animal glue onto both veneer and groundwork and bring the two surfaces together. The hot adhesive cools rapidly, leaving a thick glue line. Reheat this with an electric iron (set on low) and a damp cloth, before using the hammer to squeeze out surplus glue.

TOP Small panels such as marquetry patterns, can be veneered in a caul press. This can be built easily in the workshop from offcuts.

LEFT A special hammer is used in traditional veneering. Drawn over the veneer after gluing, it squeezes out excess adhesive and air.

## Caul veneering

In elaborate veneering such as marquetry or parquetry (see page 182) the veneer-hammer method tends to dislodge individual pieces and spoil the pattern. In the absence of a purpose-built veneer press, you use two pieces of MDF or plywood, at least 25 mm (1 in) thick and slightly bigger than the veneer, with sash cramps.

You can also use gently curved cross bearers to apply initial pressure at the centre of the boards. This prevents air or glue from being trapped between the groundwork and the veneer. Place polythene or paper between veneer and caul faces to prevent unwanted adhesion.

## Vacuum veneering

A modern alternative to both caul and hammer veneering is the portable vacuum system. This relatively low-cost equipment gives the small workshop the facility to veneer flat boards and laminate shaped components without taking up valuable shop space. The system uses a small vacuum pump to extract the air from a plastic or rubber bag containing the work piece. As the vacuum is produced, the atmospheric pressure outside the bag exerts a force in excess of 8 tonnes per sq m (¾ tons per sq ft) on to the work piece. This pressure is uniformly achieved over the whole panel.

## Taping

If using a press or caul, tape the joints before laying veneer on the groundwork. Edges should meet perfectly before taping at 152 mm (6 in) intervals across the joint. Then apply a long strip down the joint lengthways. This taping procedure is the same for hammer veneering, although you lay the veneers first and cut through the overlapping edges with a knife against a straightedge. Remove the waste before finally taping up the joint to prevent shrinkage while the glue dries.

## Finishing

Once the glue has dried completely, use a cabinet scraper to clean up the surface. Follow this with abrasive paper, starting with 150 grit and working up to finer grades. Never use a plane on the surface of a veneer as you risk slicing through it.

A finishing sander can be used with care, although a belt sander is likely to sand through the veneer.

BELOW Laminated components can be made with a vacuum press. Layers of veneer are glued together with a shaped former beneath.

ABOVE A parquetry motif in the centre of a veneered panel. Just changing the grain direction can create an elaborate pattern.

ABOVE The three-dimensional effect in this marquetry motif is made by scorching the tip of each veneer segment in hot sand.

## Marquetry and parquetry

You can cut and lay pieces of contrasting veneer to create a picture or pattern. This is known as marquetry and can be used to create three-dimensional effects – traditional floral and wildlife scenes are popular. It is possible to make your own designs by taping layers of veneer together and cutting out the pattern on a scroll saw or with a fretsaw. The technique of cutting geometric shapes from veneer is called parquetry – the simplest example being a chess board. Graph paper is very useful when designing your own patterns, which may be built up by splicing contrasting strips together, re-cutting and re-gluing. You may need to cut and glue interlocking shapes together individually.

## Inlay, stringing and banding

Decorative inlay motifs are common in traditional furniture and are still used in reproduction pieces and for antique restoration. They can be bought ready-made from veneer suppliers and consist of delicate marquetry patterns, usually floral or pictorial, then set into either a veneered surface or solid timber.

Stringings are single, light or dark strips of wood inlaid into a surface. They create a line where the grain changes direction or contrasting veneers meet. Traditionally made from boxwood and ebony, black-dyed holly now replaces ebony. Purflings are fine enough to be bent easily and are used for decoration on musical instruments, particularly the violin family. Bandings are made from several layers of contrasting wood glued together as a slab, which is then sliced lengthways into narrow strips about 1 mm (1/32 in) thick. They can be highly decorative and are often used to create borders around a veneered surface. They are commonly edged with boxwood or ebonized stringing. Narrow veneer strips cut across the grain are called crossbanding.

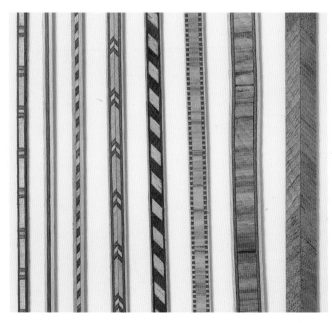

ABOVE Assorted stringing and banding for decorative straight lines. Sold by the length, they are glued into router-cut grooves.

**Further information**
Veneers pages 24–25
Sheet materials pages 26–29
Cramps pages 110–112
Scroll saws page 155
Bending wood page 183
Laminating wood pages 184–185
Glues pages 234–235

# Bending wood

A limitation when working with timber is that curved components may create areas of weak short grain, which could easily split or crack. A way to overcome this inherent weakness in wood is by steam bending, a traditional wet technique. It is used widely in making Windsor chairs and musical instruments, such as violins. Ash is favoured for chair-making; close-grained hardwoods, such as sycamore and maple, are used for instruments.

ABOVE Many hardwoods can be bent into permanent curves with a heated bending iron. Once dry, the wood retains this shape.

## Steam bending

A length of wood is heated in a steam box for up to 1½ hours, during which time it absorbs the steam and acquires a flexible, bendable nature. While still hot and flexible, the component is taken out of the steamer and very quickly bent around a former. It is cramped to the former and allowed to dry and cure overnight as it cools. This completes the first stage of drying. The component is removed from the former and kept under tension so that it does not spring back. It is then hung to dry out completely, this second stage sometimes taking several weeks.

Steam-bending boxes are not commercially available, and most equipment needs to be made in the workshop. You can make a steam box from any scrap wood for one-off bending, although exterior plywood will last longer for repeated use. Build it to suit the size of the piece of wood that you want to bend. For thin strips of wood, it is possible to use a length of plastic down pipe with a wooden bung in each end and a hose for the steam inserted through a hole in one of them. You can provide steam from a kettle, boiler or wallpaper stripper, with two bungs in the pipe and sections of tubing.

## Bending iron

A traditional tool used by musical-instrument makers, a bending iron consists of an alloy block that is cylindrical or oval in shape. An electric element inside heats it up, and the temperature is controlled by a thermostat. Timber is planed typically to a thickness of 2.5 mm (³⁄₃₂ in) and soaked in water before bending. The wood is held against the iron and carefully pulled and worked around it until a curve develops. During this process lignin particles in the wood become soft and pliable, allowing the wood to bend. A flexible metal strap is sometimes used to prevent thin wood from breaking.

### JARGON BUSTER

**Former** A mould shaped to the required curve, around which laminates are cramped while gluing. Often female and male moulds are used together, with laminates cramped in between.

### TIP

• Timber for bending should be smooth, straight-grained and free from defects. Soaking it in water for a few hours will help during bending.

**Further information**
Cramps pages 110–112
Laminating wood pages 184–185
Glues pages 234–235

# Laminating wood

Laminating is a more controllable method of curving wood than steam bending, although it involves more work. You take a shaped former or mould – not unlike that used in steam bending – and wrap thin, flexible strips (laminates) around it. The thinness of the laminates means that the process does not involve using water to soften the fibres.

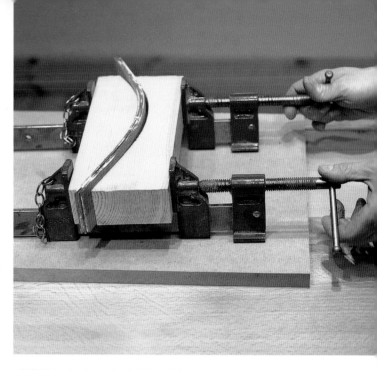

ABOVE Apply glue to both sides of the veneers, then cramp together between corresponding male and female formers.

BELOW When the adhesive has cured, cramps are removed. The laminate remains in its formed shape and edges can be cleaned.

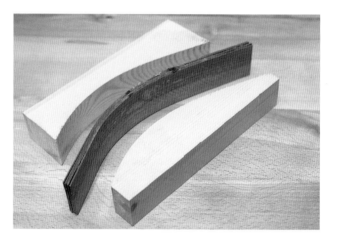

## Laminating

The easiest way to make laminates is by using 2-mm (³⁄₃₂-in) thick constructional veneers. These are available from specialist veneer suppliers, or can be cut on a band saw or table saw. You coat the laminates on both sides with glue and bend them around a former, secured in place with plenty of cramps. The cramps are necessary for holding the laminates in close contact with both the former and each other. If you do not use enough cramps there will be gaps between the laminates, causing unsightly glue lines. Once the glue has cured, which takes at least a day, you can remove the cramps. The laminated component will now hold the shape of the curved former. You can remove dried glue that has squeezed out using a sharp chisel or plane, leaving the finished laminated work piece with little, or no, visible evidence of how the shape was formed. For laminations such as contemporary table or chair legs it is possible to glue together heavier strips of solid timber, rather than veneers. When laminating larger components a vacuum press is a more efficient method. No cramps are necessary and the bag is simply folded up when not required.

### TIP

• Cut laminates longer than needed. Once glued together, you can cut the curved shape to the exact length and trim the ends with a block plane if necessary.

### JARGON BUSTER

**Face edge** The second surface to be worked when preparing timber. The face edge and face side are always at 90 degrees to each other.

**Face side** When preparing timber this is always the first face to be planed. It must be perfectly flat and straight.

**Former** A mould shaped to the required curve, around which laminates are cramped while gluing. Often female and male moulds are used together, with laminates cramped in between.

**Laminate** Thin strips of wood glued together to form a thicker, stable board. The work piece may be straight or shaped to a pattern.

# The former

You can make a former, or mould, from sheet material such as chipboard or MDF, or from solid timber. Reclaimed softwood is also ideal. Depending on the depth of the laminates you are using, it is common to build up the former in several layers, which you glue together and cramp before cutting the finished curve on a band saw. If the finished depth is relatively shallow – less than about 64 mm (2½ in) – you can cut the shape with a jigsaw, preferably fitted with a new blade.

It is a good idea to make a card template first, cutting out the required shape with a craft knife. You can then draw around this, on the former itself, with a pencil. The curve needs to be shaped accurately as the laminates will follow the sawn edge exactly. If necessary, you can tidy the curve up using a sanding drum or spokeshave.

# Band sawn laminates

To make your own laminates, fit a wide, sharp blade to the band saw and check that it is square to the table. The fence should be sturdy enough to support the depth of timber that you will use to produce the laminates. If necessary, fix a vertical piece of thick MDF to the fence to support the work.

Plane a face side and edge on the timber and determine which way you want to cut it. Raise the blade guard so that it is just above the height of the timber. With the planed surfaces against the fence and table, carefully feed the timber through the saw, using an offcut to maintain sideways pressure against the fence. Make sure you also use a pushstick, so your hands are as far from the blade as possible. When you have completed the cut, plane the freshly sawn edge of the timber again, so that it is straight and flat for feeding against the fence. Repeat the process to make as many laminates as required.

You will probably need to clean up the sawn surface of each laminate, unless your band saw produces an exceptionally clean cut with no ridges. Use either a cabinet scraper or a power sander (belt or orbital) to do this. Alternatively, coarse abrasive paper wrapped around a sanding block will do the trick, but it may be hard work. Using a plane on such thin wood is likely to make it snap.

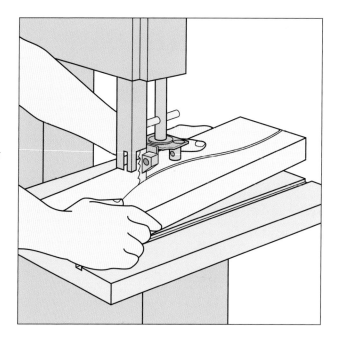

ABOVE A former can be made from solid timber or glued layers of MDF. Male and female components are cut on the band saw.

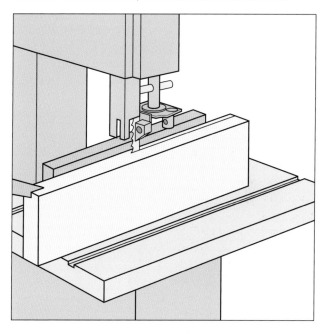

ABOVE Laminates can be sawn from solid timber on the band saw. Cramp a backing board to the table or make a suitable jig.

## Further information
Veneers pages 24–25
Cramps pages 110–112
Band saws pages 152–154
Veneering pages 178–182
Bending wood page 183
Glues pages 234–235

# Woodcarving

Woodcarving can be described as three-dimensional drawing in timber. Although almost anyone can learn the basic manual skills required, carving is undoubtedly aided by a natural artistic flair. Once you have grasped the fundamental rules and attempted a few simple projects, you will be able to explore your own ideas, free from the structural constraints of cabinet-making, where form, shape and detail are paramount.

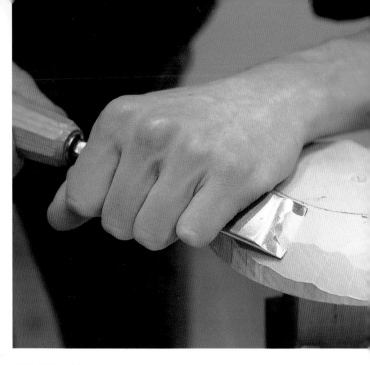

ABOVE Good hand-tool control is advantageous in woodcarving. For best results, blades must be really sharp and work held solidly.

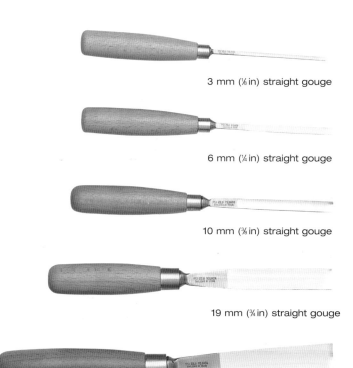

3 mm (⅛ in) straight gouge

6 mm (¼ in) straight gouge

10 mm (⅜ in) straight gouge

19 mm (¾ in) straight gouge

37 mm (1½ in) alongee gouge

**TIP**
• Store carving tools in a canvas or leather tool roll. As well as keeping them together, it protects their sharp cutting edges and your fingers.

## Woodcarving

Woodcarving can be divided into two categories: two-dimensional relief work and three-dimensional, in-the-round carving. Traditionally used for wall panelling and decoration, relief carving is seen from one side only and so is usually carried out on a flat piece of timber. Background wood is cut away to create lettering, geometric or pictorial images. In-the-round carving is generally done from a solid timber blank, with the result viewed from all sides. Depictions of figures, animals and freeform sculptures are typical.

## Hand tools

Most carving tool suppliers carry a comprehensive stock of different types of tools. Well-balanced, finely-ground tools with high-quality steel blades are necessary for woodcarving. Old, second-hand tools from well-established makers are a good purchase, often being of higher quality than many new tools currently available. Most manufacturers supply tools with box, ash or rosewood handles, with or without steel or brass ferrules. You can easily buy separate replacement handles. Hexagonal or octagonal-shaped handles ensure tools lie steadier on the bench, without the tendency for them to roll.

## Gouges and chisels

Carving tools come in a variety of shapes and sizes, providing endless possibilities for shaping wood. Gouges are numbered according to the amount of

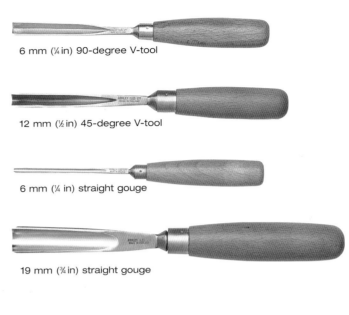

6 mm (¼ in) 90-degree V-tool

12 mm (½ in) 45-degree V-tool

6 mm (¼ in) straight gouge

19 mm (¾ in) straight gouge

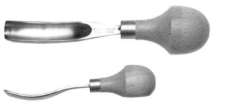

10 mm (⅜ in) curved gouge

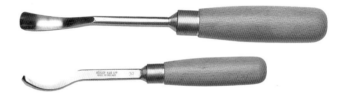

12 mm (½ in) spoon-bent gouge

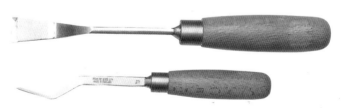

19 mm (¾ in) dog-leg chisel

3 mm (⅛ in) corner chisel

sweep or curvature across the blade. A higher number means a greater radius. There is no international standard here, so one manufacturer's 19 mm (¾ in) roughing-out tool, for example, will be a slightly different shape from another's. Big high-sided gouges, larger open-radius gouges and almost flat chisels are used mainly for heavy work such as roughing out and bulk shaping. Parting, or 'V', tools can also be used for this process, where a definite, deep and fine division is required. As you progress a carving you will need smaller versions of the tools for the refined sharpening and modelling. Gouges should only be sharpened on their outside bevel. A shaped slipstone is used to remove the resulting burr on the inside.

## Rasps, rifflers and files

A good range of abrasive tools are useful, especially when working on large sculptural pieces. Rifflers and rasps quickly smooth out heavy uneven surfaces. They have more of a ripping action than a cutting one, and although they remove heavy bumps, you will still have to do the finishing with finer rasps and files before using an abrasive paper.

## Carver's mallet

A carver's mallet has a circular head and rounded handle. The head is made from a dense hardwood, traditionally lignum vitae. Use it to strike gouges and chisels when making cuts across the grain or on difficult work.

# Power tools

## Angle grinders

With the development of the rotary Arbortech carver and similar devices, the angle grinder has become an invaluable tool for many experienced woodcarvers. The Arbortech has offset alternating teeth, with a ridge spacer between them for a smoother cut. It is particularly useful for roughing out, but is rather noisy and produces a large number of chippings. You sharpen teeth either with a chainsaw file, ceramic sharpening stone or diamond file, depending on the blade. Always wear full protective clothing when using powered carving tools such as this and use the guards provided on the machine.

## Power carvers

For the serious carver, a flexible shaft attached to an electric motor enables you to use a hand piece for fine work. You can fit a variety of small cutters, drill bits, sanders and burrs, as well as carving tools when using with a reciprocating head. You can suspend the motor above the bench and operate by a foot pedal.

## Mini power tools

Fitted with various high-speed and carbide cutters, mini power tools enable you to create very fine, detailed carvings in a fraction of the time taken by other more conventional tools. Bits are typically 3.2 mm (approximately ⅛ in) diameter and fitted into a collet, rather like a router.

# Holding devices and cramps

A variety of devices have been invented to hold a timber blank rigidly while carving. This is essential, as carving tools are sharp and driven into the wood either using a mallet or by hand. Whatever cramping method you use, make sure it is fitted to a sturdy bench or carver's stand. A normal woodworker's vice is unsuitable, as the work piece needs to be above the bench top. A heavy engineer's vice is better as you can mount it on the surface. You can fit the jaws with soft rubber facings to prevent damaging the timber.

Depending on the shape and size of the work piece, a dedicated carving cramp enables you to tilt it to an exact position and lock it firmly before screwing a faceplate to the underside of the timber. A holdfast is ideal for securing flat panels to the bench for carving. This is simply inserted in a hole in the bench top. You should place an offcut between jaw and work piece to prevent this becoming marked.

# Carving techniques

The processes of carving are relatively straightforward. What is important is that tools are sharp. Most carvings are constructed from sections of circles and ovals. A combination of the two produces 'S' shapes, creating high and low points to the carving to round over and scoop out. Coping with changing grain direction needs practice. Slicing helps to deal with this problem when cutting against or across the grain: slightly curl the tool to left or right to give work a cleaner cut.

Paring is the action of pushing a tool while keeping the blade flat to the surface of the wood, skimming off small amounts. Scalloping comprises making a series of shallow scoops adjacent to one another, giving a fine rippling texture to the surface. It takes time to become proficient, but the more you practise the more your work will reflect this. Natural drawing skills are an asset, and sketching is recommended. Obtain as much reference material as possible. Modelling clay is also of great benefit, allowing you to create a relatively quick, three-dimensional form from which to copy.

# Timbers for carving

The most suitable timber to choose depends on the type of carving you intend to do. Oak was once widely used for church carvings, mahogany for polished furniture and lime and yellow pine for gilded or painted items. These days jelutong is used for pattern making, while box is chosen for intricate detailed carvings, although it only grows to small diameters. Lime is ideal for the novice. It is readily available, soft and easy to work, and holds good detail.

BELOW With just a few tools and some practice you will be able to carve decorative items, such as this scallop jewellery box in lime.

ABOVE A scallop box uses basic woodcarving skills. The outside is shaped with a 30 mm (1¼ in) flat chisel using a slicing action.

ABOVE After removing much of the waste from inside with a drill bit, various sizes of spoon-bent gouges are used with the grain.

ABOVE Starting from the top and within lines, radiating flutes are cut into the outer side with 10 mm (⅜ in) and 6 mm (¼ in) gouges.

ABOVE Working from the outer edge towards the centre, shallow scoops are made with the gouges to finish the concave surface.

**Further information**

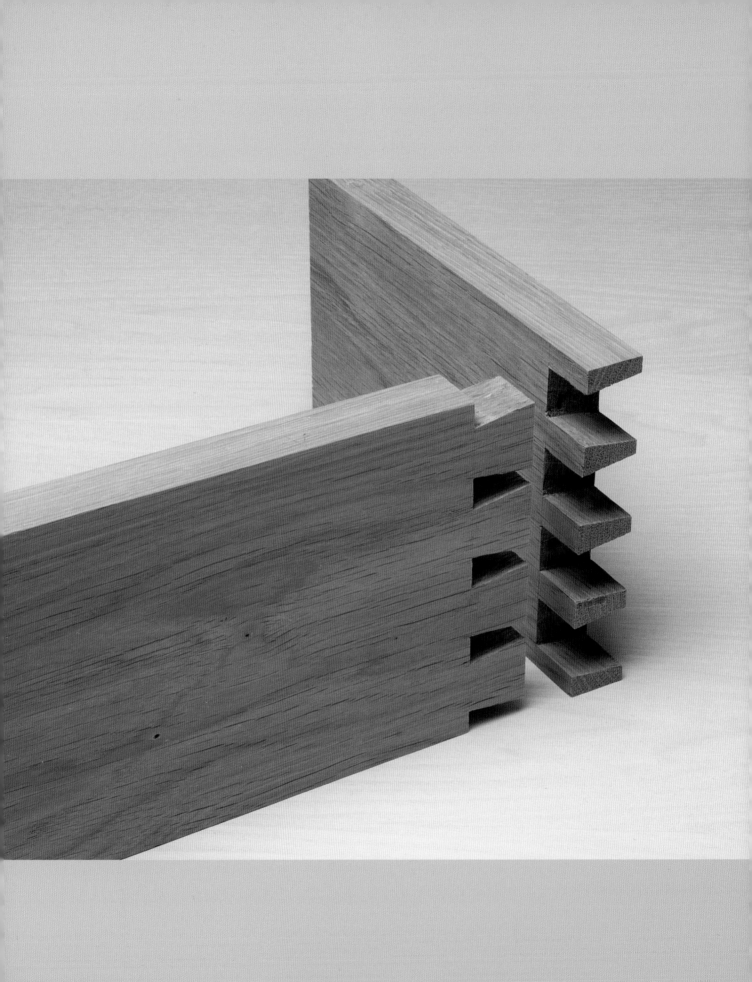

# Joints

Joints are fundamental to woodworking. Without them important structures, such as frames and carcases could not be formed, whether built from wood or man-made materials. Traditional joints have evolved over the centuries, providing solutions to various problems created by the use of solid timber. As well as providing essential strength, joints may also be decorative. Although cutting joints with power tools or machines may be faster, you will never master hand-tool skills until you have made at least some of the traditional joints by hand.

# Butt joints

The simplest way to join two pieces of wood, the butt joint has little strength and relies on glue, panel pins or nails to hold both parts together. Ends may be either square or mitred at 45 degrees – a standard joint for picture frames. Mitred frames are often decorative and can be reinforced with veneer splines. Used for making decorative boxes and lightweight frames, surfaces must be flat and ends square for accuracy in this joint.

**Tools you need**

| | |
|---|---|
| (for butt joint) | Pin hammer |
| 2H pencil | Pins or lost-head nails |
| Steel rule | Glue |
| Marking knife | Nail punch |
| Tenon saw | (additional tools for mitred |
| Bench hook | butt joint) |
| Block or jack plane | Mitre square |
| Try square | Cramps |
| Shooting board | Mitre shooting block |
| Drill | Smoothing plane |
| | Medium to fine abrasive |
| | paper |

## How to make a butt joint

**1** Mark the timber to length and square a line all the way around with a marking knife. Hold the work piece firmly on the bench hook and cut off the waste with the tenon saw. Cut on the waste side of the line, making sure you keep the blade vertical by keeping your eye in line with the back of the saw.

**2** You must now trim the end grain with a plane to obtain the best gluing surface. This can be done in one of two ways. The first is to grip the timber vertically in the vice and tighten firmly. Then, using a block plane, carefully work in from either side towards the middle of the timber. Check the work piece is true in both planes with a try square.

**3** Alternatively, use a finely set jack plane and shooting board. Use the plane on its side with the work piece held against a stop on the board. This

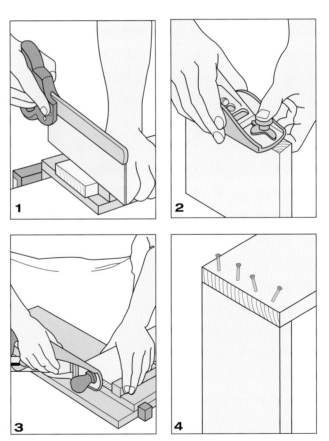

method will give more consistent results than attempting to plane a work piece held in the vice.

**4** If reinforcing the joint with pins or lost-head nails, drill pilot holes for these. For greater strength, drive pins into the joint at alternate angles. Apply glue and either cramp together or hold in the vice while driving home the pins.

# How to make a mitred butt joint

**1** Use a mitre square and knife to mark the cutting line, and continue the line around the timber using a try square. A mitre box is more accurate for guiding the saw blade than sawing the timber freehand, particularly if the timber is wide and requires a deep cut.

**2** Trim the end grain with a block plane and the timber held in the vice – cramp scrap wood behind the work piece to prevent it breaking out. A mitre shooting block is better for trimming wide boards, and should be used with a smoothing plane.

**3** To reinforce with veneer splines, cramp the joint in the vice with one mitre pointing upwards. Saw a cut into the timber, making sure it is straight and the bottom flat. Remove any dust from the slot. Cut a piece of veneer about 51 mm (2 in) and check for fit. It should fit fairly easily without being forced. If too tight, sand the spline by rubbing it on a piece of abrasive paper laid flat on the bench. Keep checking until you obtain a good fit. Glue in place and, when dry, remove most of the excess veneer with a chisel, followed by a finely set block plane.

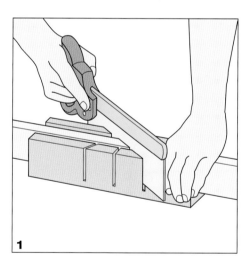

1

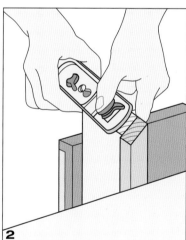

2

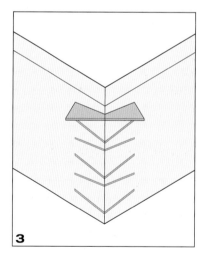

3

## JARGON BUSTER

**Mitre box** A basic wood or plastic jig for accurately cutting timber square or at 45 degrees. The work piece sits on the base of the jig between parallel, vertical sides. A tenon saw is guided by existing slots cut precisely across the sides of the jig.

**Spline** A thin rectangular strip of veneer, plywood or timber used to strengthen a joint, glued into a slot cut by a fine saw.

**Further information**

Measuring and marking tools
  pages 84–87
Saws  pages 88–93
Planes  pages 94–99
Mitre saws  pages 150–151
Glues  pages 234–235
Screws and nails
  pages 236–237

# Lap joints

Used for corners in cabinet and box construction the lap, or rebate, joint is one of the easiest to make with hand tools. It consists of a rebate cut in one component, into which the plain end of a second component is glued. The lap refers to the wood that remains from the rebate, which conceals the end grain of the second piece. Not the strongest of joints, the lap is usually reinforced with panel pins.

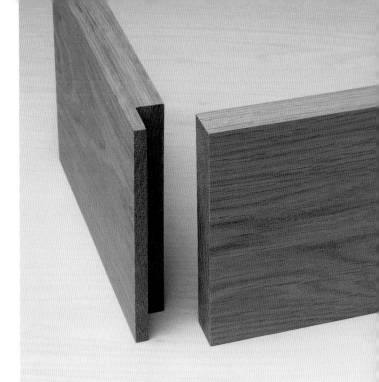

### Tools you need

| | |
|---|---|
| 2H pencil | Shooting board |
| Steel rule | Glue |
| Tenon saw | Brush |
| Marking knife | Cramps |
| Marking gauge | Pin hammer |
| Shoulder plane | Pins |
| Chisel | Nail punch |
| Try square | |

## How to make a lap joint

**1** Cut both pieces of timber to length, making the rebated piece (A) 2 mm (⅟₁₆ in) longer than its finished size. Mark the shoulder line in from one end of piece A, allowing for the extra 2 mm (⅟₁₆ in), and scribe with the knife. Continue the lines over both edges.

**2** Set the marking gauge to one-third the thickness of piece A. Working from the face side, scribe a line across the end grain and continue around both edges to reach the shoulder line. Pencil in the waste to be removed to form the rebate.

### JARGON BUSTER

**Face side** When preparing timber this is always the first face to be planed. It must be perfectly flat and straight.
**Rebate** A step formed along the edge of a piece of timber, usually rectangular in section, to accept a panel of solid wood or sheet material. Also known as a rabbet.
**Shooting board** A jig for planing edges or end grain of timber accurately. It consists of two boards glued together, the upper one narrower than the other. The side of the plane runs on the lower board, trimming the work piece that sits on the upper level.
**Shoulder** The squared end on either one or both sides of a tenon or tongue.

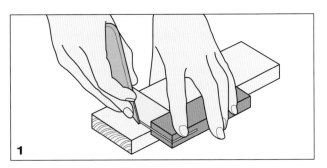

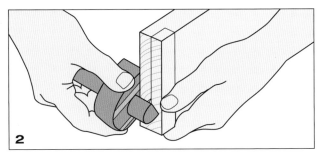

**3** Place piece A in the vice and tighten. Saw along the lap line until you reach the shoulder, taking care to cut on the waste side. Remove from the vice and either cramp piece A to the bench top or hold it against a bench hook. Saw across the shoulder line until the waste part is loose.

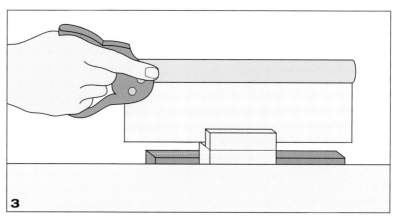

**4** Clean up the rebate with a shoulder plane or pare carefully with a chisel. Check frequently that the corner of the rebate stays square, as it is easy to tilt the plane over when used on its side. Trim the end grain of part B on a shooting board or in the vice and check that both components fit together neatly.

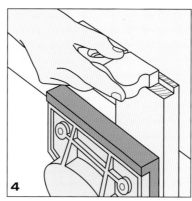
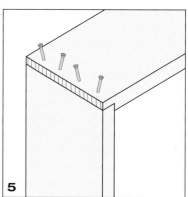

**5** Glue the joint together and apply cramps, with offcuts to prevent damage. Check with the try square held on the inside that faces are at exactly 90 degrees to each other. If reinforcing with pins, nail these in dovetail formation – that is driving the nails at alternate angles – through the lap and punch below the surface. It is easier to hold the joint in the vice for this operation.

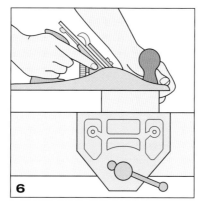

**6** When the glue has dried, hold the joint in the vice and trim the excess from the lap with a smoothing plane. Work in from both sides towards the middle to prevent the timber breaking out.

**Further information**

Measuring and marking tools
 pages 84–87
Planes  pages 94–99
Routers  pages 134–140
Glues  pages 234–235
Screws and nails  pages 236–237

## Alternative method

An accurate rebate is quick to make with the portable router, although you will get better results if you cut two or three components in one pass. Line boards up and hold them together with a sash cramp and temporarily pin (or cramp) a straight batten across them at 90 degrees. The batten acts as a guide for the base of the router, which should be fitted with a straight cutter. If the ends of the timber are sawn accurately you can use the side fence to guide the router. Alternatively, rebates can be cut safely on a router table with the machine mounted upside down.

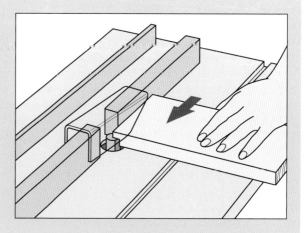

# Edge joints

Edge joints are necessary when fitting narrow, solid timber boards together to make up a wider tabletop or panel. Shaped or profiled edges increase the gluing area, add strength and make it easier to align the boards when cramping together. The joint relies on the strength of the glue, although meeting edges must still be straight and square to the face side. Glue up as soon as possible after planing, before individual boards have a chance to distort.

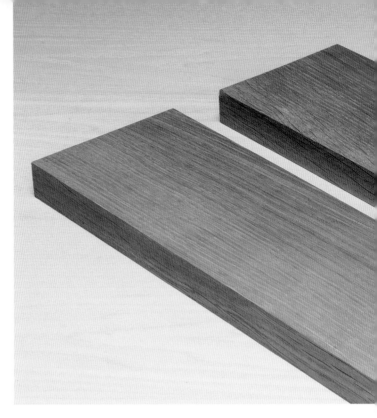

### Tools you need

| | |
|---|---|
| Bench plane | Try square |
| Sash cramps | Try plane |
| 2H pencil | Glue |
| Steel rule | |
| Straightedge | |

## JARGON BUSTER

**Face side**  A wide surface planed perfectly flat, selected to be exposed on finished work.

**Quartersawn**  Planks cut from a log radially, so that growth rings are greater than 45 degrees to the face. Exposes the best figure.

**Rubbed glue joint**  Where two straight pieces of timber are joined together without cramping. Glue is applied, both edges rubbed together and left to cure.

**Tearout**  Wood fibres tend to lift and break when planing timber in the wrong direction, or against the grain.

**Through-and-through sawing**  When a log is sliced with a series of parallel cuts, leaving only the centre boards quartersawn.

## How to make an edge joint

Plane the boards to approximate thickness before edge jointing. If they are to be cramped together, a slight hollow (convex) edge is acceptable. Additional pressure at both ends will reduce as the timber shrinks. Do not be tempted to glue together boards with rounded (convex) edges, however. Forcing the ends together by cramping will introduce stresses that could result in splitting ends.

**1** Although harder to obtain, quartersawn timber is more stable than through-and-through cut wood. Select the boards and number their sequence with a pencil. Arrange growth rings alternately to minimize timber movement. Where possible, arrange boards so that their grain runs in the same direction. This will make it easier to plane the surface once you have glued the boards together, so reducing tear out. You should also take colour variation and figuring into account, especially if the panel is to be visible.

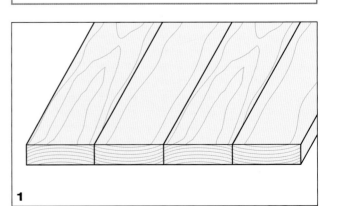

**1**

**2** Insert the first board in the vice and check the edge with a steel straightedge and try square. Using the longest bench plane possible – preferably a try plane – true up the edge. You will need to keep checking this until it is straight and square. Repeat the process on the other edge of the board. Planing two adjacent boards together gives a wider surface for the plane to run on. It is also less critical for the edges to be dead square if they are placed back to back in the vice (face sides outwards): the boards will still meet together neatly and create a flat face.

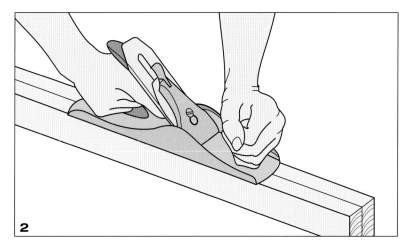

**3** Before gluing up, do a dry run with the cramps. For long boards you will need several cramps, which you should position alternately above and below the timber. Use scrap wood behind the cramp shoes to prevent damage and to keep the cramps clear of the timber surface. Apply the glue and tighten the cramps. If the boards are raised unevenly, use an offcut and tap the joints flush with a hammer.

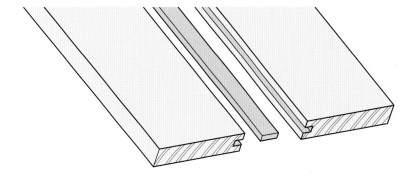

# Variations

## Loose-tongue joint

To increase the gluing area and help boards stay flush, you can add a loose plywood tongue to the joint. Cut a groove along both edges using a router fitted with a slotting cutter. Adjust the groove for width so that the plywood is a push-fit and not too tight.

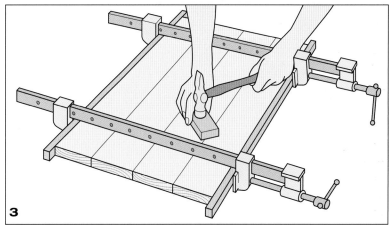

## Tongue-and-groove joint

You can cut the tongue-and-groove joint in solid timber with a combination plane, although this tool has really been replaced by the router. First cut the groove in one edge so that you can adjust the width of the tongue to match in the meeting edge. When used in rustic furniture and joinery, tongue-and-groove joints are not usually glued, so the boards are free to move with changes in humidity.

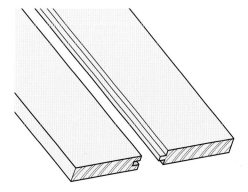

**Further information**
Timber seasoning and
  conversion pages 16–19
Planes pages 94–99
Cramps pages 110–112
Routers pages 134–140
Dowel joints
  pages 198–199
Biscuit joints
  pages 200–201
Glues pages 234–235

# Dowel joints

Dowels are a simple way to make strong butt joints in sheet materials and solid timber. Mating surfaces may be at 90 degrees or edge-to-edge. Useful in cabinet construction and for framing, dowel joints are easy and hidden. Drill the holes with a bench drill at exactly 90 degrees to faces or edges. Marking out accurately is essential: if not, parts will not mate. Metal dowel jigs enable you to repeat joints quickly and accurately.

### Tools you need

2H pencil
Steel rule
Try or adjustable square
Cutting gauge
Bench drill or electric drill mounted in stand
Dowel bit (lip-and-spur) with depth stop
Cramps
PVA glue
Brush
Hammer

LEFT Dowels are ridged so excess glue can escape. Common pre-cut dowel sizes are 10, 8 and 6 mm (⅜, 1⁵⁄₁₆ and 1¼ in ) in diameter.

## How to make a dowel joint

**1** Decide on dowel spacing: typically 25 mm (1 in) apart for frame work, 75–100 mm (3–4 in) for edge joints. Mark dowel positions on the face of the first piece of wood with a sharp pencil, measuring the intervals with a steel rule. Continue these pencil lines to the edge of the work piece using a small square.

### JARGON BUSTER

**Dowel** A short piece of cylindrical hardwood – often ramin or beech – inserted into corresponding holes drilled in two pieces of wood to be joined together. Shallow grooves allow excess glue to escape. Dowel diameter should be about half the wood thickness.
**Dowel points** Pointed metal pins used for locating and marking accurate dowel positions.
**Face edge** An edge planed straight and square to the face side.
**Face side** A wide surface planed perfectly flat, selected to be exposed on finished work.
**Lip-and-spur bit** A spiral twist drill with outer spurs and sharp point in the centre.

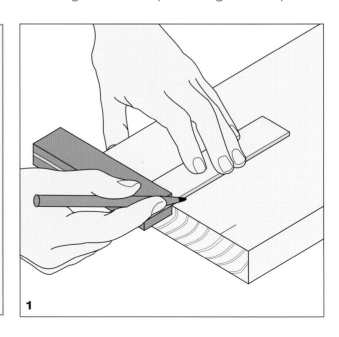

1

**2** Set the cutting gauge to half the timber thickness and run it along the end of the face side. This will give you the centre line of the joint (if the other piece is the same thickness).

**3** Align both pieces of wood and carefully transfer the dowel positions from the first to the second. Run the cutting gauge along the end grain of the second piece, and continue the marks from the face around the end grain, using the square and pencil.

**4** Adjust the depth collar on the bit and fit in the drill. Place the first piece of wood flat on the drill table, centralizing the bit above a pencil mark. Cramp the wood and plunge the bit smoothly down until you reach the depth stop. Repeat for the remaining holes.

**5** To bore the end-grain holes accurately in the second piece of wood, cramp it to the drill table or in a vice. Check with the square that the edge of the work piece is perpendicular to the drill bit. If not, the hole will run out of true, resulting in a joint that is not square.

**6** Countersink holes to help the joint go together snugly. Brush PVA glue on a dowel end and insert in a hole, tapping home with a hammer. Repeat with remaining holes. Apply glue to the protruding dowels, position the other work piece and tap the joint together. Cramp the joint until dry.

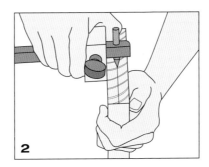

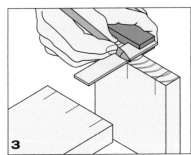

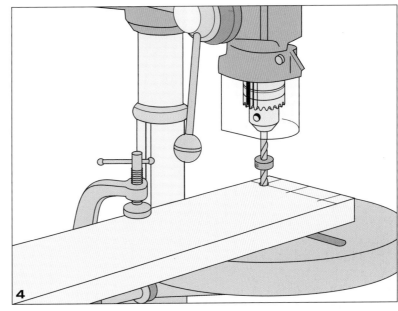

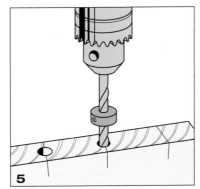

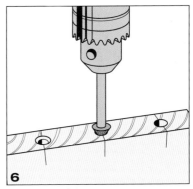

## Alternative method

You can achieve virtually foolproof marking using metal dowel points. Mark and drill the holes in the first piece of wood, as before. Tap the correct size dowel points into the holes, then align and press the two components firmly together. The points will give the exact centres of the secondary holes.

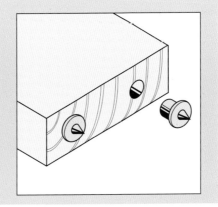

**Further information**
Measuring and marking tools
  pages 84–87
Drills  pages 104–105
Power drills  pages 126–127
Glues  pages 234–235

# Biscuit joints

This reinforced butt joint is more foolproof than using regular dowels, but it does require a portable biscuit jointer to cut a slot. A hardwood biscuit fits into a corresponding slot cut into both meeting edges and results in a fast, simple, yet strong, glued joint. You can use a router with a slotting cutter for straightforward edge-to-edge joints. Suitable for both solid timber and sheet materials, you can also use biscuits on mitred edges.

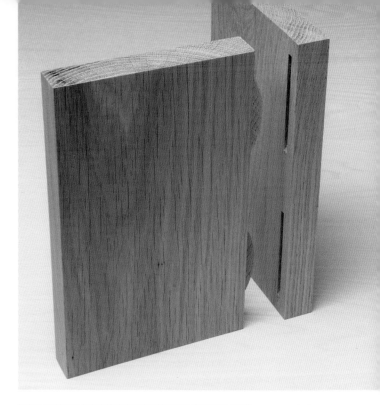

**Tools you need**

Bench plane
2H pencil
Steel rule
Biscuit jointer
Glue
Brush
Biscuits
Hammer
Try square
Cramps
Damp cloth

### JARGON BUSTER

**Biscuit** An oval-shaped dowel – made of compressed beech – inserted into matching slots in adjacent boards. Glue swells the fibres ensuring a tight-fitting joint.
**PVA** Polyvinyl acetate, a synthetic resin glue for wood. Excess can be cleaned up with water.

### TIP

• Store biscuits in an air-tight tin or jar to keep moisture out. If biscuits swell up they can become too tight for the slot.

## BISCUIT ASSORTMENT

There are three common sizes of hardwood biscuit available to suit different thicknesses of material:
**No. 0** is for timber from 6–12 mm (¼–½ in) thick
**No. 10** is for timber from 13–18 mm (½–¾ in) thick
**No. 20** is for timber from 19 mm (¾ in) and above

All biscuits are the same thickness and fit a 4-mm (⅛-in) wide slot.

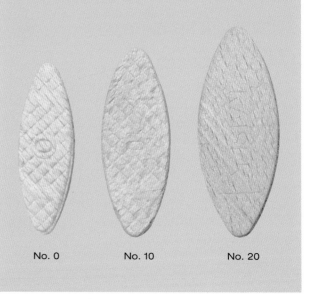

No. 0    No. 10    No. 20

# How to make a biscuit joint

**1** Plane the board edges to be jointed so they are straight and square. Check them against each other, then mark the positions of the biscuits, roughly 152 mm (6 in apart). It is sufficient to draw a pencil line across adjacent boards.

**2** Select the correct size biscuit to suit the board thickness (see left). Adjust the cutter plunge depth on the biscuit jointer and set the fence so the slot will be centralized in the edge of the timber.

**3** Rest the fence of the biscuit jointer on the board and align the guide at the front of the fence with the relevant pencil mark on the board's face. Switch on the jointer and, keeping pressure downwards on the top handle, plunge the tool forwards into the board to make the cut. Make repeat cuts as necessary along the timber and into the edge of the corresponding board.

**4** Brush PVA glue onto a biscuit, insert it into the first slot and tap home with a hammer. Work your way along the edges of both boards in the same way. Apply glue to the timber edges as well and push the boards together.

**5** Cramp the boards together and check they are flat. Use cramps above and below to avoid the panel distorting. Wipe excess glue with a damp cloth.

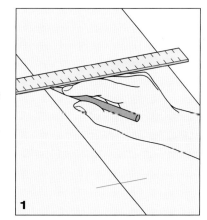

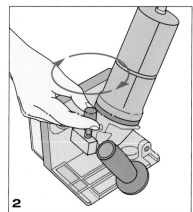

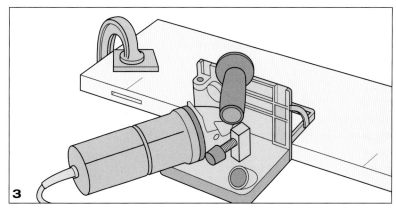

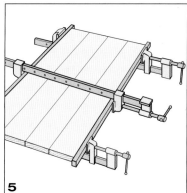

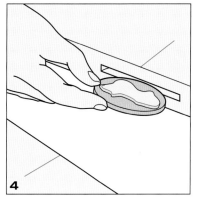

# Variation

## Corner and T-joints

**For end joints at 90 degrees,** place the fence of the tool against the end of the mating board and make plunge cuts. Biscuits are glued as before.

**For T-joints in the middle of a board,** square a pencil line across to mark the position. Either hold the tool against the line by hand or, preferably, against a guide batten cramped to the surface. This will keep all the slots in line.

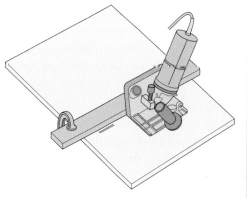

**Further information**
Measuring and marking
  tools  pages 84–87
Biscuit jointers
  pages 132–133
Edge joints  pages 196–197
Glues  pages 234–235

# T-halving joints

Used for construction such as framework and softwood joinery, halving joints have little structural integrity. Strength comes from glue or reinforcing screws, while shoulders increase rigidity. Half the thickness is cut away on one component, a corresponding section removed on the second. Wood should be straight-grained and defect-free, so you can clear waste cleanly. Variations include the corner ('L'), cross ('X'), dovetail and halving.

### Tools you need

| | |
|---|---|
| 2H pencil | Tenon saw |
| Steel rule | Chisel |
| Try square | Mallet |
| Marking gauge | Smoothing plane |
| Marking knife | Glue |
| Cramps | Brush |

## JARGON BUSTER

**Cheek**  The side of a tenon.
**Rail**  A horizontal piece of wood in a frame, usually between two vertical stiles.
**Stile**  The vertical sides of a frame.
**Stock**  Prepared timber, planed all round and ready to be worked.

## How to make a T-halving joint

**1**  Mark the width of the joint on the first piece (A) with a pencil. For accuracy, hold the second piece (B) in position and mark next to each edge. Continue the pencil lines across piece A with a try square.

**2**  Carefully mark a line around the end of piece B, which will be the tenon. Its distance from the end of the timber is the width of piece A, plus 1 mm (⅟₃₂ in) extra. Continue the pencil lines down the edges of piece B using the square. Make sure you hold the square against relevant face sides and face edges.

**3**  Using a steel rule, set the marking gauge to half the thickness of the timber. Check this for accuracy by marking from each side on an offcut. To make minute adjustments to the gauge, tap either end on the bench top, depending on whether you want to increase or decrease the gap.

**4**  Mark the sides of the joint on both pieces. Pencil in the waste sections that you need to remove with the chisel. This will prevent you from cutting into the wrong side of the wood.

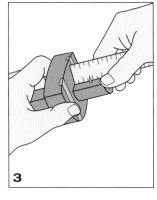

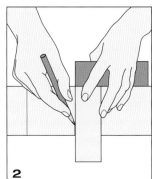

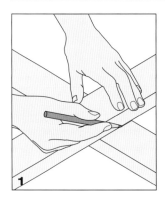

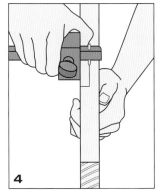

**5** Cramp piece A to the bench. Using a tenon saw, cut across the shoulders, keeping the blade just to the waste side of the pencil lines. A tip is to start the cut by scoring a line with a marking knife and chiselling a shallow 'V'. This provides a channel for the teeth of the saw to run in. With some practice, you will find this unnecessary.

**6** Use a sharp chisel and mallet to remove the waste between the shoulder lines. Make several shallow cuts, starting about 3 mm (⅛ in) down from the top. Hold the handle lower than the blade, which should be pointing up slightly. This helps to stop the wood splitting out at the back.

**7** Chop out the waste until you reach the gauged line, then turn the wood over and repeat the process from the other side. This will leave a bump, which you can pare off level with as-wide-a chisel as possible for flatness.

**8** Grip the tenon piece (B) in the vice, tilted away from you. With the saw horizontal, carefully cut down the cheek, just inside the gauged line. Reverse the work piece and cut from the other side. Reposition the tenon so that it is upright in the vice and cut down to the shoulder line.

**9** Cramp piece B to the bench and carefully pare away remaining waste.

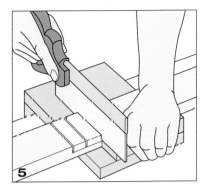

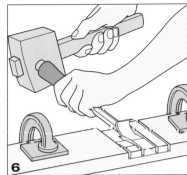

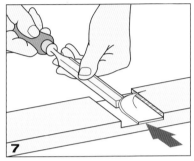

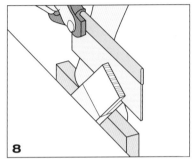

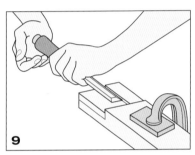

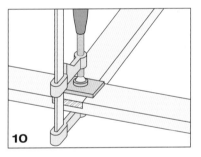

Use the chisel either with the grain or across it. Check the surface is flat, then try fitting the two halves of the joint together. If it is too tight, take a shaving off the edge of part B with a finely set smoothing plane.

**10** Apply glue, evenly, to the faces that will meet, using a brush. Cramp together, using packing pieces from scrap wood to prevent dents. Check the shoulders are tight and finally tighten the cramp. When the glue is dry, place the joint in the vice and plane off the protruding lip of the tenon.

## Alternative method

A halving joint is quick and easy to make with a router, especially if you have several identical components. Hold them together with a sash cramp and temporarily pin (or cramp) a dead straight batten across them, checking with the square that it is at 90 degrees. The batten acts as a guide for the base of the router, which should be fitted with a straight cutter.

**Further information**
Measuring and marking tools
  pages 84–87
Saws pages 88–93
Chisels pages 100–103
Glues pages 234–235

# Housing joints

Housing joints (dadoes) are used for fitting shelves and dividers in cabinets of solid timber or sheet materials. A housing is a precisely cut groove that accepts another piece of timber, usually across the grain. Structural quality is limited and it depends on a tight fit for rigidity. A dovetail housing is hardest to make, but is far sturdier, as it has mechanical strength. Either housing can be stopped so the end of the groove is not visible.

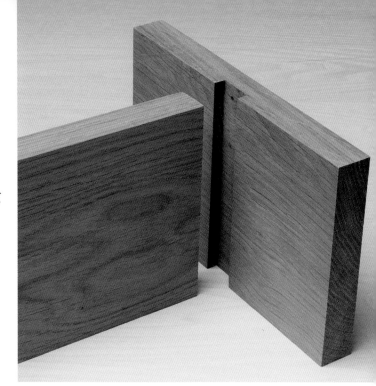

### Tools you need

| | |
|---|---|
| 2H pencil | Paring chisel |
| Steel rule | Router plane (not essential) |
| Try square | Smoothing plane |
| Marking gauge | Glue |
| Marking knife | Sliding bevel (for dovetail |
| Cramps | housing) |
| Bevel-edge chisel | |
| Tenon saw | |
| Mallet | |

---

**JARGON BUSTER**

**Dado** A wide, shallow groove across the grain. Alternative name for housing.
**Paring** Removing a thin shaving from timber with a sharp chisel, either from the surface or from end grain.

---

## How to make a through housing joint

**1** Carefully mark the position of the housing by holding the shelf component (B) on the work piece (A) and pencil in the waste. The width of the housing should be a fraction less than the shelf. Square the two lines across the face with the try square and continue them around both edges.

**2** Set the depth of the housing on the marking or cutting gauge. This should be about one-third of the thickness of the timber – deep enough to make a strong joint but not too deep to weaken the surrounding wood. Scribe the line along both edges of the housing. Holding the try square tightly against the work piece, scribe both lines with a marking knife. Make several shallow strokes rather than one deep cut, to a depth of about 2 mm (1⁄16 in).

**3** Cramp the work piece to the bench top before sawing. To provide a guide for the saw blade, open up the scribed lines to a 'V', using the chisel. Hold the chisel at about 45 degrees to the work on the inside of the housing, parallel to the line. Make a series of cuts pushing down into the incision, the blade edge 2 mm (1⁄16 in) inside the line. Do not use a mallet, which could make the cuts too deep.

**4** Open up the 'V' by working along each line, with chisel-width steps. When one side is finished, turn the work around, if necessary, and repeat along the other side. The teeth of the saw blade should just sit against the side of the incised line. Start sawing with the handle raised slightly. While cutting, gradually lower the handle until the saw is horizontal. Stop cutting when the teeth reach the gauged lines at the bottom of the housing. During sawing, check the lines on the joint edges to make sure the cut is vertical.

**5** Use the chisel and mallet to remove most of the waste. With the blade pointing up slightly, make a series of shallow cuts until you reach the gauged depth mark. Work in from each side, turning the work piece around when necessary. Both ends of the housing should now be at the correct depth, with a shallow, inverted 'V' of waste remaining in the centre. On a board up to about 178 mm (7 in) wide, you can remove this with a long chisel held horizontally. Pare the waste down with shallow cuts until the bottom of the housing is flat. Check this with a steel rule held on edge. On a wider board, use a paring chisel or router plane to clean out the housing.

**6** Check the fit of the joint and do any final trimming on the matching shelf (B). The end of this must be planed square. If the joint is too tight, carefully skim either face of the shelf with a finely set smoothing plane. Check constantly until the joint is a firm push fit. Depending on the overall length of the joint, select a suitable cramp for assembling. A bookcase will probably need a couple of sash cramps, while a G-cramp may be sufficient for a shorter joint. Use scrap wood to prevent the timber surface getting dented when you tighten the cramps. Apply glue to both pieces and check the joint is true with the try square. When the glue has dried, clean up the joint edges with a smoothing plane.

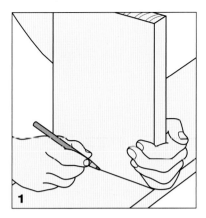

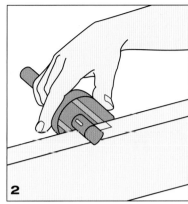

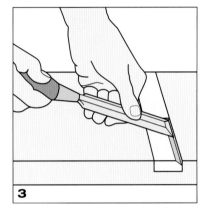

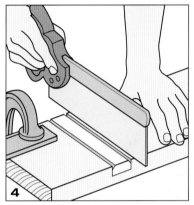

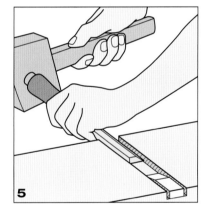

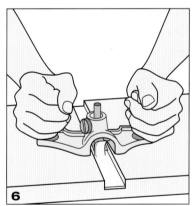

## Alternative method

A housing is an ideal joint for the router. Hold similar panels together with a sash cramp and temporarily cramp a batten across them at 90 degrees. The batten acts as a guide for the base of the router, which should be fitted with a straight cutter. Adjust the batten to match the housing width. You can also machine a groove accurately with a radial arm saw or sliding mitre saw.

**Further information**
Measuring and marking tools
  pages 84–87
Saws  pages 88–93
Chisels  pages 100–103
Radial arm saws
  pages 148–149
Mitre saws  pages 150–151
Glues  pages 234–235

# Variations

## Stopped housing joint

Instead of running the groove right across the timber, it is stopped about 10 or 12 mm (⅜–½ in) back from the front edge. The end of the shelf is notched out to match the housing by the same amount. Alternatively, the shelf may be set back from the edge of the side panel.

### How to make a stopped housing joint

**1**   Mark out in a similar way to a through housing (see page 204). Measure back the distance of the stopped part from the front edge of the work piece and gauge a line across the end of the housing. Using a chisel and mallet, chop out the waste material to form the end of the groove, removing a small amount at a time. The depth should be one-third of the board thickness. This cutout means you will be able to saw the housing from the rear edge.

**2**   Having scribed the outer lines of the housing with a marking knife, cut 'V' grooves with the chisel to guide the saw blade, as you did with the through housing joint. Remove the waste with the chisel and mallet, taking care not to damage the edges. Saw the sides of the housing and chisel out the waste carefully. Check the bottom is flat with a steel rule, and trim as necessary.

**3**   Mark the notch on the end of the shelf with the marking gauge. Continue the lines on both faces and the front edge. With the shelf held upright in the vice, remove the waste with the tenon saw. Check the shelf and housing fit together and make any adjustments carefully as needed.

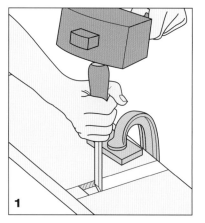

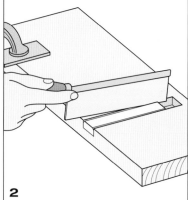

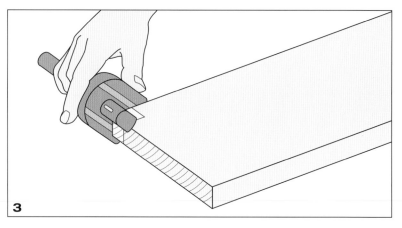

# Dovetail housing joint

Making a dovetail housing joint with hand tools is more challenging than a through housing. Although it is easiest using a router fitted with a suitable dovetail cutter, the hand-cutting technique provides good practice at controlling a chisel and tenon saw. Either one, or both, sides of the housing may be dovetailed.

## How to make a dovetail housing joint

**1** Adjust the marking gauge to one-third the thickness of the vertical panel and scribe a line underneath the end of the shelf. Continue this shoulder line around both edges and mark each one 3 mm (⅛ in) in from the lower face.

**2** Set the blade of a sliding bevel from this mark across to the outer corner of the shelf. This is the dovetail angle and should be drawn on both edges. Scribe the line with the marking knife and saw across the shoulder line until you reach the dovetail slope.

**3** Pare away the waste from the shelf with a wide chisel. A bevelled guide block will help keep the chisel at the correct angle. You can make this from an offcut and simply move it along the end of the timber as you pare the dovetail.

**4** Carefully mark in pencil the location of the dovetail housing on the side panel, squaring the lines around both edges. Then transfer the depth of the housing with the marking gauge. Using the sliding bevel, mark the dovetail slope on both edges, checking that it is the correct way round with the profile of the shelf. With the blade tilted for the lower line, saw along the sides of the housing until you reach the bottom. Again, an angled block is useful here to guide the saw. With a bevel-edge chisel, cut away the waste and clean up with a router plane.

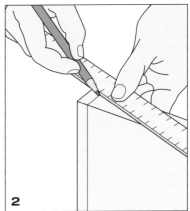

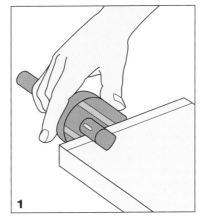

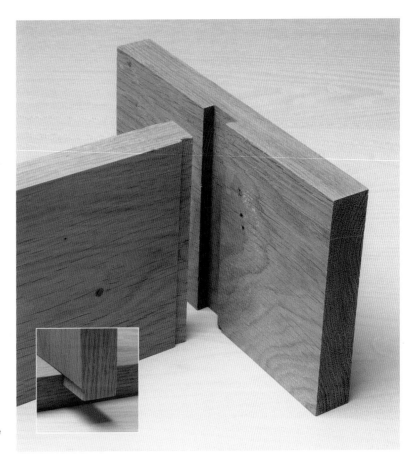

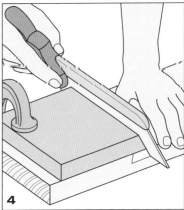

# Mortise-and-tenon joints

A framing joint used in carpentry and joinery, the mortise and tenon has great mechanical strength and creates a large gluing area. A rectangular tenon sawn at one end of a rail slots into the mortise, an elongated hole in the other part. The rail is usually horizontal and the stile vertical. Mortise and tenon are generally one-third the thickness of the timber.

## Tools you need

| | |
|---|---|
| 2H pencil | Mallet |
| Steel rule | Cramps |
| Try square | Tenon saw |
| Mortise gauge | Smoothing plane |
| Marking knife | Glue |
| Mortise chisel | |

## How to make a through mortise-and-tenon joint

**1** After selecting appropriate face sides and edges, mark the position of the joint on both pieces of timber with pencil and try square. The mortise chisel should be about one-third the thickness of the timber. In practice, this is rounded up to the next chisel size. Adjust the two pins on the mortise gauge until they are the same width as the blade. To ensure the joint is centralized in the timber, slide the stock on the gauge so that the pins mark the timber precisely the same distance from either side. Check by lightly pressing the pins into the wood, and readjust the stock if necessary, tightening once the setting is correct. This setting is used to mark out both the mortise and tenon, so treat the tool with care to avoid disturbing the adjustment.

**2** Scribe the gauge lines for the mortise between the width marks on the stile (B). Mark lines on both edges, always using the tool from the face side. Without disturbing the setting, mark out the tenon on part A. The gauge lines should continue along the end grain.

**3** Cramp part B to the bench top, preferably so that the mortise sits directly above the bench leg. Start the cut with the chisel about 3 mm (⅛ in) in from the marked lines at one end, the bevel facing into the middle of the joint. Keeping the blade vertical and square to the work, strike the chisel with the mallet. Cut to a depth of about 3 mm (⅛ in), counting the number of blows to the chisel. Move the blade along

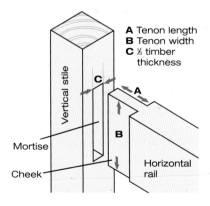

A Tenon length
B Tenon width
C ⅓ timber thickness

Vertical stile

C

A

Mortise

Cheek

B

Horizontal rail

1

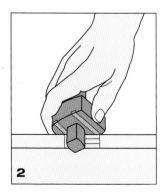

2

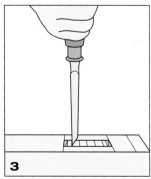

3

the mortise and repeat in 3 mm (⅛ in) steps. Making the same number of blows each time means the depth will remain constant across the width. Stop when you are 3 mm (⅛ in) away from the opposite end of the mortise.

**4** Clean out the chippings, using the chisel with the bevel side face down. Lever the blade against the short section of waste at each end of the mortise. Now make another series of cuts across the width, removing the waste in the same way. Continue cutting in steps until you have reached just over half the depth of the mortise.

**5** Remove the waste at each end of the mortise by holding the chisel vertical. Keep the blade just inside the marked line, with the bevel facing inwards. Strike with the mallet and chop down to just over half the depth. Turn the work piece the other way up, tip out the loose chips and brush any debris from the bench top. Cramp the work piece down again and start afresh from the other side. This prevents the wood from splitting out at the bottom of the mortise. Assuming you have kept the chisel vertical, the final cuts will match up with those on the reverse.

**6** When cutting the tenon rail to size, leave a fraction extra on its length. You will plane this off once the joint is assembled. In furniture construction the tenon rail (A) is often thicker than the stile (B). If so, you will need to reset the mortise gauge to mark out the tenon. The two pins remain the same distance apart, however, as these still match the width of the chisel blade.

**7** Scribe the shoulder lines of the tenon with the knife and square. Mark the waste (the cheeks) in pencil. Set the rail (A) upright in the vice and make several horizontal saw cuts on the waste side of the gauged lines to a depth of about 3 mm (⅛ in).

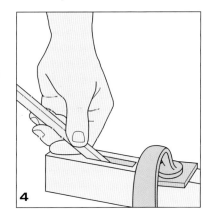

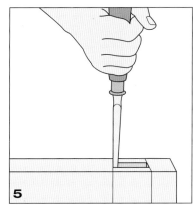

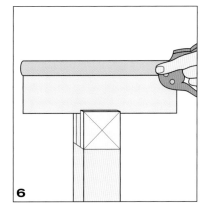

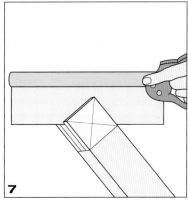

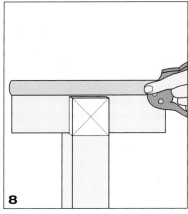

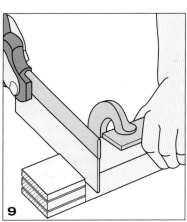

**8** Adjust the rail so that it is facing away from you at an angle of 45 degrees. Continue sawing down both gauged lines until you reach the shoulder mark. Remove the rail and turn it around so that it is again facing you at an angle of 45 degrees. Again, saw down until you reach the shoulder.

**9** You will now have sawn lines along both sides and across the top. Reposition the rail in the vice

so that it is upright. Finish cutting down both cheeks to the shoulder line. Hold the tenon rail flat on the bench hook and saw carefully across the shoulder lines to remove the waste. Turn the rail over and repeat on the reverse side. Try inserting the tenon into the mortise before gluing. You may need to pare the cheeks carefully with the chisel to remove any high spots. Do this with the timber either cramped to the bench top or held in the vice.

# Variations

## Stub mortise-and-tenon joint

Often used in furniture-making, the stub, or stopped, mortise-and-tenon joint is a neater alternative as the end grain of the tenon is not visible. This stops short of the outside edge of the stile, so the mortise is known as 'blind'. Mortise depth should be about three-quarters of the width of the stile, so there is a sufficient amount of wood remaining.

## How to make a stub mortise-and-tenon joint

**1** Measuring three-quarters of the timber width from the end of the rail (A), scribe the shoulder line of the tenon all the way round with the marking knife. Adjust the mortise gauge to the chisel width and make sure the pins are central on the work piece. Gauge the lines around the tenon and across the end grain, then pencil in the waste. Place the rail (A) on the inner edge of stile (B) and mark the width of the mortise. Continue these lines across with the square, then scribe the mortise between them with the gauge. Pencil in the waste.

**2** To make sure you do not cut the mortise too deep, wrap masking tape around the blade of the chisel, allowing about 1.5 mm (⅟₁₆ in) extra depth. This is so that the tenon does not foul the bottom of the mortise when the joint is assembled.

**3** With the stile cramped to the bench top, chop out the mortise from the inside edge. When the tape on the chisel is level with the timber, you have reached the full depth. Clean out the waste, making sure the bottom of the mortise is level. Saw the tenon in the same way as for the through tenon (see page 209). Check the tenon fits into the mortise and adjust with the chisel if necessary before gluing.

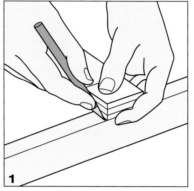
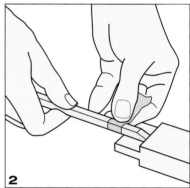
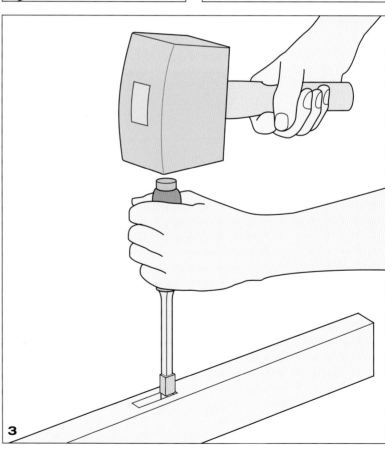

# Haunched mortise-and-tenon joint

Corners of framework can present a problem when mortise-and-tenon joints are used, particularly if the top edges must finish flush with each other. A full-width tenon is actually a bridle joint (see page 213). Because the resulting mortise is open-ended, the joint becomes much weaker. By introducing a haunch, the tenon width is reduced and the mortise does not extend to the end of the stile. A haunch can be either square or sloping, and helps prevent the frame from twisting. This joint is commonly used in joinery for door and window construction.

Where stiles and rails are rebated or grooved, a square haunch is used. Where a groove runs around the inside edges of a frame, the groove normally extends all the way along each edge. The tenon's square haunch fills the outside end of the joint as well as the groove. Shoulders are usually staggered to accommodate rebates on framework.

In cabinet-making, where appearance is important, the sloping haunch is often used. Unlike the square version, this haunch is not visible once the joint is assembled. It is commonly used between the seat rails and legs in chair construction.

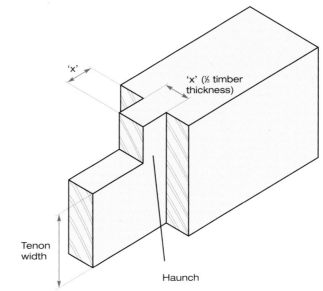

'x'

'x' (⅙ timber thickness)

Tenon width

Haunch

## TIPS

• Always cut a mortise before sawing the tenon. You can adjust the tenon to fit the mortise more easily than vice versa.
• Always use a mortise chisel when cutting the joint by hand. Other chisel blades are less sturdy and could break.

**Mortise-and-tenon joint for grooved frame**

**Mortise-and-tenon joint with sloping haunch**

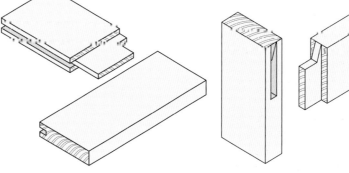

## Wedged mortise-and-tenon joint

To strengthen through mortise-and-tenon joints, wedges can be driven into the ends of the tenons. This also prevents them opening up on items of joinery such as doors, which are subjected to heavy use. Before assembling the joint, the ends of the mortise are enlarged with sloping cuts. Saw cuts are then made in the end of the tenon, and the wedges driven into these slots when gluing up. The tenon is splayed outwards, locking the joint together. Ends of the wedges are sawn off once the glue has dried.

## Twin mortise-and-tenon joint

Where the mortise is cut into the face of the timber, rather than into the edge (as in the double version, above), a twin mortise-and-tenon joint provides extra strength. The tenons sit alongside each other, rather than being stacked one above the other. This time there is no haunch between the tenons and the gap between them should ideally be the same as their thickness. Carcase construction may call for a multiple version of the joint, which has several tenons. Here, a stopped housing may be introduced to increase strength further.

## Fox-wedged mortise-and–tenon joint

When a stub mortise-and-tenon joint needs extra strength, wedges can be inserted into the tenon. Unlike wedges driven in from the outside, these must be cut to length and width precisely. Once the joint is cramped together it cannot be taken apart.

**Further information**

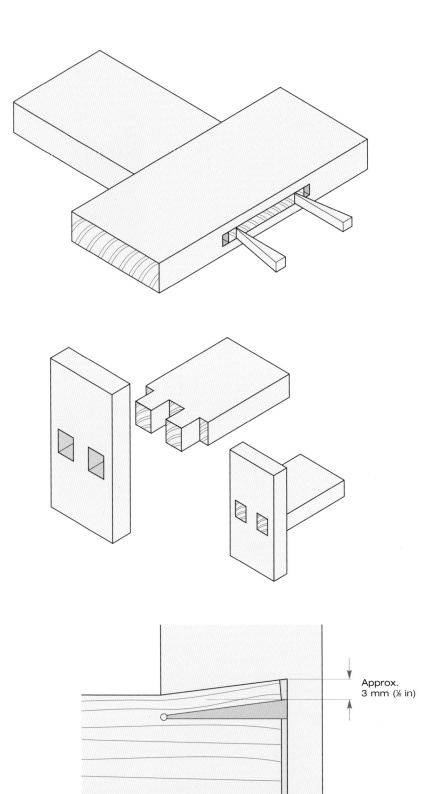

Approx.
3 mm (⅛ in)

# Bridle joints

A bridle joint is very similar to a mortise-and-tenon joint, but cut in reverse. Removing the waste is more akin to cutting a halving joint. The tenon is usually one-third the thickness of the stock, although in reality this is rounded up to the closest chisel width. Both corner- and T-bridle joints are used in narrow framework construction. Components are marked out in the same way as a through mortise-and-tenon. It is important to pencil in the waste areas before cutting, otherwise you may find yourself creating the wrong joint.

## How to make a bridle joint

**1** With a suitable drill bit, bore through the end of the mortise, close to the shoulder line. When you have drilled just over half the depth, turn the work piece over and bore from the reverse edge to prevent breakout.

**2** With the work piece upright in the vice, saw down to the shoulder lines. Pare any remaining waste away carefully with the chisel, working with the work piece flat on the bench. When making a T-bridle joint, you cut the tenon rail from both faces, as with a housing joint. For a corner bridle joint, cut as a normal through tenon.

1

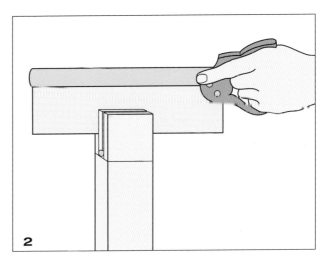

2

# Dovetail joints

The traditional dovetail joint is used by cabinet-makers, carpenters and even boat builders. It is often a demonstration of quality of craftsmanship in using hand tools. The real advantage of the dovetail is its great mechanical strength and the fact that it provides a good surface area for glue. Arguably more complex than other joints to make by hand, the most common varieties can also be made using a router and dovetail jig.

**Tools you need**

| | |
|---|---|
| 2H pencil | Bevel-edge chisel |
| Steel rule | Mallet |
| Cutting gauge | Marking knife |
| Try square | Hammer |
| Sliding bevel or dovetail | Masking tape |
| template | Glue |
| Dovetail saw | Brush |
| Coping saw | Smoothing plane |
| Cramps | |

## DOVETAIL ANGLES

The dovetail joint consists of two distinct parts: the dovetails – so called because of their fan shape – and the pins, which fit between them and also form the outer edges of the joint. The spaces between the pins are known as sockets. Dovetails are usually bigger than their corresponding pins, and the bevel angle differs depending on the timber used. For softwoods the slope is 1:6, while for hardwoods it is 1:8.

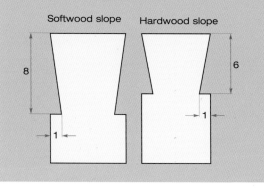

Softwood slope    Hardwood slope

## JARGON BUSTER

**Dovetail** A joint consisting of a set of tails that interlock with pins in the corresponding piece.
**Face edge** An edge planed straight and square to the face side.
**Face side** A wide surface planed perfectly flat, selected to be exposed on finished work.
**Shoulder** The squared end on either one or both sides of a tenon or tongue.
**Socket** The space between a pair of pins in a dovetail joint.

## How to make a through dovetail joint

**1** Cut and plane the ends of the timber square, allowing an extra 1 mm (1/32 in) on the length of each piece. This will allow you to clean up the joint with a plane after assembly. Mark the shoulder-line positions on both pieces. Set the cutting gauge to these marks and scribe a line around the end of the tail piece (A). The cutting gauge is used in preference to a marking gauge, as its small knife blade produces a clean-cut line across the grain. On the pin piece (B) mark only the sides with the gauge. Use a pencil and square on the faces here, as gauged lines would be visible after the joint is glued up.

# DOVETAIL SPACING

Dovetail spacing is largely a question of structural and aesthetic balance. The outer pins should not be too small, or they could break off. Softwood joints need fewer tails than hardwood ones. Accurate marking of the pins is one of the secrets of a neat dovetail joint, which you can achieve by scribing the pins directly from the cut tails. Alternatively, you can cut the pins first and use these to scribe the tails. Practice will help you decide which method you prefer.

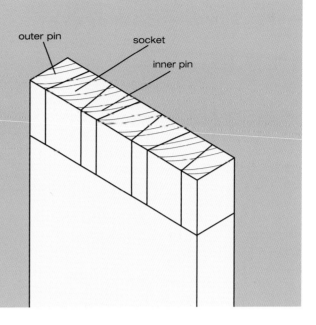

outer pin
socket
inner pin

**2** Use either a sliding bevel or dovetail template to mark out the tails on part A. Measure 6 mm (¼ in) in from each edge and divide the distance between them equally. Mark these points on the end of the timber, then add 3 mm (⅛ in) either side. This gives the spacing between each tail. Square the lines across the end, and mark the slope of the dovetails with the sliding bevel or template. Shade in the waste to be removed between the dovetails. This is crucial, as it is easy to saw on the wrong side of the pencil lines.

**3** Insert part A in the vice, tilted so that the dovetail bevels on the right side are vertical (if you are right-handed). Start cutting with the saw pointing upwards for the first two or three strokes. Level out the saw and cut down each tail until you reach the shoulder lines. Tilt the timber the other way and saw the left sides of each tail.

**4** Remove most of the waste with a coping saw. Start cutting in line with the dovetail bevel, changing to a horizontal cut after a few strokes. Aim to remove as much waste as possible without the blade touching the shoulder line. Check the saw cut on the reverse face to make sure the blade is level.

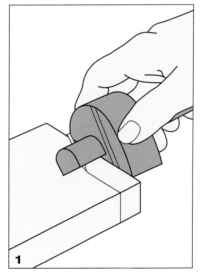

1

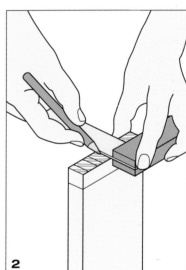

2

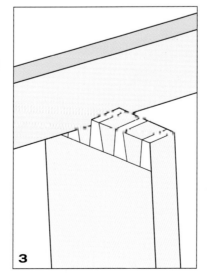

3

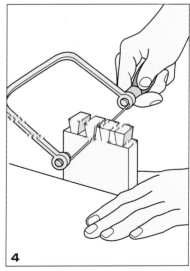

4

**5** To remove the waste from the outside edges, cramp the work horizontally in the vice and saw down to the shoulder line.

**6** Cramp the work piece to the bench top with a piece of MDF or plywood underneath. This protects the bench and prevents breakout on the reverse side of the joint. A square-section offcut cramped to the face, aligned with the shoulder line, will help to keep the chisel vertical. Hold the chisel firmly against the guide block and strike the handle with the mallet. Continue cutting down until you reach the offcut.

**7** Hold the pin work piece (B) upright in the vice, so it protrudes above the bench top by the height of a suitable tool such as a plane. Lay the plane on its side

behind the work piece so that the dovetail piece (A) can rest level on top. Hold the dovetail firmly in position and scribe around the tails carefully with a marking knife. Fill the scribed lines in with pencil, as they can be difficult to see. Using a small try square held against the end of the work piece (B), continue the lines on to the face. Shade in the waste areas as you did with the tails. You can mark both sides of the timber in this way, although this is not essential.

**8** Saw the pins in the same way as the tails. You must do this accurately, as there is no room for error. Cut carefully, keeping the saw level, until you reach the shoulder line. It is easier to cut the pins so that the blade just shaves the line than to leave waste that must be trimmed back later.

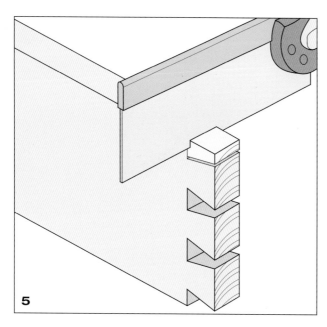

5

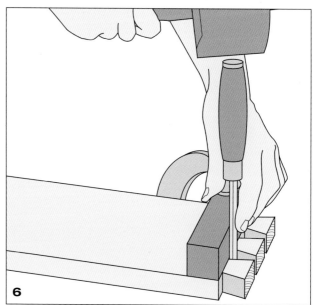

6

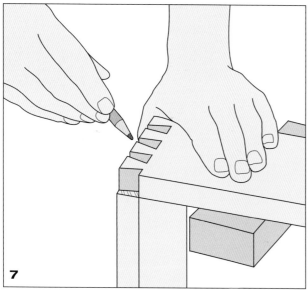

7

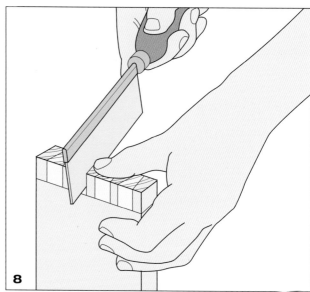

8

**9** Now remove the waste between the pins with the coping saw. Keep checking the blade position at the back of the joint so that it does not wander too close to the scribed line. This time allow for the bevelled shape of the pins as you cut. Alternatively, lay the work piece flat on the bench top and cramp the guide block to the shoulder line again. Pare away the waste gradually with the chisel, working from both sides in towards the middle. Make the final cut by holding the blade against the block and striking the chisel with the mallet. Clean out any waste still in the socket corners with the blade held at the same angle as the pins.

**10** To check that the joint will fit together snugly, cramp the pin part (B) upright in the vice. Hold the dovetail part (A) in place and tap it gently with a hammer and an offcut resting on the tails – this applies firm, even pressure without causing damage. If the joint begins to go together evenly, you can take it apart. Do not completely assemble yet, as a

dovetail joint is a close fit and should only be fully driven home once. If the joint does not fit evenly, check where the tight spots are and gradually ease them back with the chisel. Dovetails should be snug, but not too tight or they will split.

**11** Wrap masking tape around both pieces of timber up to the glue lines. Brush on glue to all parts of the joint that will be in contact, allowing it to soak into the surfaces to create a good bond. Assemble the joint using the hammer and offcut to drive it home. Cramp up and check the inside faces are square.

**12** When the glue has dried, remove the masking tape. With the joint held firmly in the vice, clean up the end grain with a finely set smoothing plane. Work at an angle of about 45 degrees from the outside of the joint in towards the middle. This cutting angle overcomes the problem of opposing grain directions and prevents breakout.

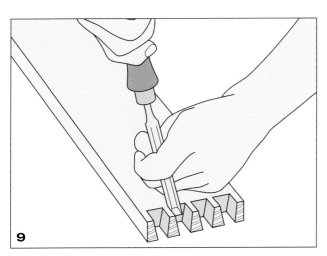

9

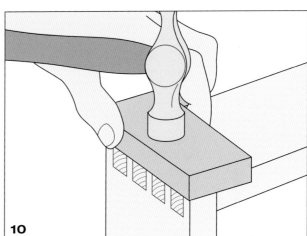

10

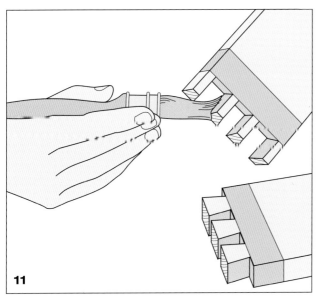

11

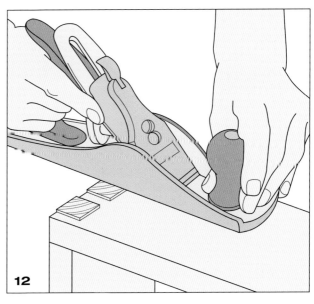

12

# Variations

## Lapped dovetail joint

A typical use of the dovetail joint is for drawers. The lapped dovetail stops short of the front face of the timber, so that end grain is not visible when the drawer is closed. This is more difficult to make than a through dovetail, as more of the waste is chiselled away rather than sawn.

### How to make a lapped dovetail joint

**1** Determine the thickness of the lap before you cut the dovetail part (A) to length. It should be about one-third the thickness of the stock. Saw the pin part (B) 1 mm (1⁄32 in) longer, and plane the ends of both pieces square. Adjust the cutting gauge to the tail length, allowing for the lap thickness. Gauge the shoulder line around part (A). Set out the dovetail positions and pencil in the waste. Cut the tails in the same way as making a through dovetail joint.

**2** Gauge the lap line across the end of the pin part (B) from the inside face. Reset the gauge to the thickness of the tail part (A), plus an extra 1 mm (1⁄32 in). This will allow you to plane the end grain flush after assembly. Mark the shoulder line across the inside face of part (B). With the pin piece (B) upright in the vice, lay part (A) on top and mark out pins from the tails with a knife. Square the lines over the inside face to the shoulder line.

**3** With part (B) held in the vice, cut along the waste side of the pins. Keep the saw at an angle and stop when you reach the shoulder and lap lines. Saw into the corners to start removing waste.

**4** Cramp the work piece to the bench with a piece of MDF underneath. Using a mallet and chisel, chop out the waste to form the sockets. Cut vertically across the grain just in front of the shoulder line, and horizontally into the end grain. Trim the corners with a narrow chisel and pare downwards at the shoulder line.

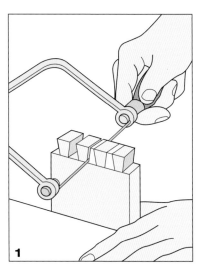

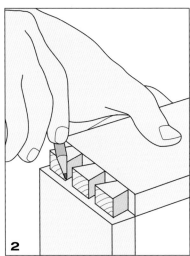

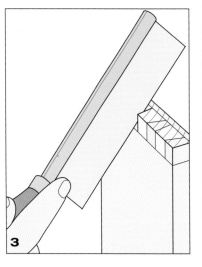

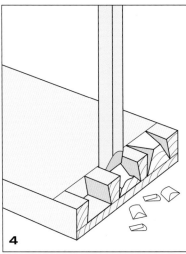

## Rebated dovetail

Through dovetails present a problem when making boxes. If top and bottom panels are rebated in, then gaps will show at the corners where the rebates continue to the end of the timber. The solution is to extend the shoulder of the tail piece to fill the rebate. Careful marking out of the rebate before setting out the dovetails will help to get a good joint. The rebates are planed or routed after cutting the dovetails.

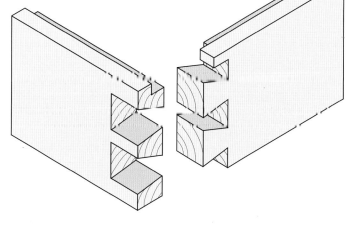

## Secret mitred dovetail

Used sometimes in fine cabinet-making work, the secret mitred dovetail appears to be a normal mitre joint from the outside. Its construction is hidden when the joint is assembled. Both parts have to be identical in thickness and must be cut precisely to length. Pins are cut first and the tails marked out from these. The actual mitre is pared with a chisel, although it is neater when cleaned up with a shoulder plane.

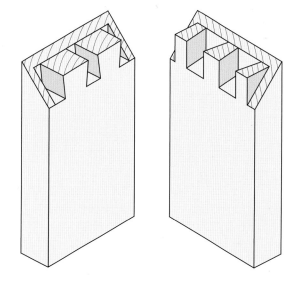

## Bevelled dovetail

One of the most difficult joints to make, the bevelled dovetail is used when the sloping sides of a frame meet at a compound angle (where adjacent sides are both sloping). It is essential to make a drawing of the elevation, so that you can calculate the shape of each component before marking out. Each piece of timber must be the same thickness and is cut oversize in both width and length.

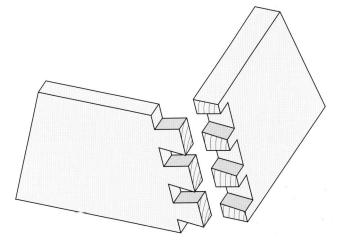

**Further information**
Measuring and marking tools
  pages 84–87
Saws  pages 88–93
Glues  pages 234–235

# 10

# Preparation and finishing

The purpose of a finish is to protect the wood from heat, moisture and general wear and tear, as well as to enhance its beauty. It is important that finishing materials are compatible: if staining timber, for example, make sure your selected finish can be applied over the top. Before any finishing takes place, surfaces must be thoroughly prepared. This normally involves sanding, which means a certain amount of hand work. Then you can apply a finish, be it traditional oil, wax or polish, or a more contemporary lacquer. Always read the instructions on the container before you begin and follow any health and safety recommendations.

# Abrasives and sanding

Most completed pieces of furniture or joinery need sanding once they have been carefully planed or scraped. Never skimp on the time spent on preparation before applying a finishing coat. Thorough sanding may be tedious, but it will ensure that the beauty of the wood is revealed fully when a finish is eventually applied.

ABOVE A range of abrasives can be used when preparing wood for final finishing.

BELOW From left to right: Silicon carbide, glasspaper, aluminium oxide and punched sheets for power sanders.

## Abrasive paper

The three main types of paper used by furniture-makers are garnet, aluminium oxide and silicon carbide. The grade, or coarseness, of abrasive paper is identified by a number printed on the back, and those most used by cabinet-makers are 80, 100, 120, 150, 180, 240 and 320 grit. Irrespective of type or grade, abrasive paper is sold in standard sizes, measuring 280 x 230 mm (approximately 11 x 9 in). It is normally folded and torn into four pieces for wrapping around a block for sanding by hand. Work systematically through the grades, from coarse to fine. This ensures scratches are removed, which would show up under a finishing coat.

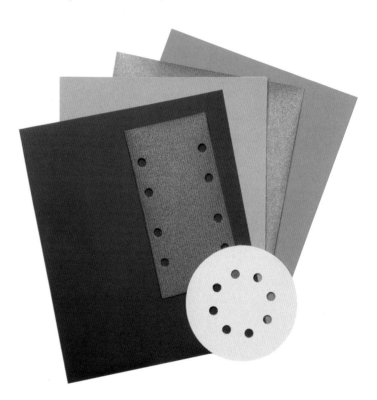

### Garnet

Garnet paper is made from crushed stone particles, which are harder and last longer than glass. A good choice for sanding by hand, sheets are orange in colour. It is made specifically for sanding hard and softwoods and comes in grades from 40 to 320 grit.

### Aluminium oxide

Most suitable for power tools and sanding machines, aluminium oxide is available in coarser grades, from 40 to 320 grit. Particles are harder than garnet and suitable for metals and fillers, besides wood, and also for sanding by hand. The most economical way to buy it is in roll form, with widths of 90 and 115 mm (3½ and 4½ in). Lengths can be up to 100 m (approximately 327 ft). Coarser grades with a heavy backing paper for machine use have a tendency to crack when folded, so cut with a knife.

### Silicon carbide

The hardest abrasive of all, with particles almost as tough as diamond. You can use it on hard materials such as glass, as well as lacquers and paints. The most expensive abrasive, silicon carbide paper is flexible and lubricated with a fine dust, rather like talcum powder. It is ideal for final hand sanding of varnishes and lacquers, with grades from 60 to 500 grit.

# Other abrasives

## Wet-and-dry paper

Used with soap and water as a lubricant, waterproof wet-and-dry paper is used to cut back coats of varnish or lacquer before applying subsequent ones. Available in grades from 80 to 1,200 grit. 400 grit is suitable for most finishes. Musical-instrument makers and fine cabinet-makers often use much finer grits, so that no scratches are visible under the final finishing coat.

## Glasspaper

Traditional glasspaper is relatively soft and the particles of glass wear rapidly. As a result, it clogs quickly and has a short lifespan. Flour paper is the finest grade ('00') and is sometimes used for de-nibbing. Still sold in many hardware stores, glasspaper has long been superseded by far more effective abrasives.

## Nylon fibre pads

Resembling pan scourers, resilient nylon-fibre pads are available with bonded aluminium oxide or silicon carbide particles. Resistant to clogging, they mould themselves to any shape and can even be washed under the tap. They are comparatively unaggressive, come in grades from 60 to 1,500 grit and are excellent for de-nibbing coats of lacquer or applying wax polish. Grades are distinguished by different colour pads.

## Steel wool

Steel, or wire, wool is available in several grades from '4' at the coarse end (for stripping) to '0000' at the fine end for cutting back and final finishing. It is very resistant to clogging and will follow the contours of even the most complex moulding.

## Grit grades

Abrasive particles are graded during manufacture by passing them through mesh of various sizes. The grit number relates to the number of particles per unit area and is an international classification. The higher the number, the finer the grade of abrasive.

Nylon fibre pads

Steel wool

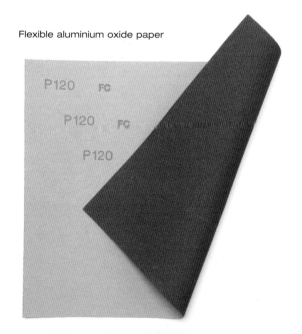

Flexible aluminium oxide paper

---

### JARGON BUSTER

**Cutting back** When a finish is applied, the grain is raised or the surface coating itself is uneven. This requires the finish to be smoothed down or 'cut back' between coats using a gentle abrasive.

**De-nibbing** The process of lightly sanding a varnished or lacquered surface between coats to remove dust particles.

**Tack cloth** A fabric cloth impregnated with resin to collect dust particles from a surface.

# Sanding techniques

## Sanding by hand

Before using abrasive papers it is often necessary to use a cabinet scraper to remove fine tears and blemishes. A cork sanding block will ease this task and increase the life of the paper. Always sand with the grain, working up through the grits. For most woodwork projects, start at about 120 grit and move up to 240 grit. As paper becomes clogged, tap the sanding block against the bench to clear the dust. As a final touch, use a piece of worn, fine-grit paper to take the edge off any edges and corners. When you have sanded with the finest grade of paper, wipe a cloth lightly dampened with water over the surface of the wood. This causes the fibres to swell, and allows you to give a final sanding with the same grade of abrasive for a superior finish.

## Power sanding

Portable power sanders are ideal for initial sanding of surfaces and are fast, but they do have drawbacks. Belt sanders are aggressive and can quickly sand through veneers, or leave gouges in a surface. Even random orbital sanders can leave light scratches, and should always be followed by hand sanding. Combination and disc sanding machines are useful for initial sanding of components and edges and are particularly good for cleaning up end grain to make sure it is square.

# Final preparation

For finishing, your working area should be warm (15°C/59°F), well lit and ventilated. Both project and workshop should be thoroughly cleaned and vacuumed. Get as much dust out of the grain and pores as possible, particularly where dark and pale woods are used alongside each other. A tack cloth is ideal for this. You must also remove all traces of wax and silicon used to lubricate tools during construction. Clear an area of the workshop for your finishes, making sure that you have plenty of rags, mixing sticks and containers to hand.

## Masking and finishing

On complex pieces it may be easier to finish components before final assembly, especially internal surfaces of carcases that may be difficult to access once glued together. If you choose to do this, mask off gluing surfaces first. If not, there is a risk that joints will not hold when glued. Apply the finish in sequence: start with corners and undersides, ending up with the primary surfaces.

ABOVE Moulded edges are trickier to sand than flat surfaces. Use dowelling, a flexible sanding pad or your fingers to back the paper.

BELOW Abrasive paper is normally folded and torn into four pieces for wrapping around a block for sanding by hand.

**Further information**
Essential toolkit  pages 74–75
The work environment  pages 66–67
Health and safety  pages 68–69
Spokeshaves and scrapers  pages 113–115
Power sanders  pages 128–130
Sanders  pages 164–165

# Fillers and stains

Before applying a finish you often need to fill the grain and stain the timber, depending on the colour and effect you want. Small defects in the surface, such as splits or tears, can be concealed. Stains can alter the colour of timber dramatically or can be quite subtle, while still allowing the grain to show through.

Two-pack wood filler

Wood filler and stain

Natural grain filler

Wax filler sticks

## Fillers and stoppers

A filling knife has a flexible steel blade and is the best tool for applying fillers and stoppers to a surface. Press the filler into the wood with the blade and drag it across. When dry, sand the filler flush with the wood.

## Grain and wood fillers

Ring-porous hardwoods may need their open grain filling if a smooth, piano-like finish is required. Although open grain can provide a more natural texture, this effect is not always appropriate. Grain filler is generally a thin cellulose-based paste, which you work across the wood with a cloth, driving it into the pores. When dry, you sand it ready for applying a finish. You can buy fillers in colours, as well as clear. You can obtain interesting effects by using a filler that contrasts with the timber colour. Most grain fillers are ready mixed, although you can get them in powder form and mix with water.

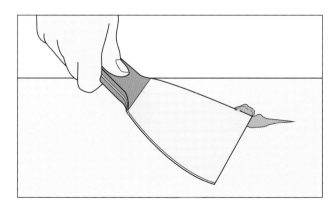

ABOVE Force filler or stopping into cavities with a flexible knife, until proud of the surrounding wood.

Stiffer than grain filler, wood filler is generally used on small defects. It comes in a range of timber-effect colours, although it is possible to add a compatible wood stain. Ready-mixed fillers may be spirit or water-based and sold in tubes or tins. Cellulose fillers usually come in powder form to mix with water.

## Stopper

Two-part chemical fillers consist of a hardener and resin, and are suitable for filling large holes quickly. Once mixed, they set hard in just a few minutes and can then be sanded. Other stoppers are ready-mixed. Some are suitable for exterior as well as interior use.

## Shellac sticks

Traditionally used for filling defects, solid shellac sticks come in a range of timber colours. You simply melt the stick with the tip of a soldering iron and drip the liquid into the crevice. Use a filling knife moistened with water to force the shellac down firmly.

## Wax sticks

Wax sticks are suitable for filling small blemishes. You shave a small amount off the end with a knife and press into the surface. You should only use these sticks under a wax-polish finish. A range of colours is available.

## Knotting

Certain softwoods can exude resin – particularly from knots – even after a finish has been applied. You need to seal them with knotting, a shellac-based sealer that prevents bleeding. Only use knotting under a paint finish, as it stains the surrounding wood.

ABOVE Hardwoods, such as oak, generally accept stain more evenly than softwoods, which can appear blotchy.

ABOVE The result of the fuming process on European oak. The lower sample has been left untreated.

# Stains

Stains can enhance bland timbers and add depth, while still allowing the grain to show through. You can buy them in powder, spirit and acrylic (water-based) forms, which you then mix with other colours. Make sure the brand and type are the same, however. Most stains are ready-mixed, and those in powder form are generally stocked by specialist suppliers rather than hardware stores. Colours do not always penetrate deeply so take care not to sand through the stain when finishing. Apply stain evenly with a quality paintbrush or a clean, lint-free cloth, working with the grain. Make sure that wet edges are blended together rapidly. Always wear gloves for this process.

## Oil stain

Ready-mixed oil stains contain white spirit or naphtha and can interfere with subsequent finishing coats unless you apply a a sanding sealer. Oil stains do not raise the grain and give good results, however.

## Water stain

Easier to dilute than other types, water stains penetrate the wood well and dry more slowly. As a result, they are easy to apply and will accept most finishes over the top. Available ready-mixed or as aniline powder to mix with warm water.

## Spirit stain

Spirit stains are dissolved in methylated spirit and dry rapidly. This means it can be difficult to cover a panel without getting streaked, overlapping edges. Available ready-mixed or as a powder, spirit stain is trickier to apply than other types.

## Fuming

Some timbers darken when exposed to ammonia fumes. The effectiveness of the process varies from species to species, but oak is a classic example that is often fumed. The colour depends on how long the timber is exposed to ammonia fumes: for a very dark brown the ammonia will have to be changed several times. To fume a piece of furniture, either make a temporary fuming tent from clear polythene or modify a cupboard by blocking up all the ventilation. Place the piece inside with a shallow dish of ammonia and check the colour periodically.

## Bleaching

Bleaching makes wood paler, and is often used to turn several pieces that may not match in terms of colour to a uniform state before staining them. A two-pack bleach kit commonly available consists of a solution of caustic soda and hydrogen peroxide, and is effective to varying degrees on a wide variety of timbers. The extent of the colour change depends on the timber and the number of applications. Oxalic acid is a milder alternative. It is also a good reviver of timber and will remove many stains, including iron, ink and water.

**TIP**

• Always wear thin vinyl or latex protective gloves when using chemicals. Available in quantity packs, disposable pairs are inexpensive to buy.

**Further information**
Timber selection  pages 12–15
Veneers  pages 24–25
Sheet materials  pages 26–29
The work environment  pages 66–67
Health and safety  pages 68–69
Abrasives and sanding  pages 222–224
Lacquers  pages 230–231

# Polish, wax and oil

Having prepared your surfaces, you can select and apply an appropriate finish. Waxes and oils are easy to use and it is possible to obtain an impressive satin finish with little experience. French-polishing is not so straightforward, and takes much practice to develop the necessary skills to perfect the technique.

ABOVE Oils penetrate the grain to create a rich finish, particularly with timbers such as oak.

## Polish

French polish is the most traditional of finishes, and has been used in Europe since the 16th century. Although largely superseded by the development of modern finishes, it is still used in antique furniture repair and restoration. It gives a deep, gloss finish, which is nevertheless fairly delicate compared to more modern coatings. The French-polishing process is a laborious and skilled technique that has evolved into a specialized trade. Most polishes are based on shellac, a resin derived from secretions from the lac beetle, a parasite found on trees in India. The manufacturing process usually results in shellac flakes that are dissolved in industrial alcohol.

There are several types of polish – some giving a slight tint to the timber. Button polish is made from high-quality shellac and gives a golden tone to the wood. Garnet polish gives a darker brown tint. White polish alters the colour of most woods less than button and garnet, while transparent polish is the clearest of these finishes. You apply French polish with a rubber, each coat slightly dissolving the one underneath so that they blend together. A common use for shellac is in the form of sanding sealer, used as a base for a wax finish.

Button polish

Knotting

French polish

---

### JARGON BUSTER

**De-nibbing** The process of lightly sanding a varnished or lacquered surface between coats to remove dust particles.

**Rubber** A folded cloth filled with cotton wool or lint wadding, which has been charged with polish. Applied to timber with figure-of-eight and circular movements.

Liming wax

Paste wax

Coloured wax polish

Wax polishing brush

ABOVE Liming wax is applied to bare wood with a cloth, after rubbing the surface with a wire brush to open up the grain.

ABOVE After about ten minutes the excess wax is removed with a hard cloth.

# Wax

Wax provides a beautiful finish for wood, but used alone it gives almost no protection from heat or moisture and also results in a fairly dull finish. You can achieve greater protection and a richer effect if you use it over a base of sanding sealer, varnish or oil. Traditionally, furniture wax has been made from a blend of beeswax and turpentine, sometimes with extra ingredients such as carnauba wax to improve its performance. A wide range of timber colours is produced, as well as clear waxes. Apply paste wax with fine steel wool or cotton cloth, and buff up to a satin finish with a cloth or special brush. Apply liquid wax with a soft cloth, either onto bare timber or over a sanding sealer.

## Liming wax

Liming emphasizes the grain and gives a lighter overall effect. It is only effective on ring-porous timbers such as oak, elm and ash, highlighting the grain by leaving a white deposit. On close-grain timbers such as maple, the wax will not penetrate the pores so the effect is limited to crevices and corners. The wax is generally sold ready mixed in tins. Before using liming wax, first rub the timber with coarse steel wool or wire brush to open up the grain. Apply the wax with a cloth, rubbing it well into the crevices. After a few minutes remove the excess with a hard cloth. Finally, polish with 0000-grade steel wool.

# Oils

Although applying traditional linseed oil is a lengthy process, contemporary oil finishes are quick, simpler to use and generally produce a harder coating. They offer moderate protection from heat and moisture, but are easy to repair when necessary. You can apply oils with a rubber or a good-quality paintbrush. At least five coats are necessary initially, which you should maintain with a reapplication at least every six months. Furniture oils tend to include ultraviolet absorbers to reduce the harmful effects of sunlight, and those for exterior use may have biocides to prevent mould.

## Linseed oil

The traditional oil finish, linseed comes in raw and boiled versions. Boiled linseed oil dries more quickly than the raw type, although adding pure turpentine speeds up drying. These oils require many coats to build up to a gloss finish. As overnight drying is required between coats, the process can take weeks if you want a gloss finish. Because linseed oil takes a long time to dry, there is a tendency for it to attract dust.
De-nib surfaces between coats to remove particles.

## Tung oil

Resistant to heat and water, tung oil is the most durable oil finish. Also called Chinese oil, it is made from nuts produced by the tung tree and blended with synthetic resins to improve the hardness. It penetrates well and gives an excellent finish, especially if surfaces are lightly sanded between coats.

## Danish and teak oil

Good for a durable matt or satin finish on indoor and outdoor furniture, Danish and teak oils contain special vegetable oils, resins and driers. Danish oil will give more of a satin finish than teak oil, which will develop a gloss with a few coats. They both contain tung oil.

# Texture

An alternative way of emphasizing the nature of wood is to pick out the grain pattern and surface texture. Resulting in pieces that are more difficult to clean, these processes are generally restricted to pieces that are not constantly handled.

## Sandblasting

The process wears away the softer fibres to create an effect similar to driftwood. The surface quality depends on the grit type and the power of the machine. You can create interesting effects by masking off areas.

## Scrubbing

Scrubbing some timbers with caustic soda picks out the grain like sandblasting, but without leaving hard edges. Success varies between species. The scrubbing solution is very caustic so it is essential to take adequate safety precautions.

## Scorching

Lightly scorching timber leaves a very smooth and soft texture on even the roughest of woods. It is very quick to achieve and you can do it on any timber, even when unseasoned. It is particularly applicable to rough carving and more sculptural work, as the grain is lost and the form emphasized.

ABOVE A selection of traditional and contemporary oils: (A) finishing oil; (B) boiled linseed oil; (C) Organoil; (D) Danish oil; (E) teak oil; and (F) lemon oil.

ABOVE A blow torch can be used to lightly scorch timber to create a smooth-textured surface.

---

**TIP**

• Owing to the risk of spontaneous combustion, cloths used for applying finishes should be disposed of carefully. They should be laid out to dry outdoors, before soaking in water and throwing away.

**Further information**

# Lacquer

'Lacquer' and 'varnish' are collective names for synthetic clear coatings. These are durable finishes and can broadly be subdivided into solvent- and water-based products. There are many products available for both interior and exterior use, some having a flexible film.

Yacht varnish

Acrylic varnish

## Polyurethane

Among the most popular of brush finishes, polyurethane varnishes are available in gloss, satin and matt. Particularly tough and ideal for everything from floors to furniture, polyurethane is easy to apply. Available in wood tints as well as clear, drying times are relatively slow. Typically touch-dry in two to four hours, they need to harden for up to eight hours before re-coating. Drying times depend on workshop temperature and humidity, reaching full hardness within 24 hours. White spirit is generally used for thinning the finish and cleaning equipment.

### CHOOSING LACQUER

Solvent-based lacquers perform marginally better than acrylics. A much slower drying time means fewer brushstrokes, but dust particles can be a problem. Water-based, acrylic lacquers dry faster and are generally safer and more pleasant to use. On large areas it is hard to avoid brushmarks appearing, as it is difficult to keep all edges wet for blending together. The advantage of acrylic finishes is that you can apply all the coats in one day, de-nibbing between each one as necessary.

### JARGON BUSTER

**De-nibbing** Lightly sanding between coats to remove dust particles.
**Rubber** A folded cloth filled with wadding. Used to apply French polish or varnish.
**Solvent** The liquid in which a substance can be dissolved to create a solution.

## Acrylic

Very fast drying, acrylic varnish is water based, so brush cleaning means simply running it under the tap. Although milky in appearance when applied, acrylic varnish dries to a clear finish within about 15 minutes. It can be recoated after two hours. Available in gloss, satin and matt finishes, as well as wood-tint effects, this is a durable coating that is resistant to alcohol and water.

## Cellulose

The advantage of nitrocellulose (cellulose) lacquer is its rapid drying time, making it extremely popular throughout the furniture industry. Although superseded by more advanced finishes, it is still a favourite for spraying. You can apply cellulose by brush, but have to work very quickly.

## Melamine

A two-pack coating containing melamine and mixed with a hardener. This produces a thick, tough finish that is particularly heat- and water-resistant. Touch-dry within about one hour, it can take up to a week to cure fully. You can apply additional coats once the previous one is touch-dry. Ideal for kitchen worktops and toys.

## Yacht varnish

Yacht varnish is based on tung oil and is renowned for its high-gloss appearance. Able to withstand saltwater, this extremely durable finish is good for exterior use, particularly in coastal locations. Drying time is about 12 hours.

# Exterior varnish

Exterior varnishes contain ultra-violet inhibitors, which slow down the deterioration of the coating. Most finishes for outdoor use are slightly flexible and move with the wood, so peeling and blistering should not be a problem if applied correctly. This is ideal for joinery, such as doors and windows and garden furniture.

# Aerosol sprays

Cellulose and acrylic lacquers are available in aerosol form, convenient for spraying small items and turned or carved work where thin coats are necessary to prevent runs. Dry in a few minutes, you can spray all the coats necessary in a couple of hours.

# Brushes and rubbers

To apply a lacquer, either use a soft bristle brush or make up a disposable rubber from folded cotton. Clean brushes immediately after use with the correct thinners, or water if using an acrylic finish. Spraying is an alternative technique, but specialist equipment is necessary, as well as an area for spraying.

ABOVE To make a disposable rubber for applying a shellac-based polish or oil, wrap a wad of lint in a clean piece of cotton sheet.

**TIP**

• Try to do any wood finishing at the end of the day, when you are unlikely to create more dust and can shut the workshop door. If using fast-drying finishes, this is less of a problem.

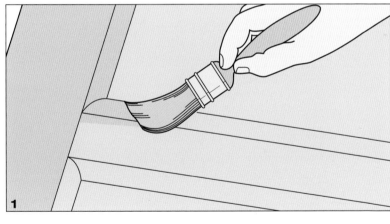

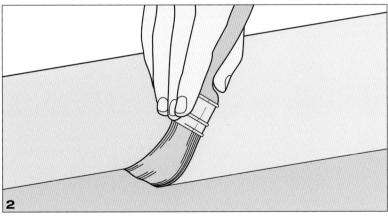

## How to apply lacquer

**1** Having prepared the surface adequately, thin down your first coat with an appropriate solvent. Using a good-quality bristle brush, apply the lacquer to corners and mouldings first, then larger, flatter areas. Use a narrow brush (about 13 mm/½ in) for mouldings, and a wider one for bigger surfaces (about 51 mm/2 in).

**2** Brush lacquer in the direction of the grain, blending in wet edges quickly so they do not start to dry out. When dry, de-nib with 320-grit silicon-carbide abrasive paper and remove the dust. Apply further coats. When fully hardened, buff the final coat with a soft cloth or rub with fine steel wool for a satin finish.

### Further information
The work environment  pages 66–67
Health and safety  pages 68–69
Abrasives and sanding  pages 222–224
Polish, wax and oil  pages 227–229

# 11

# Adhesives and fittings

Almost every piece made involves hardware of some sort during its construction, if only for making a jig or template. At the very least, you will use glue, of which there are several to choose from. Handles and knobs can affect the appearance of a piece of furniture radically, so choose carefully. A wide variety of hinges and catches allow you to fit virtually any type of door correctly, no matter how traditional or contemporary the design. Although you may not always find what you want from a local hardware store, specialist mail-order suppliers and the Internet make the ordering and selection process relatively straightforward.

# Glues

Modern technology has resulted in a vast range of sophisticated adhesives. Each is designed for bonding specific materials and several types are used in woodworking. You may need additional glues for metals, plastics or inlay materials. It is also a good idea to keep a selection of adhesives for emergency repairs and general maintenance work in the workshop and around the home.

ABOVE Apply glue with a clean brush to a prepared surface that is also dust- and particle-free.

## Polyvinyl acetate (PVA)

The most commonly used woodworking glue is PVA, which is a cold-setting adhesive. A good all-round glue with water-resistant properties in some types, it remains slightly flexible, even when set, allowing some movement of timber. It is easy to clean up with a damp cloth or paper towel. However, its high moisture content can make larger areas of veneer difficult as the moisture is absorbed within the veneer, leading to curling. If using cellulose-based polish, you will find the solvents mix with the PVA and can cause unsightly swelling on the glue line, called 'creep'. Aliphatic resin (yellow) glue is a sophisticated PVA which has a fast initial grab, with a shorter cramping time necessary.

## Resin

One of the most permanent and reliable of glues is synthetic resin, otherwise known as urea formaldehyde. Many brands are two-part adhesives: the glue is brushed to one joining surface while the hardener or catalyst is applied to the other. For the small workshop, mixing resin glue in powder form with water is easy

**TIP**

• Unless you are likely to be using large quantities for a project, always buy glue in small packs. Most have a limited shelf life, so you could end up wasting glue that is past its best.

(the powder incorporates the hardener). A general guide for resin glue shelf life is about three months, in dry conditions.

## Polyurethane

Polyurethane glue creates an exceptionally strong bond in a wide range of materials besides wood, including metals, ceramics and most plastics. It cures when exposed to moisture in the air, so shelf life is shorter than most other glues. Squeezed-out glue foams as it dries and can be chipped away before sanding. Used extensively for boat building, polyurethane glue is relatively expensive compared to PVA.

## Animal glue

Made from the bones and skins of animals, this glue has been used for centuries and is still preferred by antique restorers, musical-instrument makers and those making reproduction furniture. Traditionally, animal glue is used in granule (pearl) or sheet form, soaked in water and heated – usually in an electric glue pot. You can also buy it in liquid form.

Although animal glue requires some preparation, the real advantage is that it is reversible: you can ease joints apart with a pallet knife and hot water. This makes it popular with luthiers, where awkward repairs may be needed later during the life of the instrument. Disadvantages include instances where air conditioning reduces the humidity levels upon which this glue relies. Many genuine antiques have lost their marquetry veneer owing to the dry environment in which they are kept. If in doubt, leave a bowl of water under a radiator to maintain the humidity needed for this type of glue.

Powdered resin  White PVA

Polyurethane glue  Dark PVA

Two-part epoxy resin glue

## Contact adhesive

Contact adhesive is latex based and relies on both surfaces being coated and meeting when touch-dry – about 15 minutes – to form an instant bond. Although unsutable for most woodworking tasks, it is used widely by kitchen and shop fitters for gluing plastic laminates to worktops and cabinets. In the workshop it is ideal for building projects, such as router tables or jigs, that need a laminate surface for durability. If used for veneering, the tension within the glue can pull veneers open in time and edges are likely to lift slightly, especially where humidity levels are high. You need a more permanent adhesive in cases where wood meets wood.

## Epoxy resin

A two-part adhesive, epoxy resin provides incredible strength when bonding a wide range of materials, including metals and some plastics. Here, you mix glue and hardener in very small quantities, as working time can be just a few minutes before it starts to set. Epoxy is also available in syringe format for dispensing equal amounts of glue and hardener. This option is expensive but invaluable for repair jobs or gluing decorative inlays.

Superglue

## Cyanoacrylate

Also known as 'superglue', cyanoacrylate glues create a bond in seconds with the right materials. Useful for small repairs, such as chipped or lifting wood fibres, you only need a few drops. Available in liquid or gel form, cure times of some superglues can be increased by using a spray accelerator. Although it is easy to glue fingers together accidentally, de-bonders will soften and release any joint. This option is very expensive.

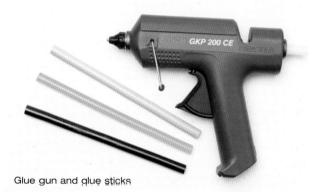

Glue gun and glue sticks

## Glue guns

An electric glue gun distributes hot-melt glue in a continuous bead, and is very useful for mock-ups and temporary holding purposes, such as turning small items on the lathe. You feed a glue stick into the back of the tool and dispense it by pulling the trigger. Operating temperatures make glue-gun tips very hot, so make sure safety is a priority.

### Further information

# Screws and nails

Screws are used widely in furniture-making and joinery, while nails are the most basic fixings of all, used mostly for carpentry and construction. Screws are stronger and take longer to fit, usually drilling clearance holes first. With nails, you simply hammer them in, punching them below the surface to conceal them.

ABOVE Although generally pre-packed these days, nails and panel pins may still be sold by weight.

## Screws

Screws for wood vary greatly in pattern, size, quality and purpose. Their appearance may not be important in many situations, but invariably for furniture- or cabinet-making they should enhance the finished piece. Solid brass screws are commonly used for furniture fittings. Screw heads can become damaged easily by using the wrong tool, so always use the correct type and size of screwdriver. A traditional wood screw has a single slot in the head and is countersunk, allowing you to insert it into wood so that it sits flush with the surface. More recent patterns have a cross-headed slot, which offers a better grip when driving or unscrewing them. Most common are Pozidriv screws, similar to the earlier Phillips pattern, but with added shallow grooves between the slots. Newer patterns include T-star and square-headed screws, which require special screwdriver blades to drive them. Hex screws are frequently used in the assembly of woodworking machines and are tightened with a special key.

Threads are designed for driving and fixing screws into various materials. Traditional wood screws have tapered shanks and fit tightly through clearance into pilot holes. Modern screws have parallel shanks, for driving into wood, often without pilot holes. These are less likely to split the wood and are ideal for use with cordless drill/drivers. Screws for MDF have coarse, single threads on their shanks and twin-threaded sharp points for starting. By comparison, chipboard screws have shallower threads. For exterior use, screws should be zinc plated or treated to prevent corrosion (passivated).

Slotted countersunk screw

Round-head screw

Pozidriv screw

Split point and rifled thread

Surface-mounted screw cup

Recessed screw cup

**TIP**

• When inserting a screw into hardwood for the first time, dip the thread into wax or grease to make it easier to drive home.

## SCREW GAUGES

Screw gauge refers to the shank size, although these are not precise diameters. Screws are available in both metric and imperial gauges, with each requiring a clearance hole for the shank and a pilot hole for the tip. Generally, you should select a screw size that is three times the thickness of the smallest piece of timber it has to pass through. Hardwoods tend to need bigger clearance holes than softwoods. Note that metric/imperial conversions are approximate.

| metric | imperial | pilot hole | clearance hole |
|--------|----------|-----------|----------------|
| 3.0 | No. 4/5 | 1.5 mm (1/16 in) | 2.5 mm (7/64 in) |
| 3.5 | No. 6 | 2.0 mm (3/32 in) | 3.5 mm (5/32 in) |
| 4.0 | No. 8 | 2.5 mm (7/64 in) | 4.5 mm (11/64 in) |
| 4.5 | No. 9 | 3.0 mm (1/8 in) | 5 mm (3/16 in) |
| 5.0 | No. 10 | 3.5 mm (5/32 in) | 5.5 mm (13/64 in) |
| 6.0 | No. 12/14 | 3.5 mm (5/32 in) | 6.0 mm (1/4 in) |

## JARGON BUSTER

**Counterbore** The process of drilling a hole so that the screw head lies beneath the wood surface when inserted; usually concealed with a matching wood plug.

**Countersinking** The process of enlarging a clearance hole opening to accept the countersunk screw head.

**Countersunk** Refers to the underside of the head of a wood screw, which is bevelled to sit inside a corresponding recess in the timber.

**Phillips** A screw pattern with a cross-headed slot.

**Pozidriv** A screw pattern with a cross-headed slot, plus additional shallow grooves.

**Torque** The twisting force when driving a screw; measured in Nm with power tools.

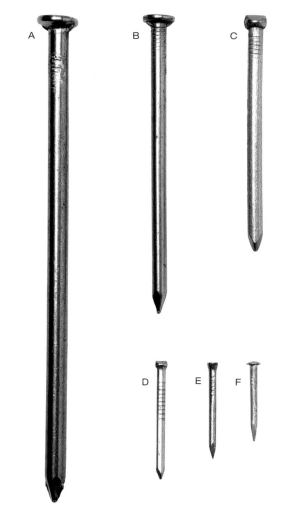

ABOVE A selection of nails and pins: (A) and (B) round wire nails; (C) and (D) oval nails; (E) Steel panel pin; and (F) brass pin.

# Nails

Nails are often used in the workshop when building jigs or temporary structures. A selection of round-head, lost-head and oval nails is useful. When selecting a size, choose one that is three times the thickness of the smallest piece of timber. Panel pins are frequently used in carpentry and joinery work when fixing battens and other small mouldings while glue cures. They are available in a brass finish as well as steel. Smaller veneer pins are suitable for applying fine decorative mouldings to furniture.

**Further information**
Drills  pages 104–105
Screwdrivers  pages 106–107
Hammers  pages 108–109
Cordless tools  pages 120–123

# Hinges

Most doors rely on hinges of some sort to open, whether for a tiny cabinet or a large pair of gates. How neatly they are fitted is a reflection of the quality and care that has gone into building the rest of the project. Always choose the correct hinges and take your time to install them properly. If unsure about marking out or how they work, try fitting them to an offcut first.

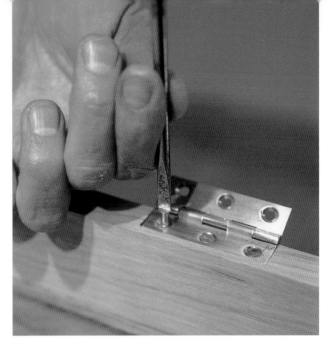

ABOVE Neatly-fitting hinges can make a piece of furniture. Use the correct type and take care when marking out and cutting recesses.

Cylinder hinge

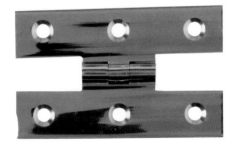

H-hinge

Desk-strap hinge

## Types of hinge

The most common hinge is the butt, used on doors of all descriptions from fine cabinets to house entrances. Available in a wide range of sizes, they are normally made from mild steel or solid brass. Plated finishes are suitable for exterior use, while decorative antique finishes may suit certain styles of furniture.

Variations on the butt hinge include backflap, table and counter hinges, with deeper flaps suitable for attaching folding tops on pieces of furniture. The piano hinge is a continuous strip for cabinet doors and flaps. Sold in lengths of 1 and 2 m (approximately 39½ and 79 in), you simply cut it to size with a hacksaw. Designed for lightweight doors, flush hinges do not need to be recessed as they are mounted directly on to a surface. Soss hinges are far more complex, requiring special routed recesses to accommodate the completely concealed hinge mechanism.

Cylinder hinges enable a door to be opened to 180 degrees and are hidden from view when closed. They are fitted into precisely drilled holes in the wood. One of the most common hinges for cabinets is the surface-mounted, self-closing type used by kitchen fitters. This hinge has the benefit of being relatively straightforward to fit and, once fitted, enables the position of the door to be adjusted in all directions.

Piano hinge

# Surface hinges

When choosing the type of surface hinge to use you must first determine whether the door will be:

Full overlay – overlapping the carcase, as in the case of a single cabinet door.

Half overlay – where two doors meet at the centre of a frame member.

Inset – where the door fits inside the carcase.

All three positions are possible but each requires a different version of the same hinge, so take advice before ordering your hardware.

Steel backflap hinge

# Bradawls

Marking the position of small screws can be critical when it comes to fitting hinges and other cabinet fittings. A bradawl or awl is easier to control than a cordless drill. An awl has a square blade with four faces that come to a sharp point. Use this point to locate the position of the screw. Once marked, you drive the awl into the wood to create a pilot hole for the screw. You can also use the awl to modify an existing pilot hole that is slightly out of place: simply lean the tool over. A bradawl's tip is like a tiny screwdriver blade, which is twisted into the grain when making the hole.

Self-closing cabinet hinge

Brass butt hinge

---

### JARGON BUSTER

**Knuckle** Where the two halves of a butt hinge join. A pin through the knuckle enables them to pivot.

**Leaf** The flap on a butt hinge that is recessed into the wood.

---

### TIPS

• When fitting hinges with brass screws, use a duplicate set of steel screws of the same size. Brass screws are softer and would invariably break off or become damaged during the fitting process. Instead, position and fit the hinge using the steel screws and swap to the brass screws when everything fits well.

• When fitting butt hinges, line the slots of the screws up for a neat appearance.

Brass butt hinge

**Further information**
Measuring and marking tools  pages 84–87
Drills  pages 104–105
Screwdrivers  pages 106–107
Cordless tools  pages 120–123
Pillar drills  pages 160–161

# How to fit brass butt hinges

**1** On a frame and panel door, position the top of the upper hinge level with the bottom of the upper rail and the bottom of the lower hinge in line with the top of the lower rail. Use a pencil and try square to mark out. Place the hinge on the door edge, and mark precisely with a knife.

**2** Set a marking gauge to the dimension from the centre of the hinge knuckle to the back of the leaf.

**3** Gauge a line on the edge of the door between the cut lines. This marks the position of the recess for the hinge flap.

**4** Use another marking gauge if possible. If not, readjust the tool to the thickness of the hinge flap and scribe a line on the face of the door.

**5** With the door gripped firmly in the vice, hold a chisel vertically with its cutting edge on one of the knifed marks denoting the hinge recess. With the blade bevel facing inwards, strike the tool with a mallet. Repeat at the other end of the recess. Do the same along the back edge of the recess.

**6** Make a series of vertical cuts across the recess, striking the chisel the same number of times in each position to maintain a consistent depth of cut.

**7** Carefully chisel out the waste by holding the chisel horizontally and pushing it across the previously cut marks. Clean out the wood down to the gauged line and check the hinge fits exactly into the recess. Trim if necessary with the chisel.

**8** Mark the screw-hole centres. Depending on the size of the screws, either drill pilot holes or use an awl. Fit the hinge first with a set of steel screws, followed by brass ones if appropriate. Lubricate brass screws using candle wax or petroleum jelly.

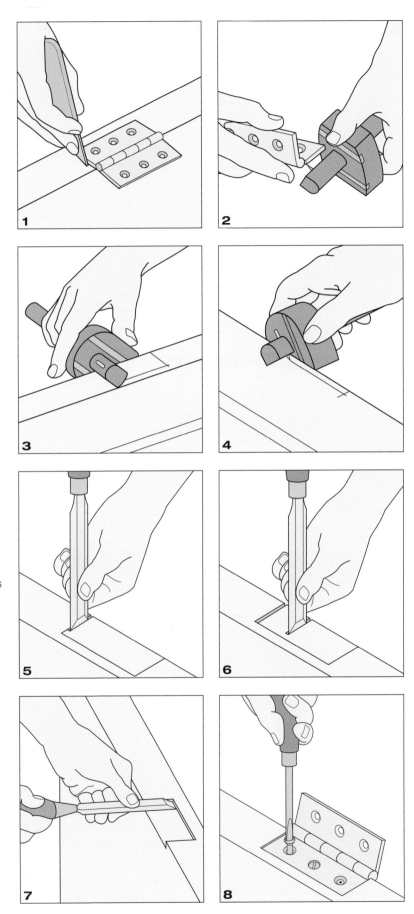

**9** With the hinges fitted, offer them up to the carcase and mark their corresponding positions. Mark the screw location for the centre hole of the hinge flap and insert a steel screw. You may find it helpful, while fiddling with the lower hinge, to secure the upper one temporarily by driving an awl into one of the screw holes.

**10** Make a knife line around the hinge and cut out the recess as before. Make any adjustments necessary and, again, use steel screws first. Once you have hinged the door it may be necessary to take a few more shavings from around the edge of the door in order to get an even clearance all round. This is best done after fitting the hinges. Only when the hinge is fitted to your satisfaction use the set of brass screws.

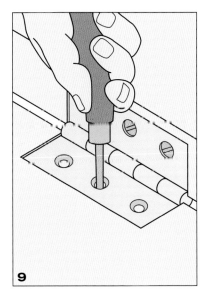

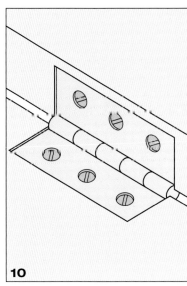

# How to fit self-closing surface hinges

The great advantage of surface-mounted doors, as used in fitted kitchens, is that they are much easier to install than doors fitted inside a carcase opening. One of the most convenient, and elegant, solutions to hinging this type of door is to use self-closing surface hinges. These are also known as concealed cup hinges and usually require a 35 mm (1⅜ in) diameter drill bit.

**1** Using the correct drill bit, bore a shallow hole on the inside of the door. Use either a pillar drill or power tool mounted in a stand for accurate holes.

**2** Once the recess has been drilled, screw the hinge to the door.

**3** With the rear part of the hinge now in place, offer up the door to the carcase. Mark the position of the screw holes using an awl.

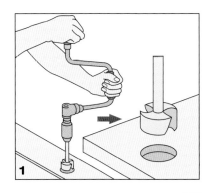

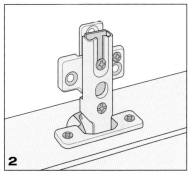

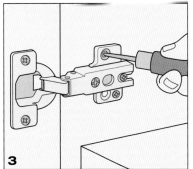

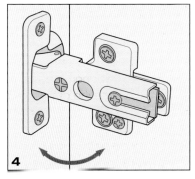

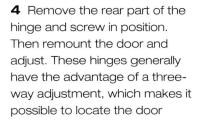

**4** Remove the rear part of the hinge and screw in position. Then remount the door and adjust. These hinges generally have the advantage of a three-way adjustment, which makes it possible to locate the door

position precisely. This is especially useful when hanging a series of doors where it is important to line them all up exactly and make sure there is an even gap between the two closing stiles.

# Furniture fittings

Knobs and pulls, cabinet and drawer handles can be a furniture-maker's nightmare. They are the means by which you lend style and distinction to a piece of furniture, yet the temptation is always to leave them until last. By doing this, you inevitably limit yourself to increasingly narrow choices and options.

ABOVE The choice of handles and other fittings will affect the overall look of a project. If possible, select these at the design stage.

## Knobs and handles

There is a vast range of knobs, handles and drawer pulls available from shops, mail-order catalogues and over the Internet. Alternatively, you can rout, or even carve, them in your own workshop. Choices generally fall into two categories: knobs or handles that are applied to a surface; and drawer or door pulls or handles that are incorporated into the design of a piece of furniture.

### Applied knobs and handles

These knobs and handles are surface mounted, usually with a screw fitted from the back of the door or drawer. In the case of traditional wooden knobs they may simply have a dowel behind, which you glue into a hole drilled in the drawer front or door. There are many styles of knobs and D-handles, in hard- and softwoods, metals and plastics.

### Built-in pulls and handles

Handles incorporated into a piece of furniture are not necessarily complex, but can certainly be effective. One option, for example, is to rout finger holds in the bottom edges of drawers, creating visual interest as well as fulfilling a practical need. Another type of routed handle is that produced by using a router to create a curved moulding at the back of an applied handle. Router bits are available for cutting recesses into drawer fronts, door stiles and rails. They are generally used with a template and a guide bush fitted to the router to form the shape of the recess required.

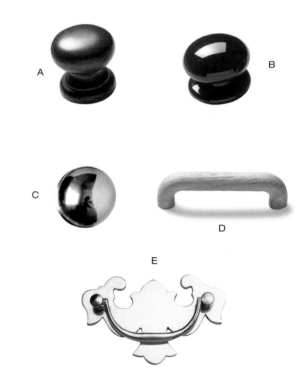

ABOVE A selection of knobs and handles suitable for drawers and cabinet doors: (A) stained hardwood knob; (B) ceramic knob; (C) brass knob; (D) oak D-handle; and (E) traditional brass drawer handle.

## TIP

• When judging visual placement of door or drawer handles and knobs, fit them to an offcut before drilling holes in a finished project.

# Door catches

You may not always want to emphasize such fittings as door catches, latches and hinges, and might be concerned that they serve their function effectively and discreetly. In a few cases, however, you might choose them to enhance a particular period or style. High-quality fittings tend to be made from drawn brass.

Some form of latch or catch is required to hold a door closed. One of the earliest types of latch was a wooden Sussex or Suffolk latch, operated either by lifting a small wooden bar that goes through the door and raises the latch, or by putting a finger through a hole to lift it. This type of latch is very simple and could be added to any type of door.

You might use bolts where the closing stiles of two doors meet. Almost invariably one door is held shut with the second one closing against it. Brass, surface-mounted bolts are popular and used in both period and contemporary furniture. These will fit neatly onto the edge or the back of a door and locate in a metal plate attached to the carcase.

Magnetic catches are another way of holding a door closed and come in several forms. One solution is a small magnetic barrel that fits into a hole drilled in the front of a divider panel or the edge of the carcase, leaving only a small black disc visible. You fit an equally small metal plate to the inside of the door, which attracts the magnetic surface of the catch.

Ball catches are another option and consist of two opposing balls, which are each fitted against spring resistance. The balls capture a brass fitting, which is attached to the door. Making this fitting work smoothly requires some patience. You may find the fitting on the door needs filing, while the springs that hold the balls against the door catch may need adjusting for tension.

Push latches are popular where an exterior handle is not wanted on a cabinet door, for example. Here, you attach a small plastic fitting to the back of the door. When the door is pushed firmly inward the catch allows the door to move inside the cabinet by 5–10 mm (³⁄₁₆–³⁄₈ in). The door is then thrown forward by a spring mechanism within the catch, which enables you to get a hold on the corner of the door and open it.

# Door locks

Traditional cylinder locks are frequently used on cupboards and drawers. They may be surface mounted or recessed into the backs of doors or drawer fronts and operated with keys. Fall locks are used to secure the flaps on bureaus and desks. Good-quality locks are made from drawn brass.

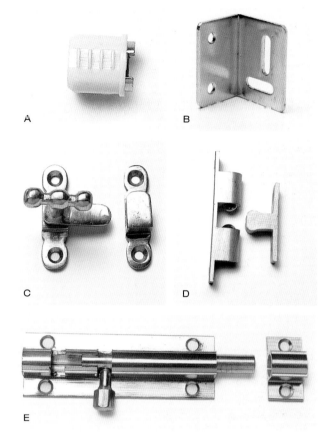

ABOVE A selection of furniture fittings: (A) magnetic catch; (B) shrinkage or stretcher plate; (C) traditional brass turn latch; (D) brass ball catch; and (E) surface-mounted brass bolt.

# Stays

To prevent a folding flap dropping down too far, fit a stay to the inside of a cabinet, with the opposite end of the arm screwed to the flap. You can control friction by using a sliding stay, while a joint stay is simply a folding arm. The finish may be plated steel or brass.

# Shrinkage plates

Used to mount solid timber tabletops on to supporting framework, steel shrinkage plates are easy to fit. Bent at 90 degrees, one face has elongated screw holes, which allows for timber movement across the grain. They are fitted with round-headed screws.

**Further information**
Drills pages 104–105
Routers pages 134–140

# Glossary

**Ah**
Amp hour, measurement of battery capacity. The higher the Ah rating, the longer the tool will run.

**Air-drying**
Once a trunk has been converted, logs are stacked 'in stick' in the open air to dry naturally, but protected from the rain.

**Axes**
Three mutually perpendicular directions, usually called X, Y and Z axes.

**Bastard cut**
File with coarse teeth for an aggressive cut.

**Bed**
The base of the lathe. This may be cast iron, although a machine may have circular or square-section steel bars.

**Biscuit**
An oval-shaped dowel – made of compressed beech – inserted into matching slots in adjacent boards. Glue swells the fibres ensuring a tight-fitting joint.

**Blank**
A piece of wood sawn into a disc and mounted on a faceplate for bowl turning.

**bpm**
Blows per minute. The measurement for impact drilling.

**Burnisher**
A straight, hardened steel blade set into a handle for raising the burr on a scraper. It may be oval or circular in section.

**Burr or burl**
Wild grain revealed when a growth on a tree is cut off and sliced.

**CAD**
Computer-aided design. Software replacing the traditional draughting board, paper and pencil.

**CAM**
Computer-aided manufacture. Machines (such as lathes, milling machines, etc.) controlled by a computer rather than directly by an operator. They often take their geometry information directly from a CAD model.

**Carborundum powder**
An abrasive powder used on a lapping plate to surface a tool. Lubricate with water or oil.

**Carcase**
Structure consisting of a jointed top, bottom and sides. May be built from solid timber or sheet materials.

**Catenary wire**
A steel wire stretched overhead between two points, usually buildings. Used to suspend a power cable.

**Caul**
A stiff board, flat or curved, for cramping groundwork and veneer together.

**Chamfer**
A bevel along the edge of a piece of wood, normally at an angle of 45 degrees.

**Chatter**
When the blade vibrates during planing, rather than remaining solidly locked in the plane. Causes the tool to skid across the timber.

**Cheek**
The side of a tenon.

**Chuck (1)**
Fitted to the end of the spindle, three self-centring jaws close on the bit when inserted. On a hand drill or swing brace this is generally keyless and tightened by hand.

**Chuck (2)**
Highly engineered circular steel device for holding timber on the lathe instead of a faceplate.

**CITES**
Convention on International Trade in Endangered Species monitors woods that are at risk.

**Clamp**
American term for cramp.

**Collet**
Split, tapered sleeve that grips the cutter shank. Retained by a locking nut on the end of the motor spindle.

**Coordinates**
Numbers that define positions in space using the X, Y and Z axes.

**COSHH**
Control of Substances Hazardous to Health Regulations

**Counterbore**
The process of drilling a hole so that the screw head lies beneath the wood surface when inserted; usually concealed with a matching wood plug.

**Countersinking**
The process of enlarging a clearance hole opening to accept the countersunk screw head.

**Countersunk**
Refers to the underside of the head of a wood screw, which is bevelled to sit inside a corresponding recess in the timber.

**Crosscutting**
Sawing across the direction of the grain.

**Crown guard**
Adjustable steel or plastic safety cover above the saw blade.

**Crown-cut**
Another term for through-and-through sawing (see below). Crown-cut boards display almost flat or slightly curved growth rings in the end grain. Board faces show the flame effect of the growth rings.

**Cutter block**
A cylindrical steel or aluminium block into which straight or shaped cutting blades are locked. Found on stationary surface planers and spindle moulders, but also power tools such as portable planers.

**Cutting back**
When a finish is applied, the grain is raised or the surface coating itself is uneven. This requires the finish to be smoothed or 'cut back' between coats using a gentle abrasive.

**Dado**
A wide, shallow groove across the grain. Alternative name for housing.

**Dead centre**
Similar to a revolving centre, but with no ball bearings. Must be lubricated with wax or grease.

**De-nibbing**
The process of lightly sanding a varnished or lacquered surface between coats to remove dust particles.

**Design brief**
A written plan identifying a problem and how it can be solved, within certain criteria and constraints, by a designer.

**Double-cut**
Teeth criss-cross in both directions across a file.

**Dovetail**
A joint consisting of a set of tails that interlock with pins in the corresponding piece.

**Dowel**
A short piece of cylindrical hardwood – often ramin or beech – inserted into corresponding holes drilled in two pieces of wood to be joined together. Shallow grooves allow excess glue to escape. Dowel diameter should be about half the wood thickness.

**Dowel points**
Pointed metal pins used for locating and marking accurate dowel positions.

**Drive centre**
Mounted in the headstock, sharp prongs grip the end of a spindle blank. Either two or four prongs are standard.

**Ducting**
Pipework through which sawdust or chippings pass on their way to an extractor unit.

**End grain**
The fibres that are exposed when wood is cut across the grain.

**Ergonomics**
The study of people's relationship to their working environment – particularly relevant in the design of furniture.

**Face edge**
An edge planed straight and square to the face side. The second surface to be worked when preparing timber. The face edge and face side are always at 90 degrees to each other. Both are used as reference faces for marking tools.

**Face side**
A wide surface planed perfectly flat, selected to be exposed on finished work. When preparing timber this is always the first face to be planed. It must be perfectly flat and straight.

**Faceplate**
A metal disc attached to a lathe for mounting timber blanks which may then be turned into bowls.

**Feed speed**
The rate at which timber automatically passes through a thicknesser. The slower the speed the better the finish to the timber.

**Ferrule**
Steel or brass ring that prevents a wooden handle splitting when the tang of a chisel or gouge is fixed in place.

**Fettling**
The process of preparing a tool before sharpening, to make it work more efficiently.

**Figure**
The grain pattern revealed in a piece of timber, usually when planed. The term usually refers to unusual effects characteristic of certain woods.

**Fillers**
Substances used to fill small holes and defects in timber. Usually chemicals, although sawdust mixed with glue is sometimes used.

**Flitch**
A bundle of veneer leaves.

**Former**
A mould shaped to the required curve, around which laminates are cramped while gluing. Often female and male moulds are used together, with laminates cramped in between.

**FSC**
Forest Stewardship Council

**Grit**
Abrasive sheets are graded by particle size. Each number relates to the number of particles passing through a mesh per unit area. The lower the number, the coarser the grit.

**Groundwork**
Sheet material or timber to which veneer is glued.

**Guide bush**
A steel collar screwed to the router base, enabling the tool to follow a template. The cutter passes through the middle.

**Gullet**
The valley between two teeth points.

**Hardpoint saw**
A saw on which the teeth have been heat-treated so the tips remain sharp, but which cannot be re-sharpened.

**Haunch**
Shortened part nearest the corner of a tenon that prevents the wood twisting or snapping off.

**Headstock**
The lathe's main casting at one end of the bed, through which the spindle passes. Also houses the pulleys and belts for speed change.

**Heartwood**
Hard, dense cells at the centre of a tree, providing the most stable timber.

**Holdfast**
A metal arm inserted in a collar in the bench top for holding timber flat. May have a threaded screw adjuster or be simply tapped in place with a hammer.

**Honing**
After grinding, edge tools are honed (sharpened) on an abrasive stone to produce a cutting edge.

**hp**
Horse power; 1 hp equals 760 w.

**HSS**
High-speed steel.

**In stick**
Air-dried boards are stacked as they come off the log with spacer battens, or 'stickers', spaced evenly between them.

**Infeed**
The front table on a machine that supports timber before and during a cut.

**Iron**
Another name for a plane blade or cutter.

**Jaws**
Steel fingers that expand or contract to grip a cylindrical timber blank or the spigot turned on the end of one.

**Jig**
A proprietary or workshop-built device that enables a power tool or machine to cut or shape a timber component accurately and safely.

**Kerf**
Width of cut produced by the blade teeth on a saw blade.

**Kickback**
When a work piece is ejected from a machine towards the operator by a rotating cutter or blade.

**Kiln-drying**
The process by which the moisture content of timber is reduced by more than is possible by air-drying. The timber is seasoned in an oven using a mixture of hot air and steam. This process is essential for wood destined for internal use.

**Knives**
The removable cutters on a planer or spindle moulder. There may be two, three or four per block.

**Knuckle**
Where the two halves of a butt hinge join. A pin through the knuckle enables them to pivot.

**Laminate**
Thin strips of wood glued together to form a thicker, stable board. The work piece may be straight or shaped to a pattern.

**Laminating**
The process of gluing several layers of veneer together to form a stable, curved shape without steaming and bending. (Plywood is a form of laminating, using constructional veneers.)

**Lapping plate**
A dead-flat piece of steel on which tools can be ground flat.

**Leaf**
The flap on a butt hinge that is recessed into the wood.

**Li-ion**
Lithium-ion

**Lip-and-spur bit**
A spiral-twist drill with outer spurs and sharp point in centre. Also called a dowel bit.

**Luthier**
Maker of traditional stringed instruments, such as the violin family and guitar.

**Mating surfaces**
Two flat metal surfaces that should bed together firmly, without any movement.

**Medullary rays**
Flecks evident on the face of some quartersawn timber.

**Melamine**
A durable, hard plastic coating applies to sheet materials during manufacture.

**Mitre box**
A basic wood or plastic jig for accurately cutting timber square or at 45 degrees. The work piece sits on the base of the jig between parallel, vertical sides. A tenon saw is guided by existing slots cut precisely across the sides of the jig.

**Morse taper**
The chuck spindle is slightly tapered to fit securely in the head of the machine.

**Mortise**
A rectangular hole in a piece of timber to accept a tenon. It may extend right through the wood, or can be stopped so the tenon is not visible on the outside face.

**NiCd**
Nickel cadmium

**NiMH**
Nickel metal hydride

**NVR**
No volt release. A type of safety switch.

**opm**
Orbits per minute.

**Orbital**
The action of a sanding pad moving around a central point without spinning.

**Outfeed**
The rear table on a machine that supports timber after a cut.

**PAR 'planed all round'**
A term referring to softwoods that are planed on all four sides.

**Paring**
Removing a thin shaving from timber with a sharp chisel, either from the surface or from end grain.

**Pein**
A wedge-shaped end of the head on some hammers, used to start off nails.

**Phillips**
A screw pattern with a cross-headed slot.

**pindle**
The rotating shaft that passes through the headstock, mounted in bearings.

**Platen**
The cast-alloy or plastic base plate flexibly mounted to an orbital sander.

**Pozidriv**
A screw pattern with a cross-headed slot, plus additional shallow grooves.

**ppi**
Points per inch (25 mm).

**PTFE Polytetrafluoroethylene**
A material used in industrial applications where sticking must be avoided; also used as coating on cookware.

**Pushstick**
A wooden or plastic safety device used to push narrow or small components past the blade on a saw. Prevents fingers getting too close to the moving blade.

**Quartersawn**
Planks cut from a tree radially, where the growth rings are at least 45 degrees to the face. This technique exposes the best figure.

**Rail**
A horizontal piece of wood in a frame, usually between two vertical stiles.

**RCD**
Residual current device.

**Rebate**
A step formed along the edge of a piece of timber, usually rectangular in section, to accept a panel of solid wood or sheet material. Also known as a rabbet.

**Rendering**
The process of putting colour, texture, lights, shadows and reflections on to a model, in order to make it look realistic.

**Revolving centre**
Mounted in the tailstock, its point is inserted into the end of a spindle blank. Also called a live centre, it revolves freely on ball bearings.

**Ringing sound**
The sound produced as timber components, particularly joints, are hammered together. The sound becomes solid, rather than hollow, as the surfaces mate together.

**Ripsawing (ripping)**
Cutting parallel to the grain of the timber.

**Riving knife**
A curved steel plate fixed behind the saw blade to prevent timber closing up and pinching as it passes through the blade. Slightly less than kerf width but wider than blade thickness.

**rpm**
Revolutions per minute

**rubbed glue joint**
Where two straight pieces of timber are joined without cramping. Glue is applied, both edges rubbed together and left to cure.

**Rubber**
A folded cloth filled with wadding. Normally used to apply French polish, it can also be used for varnish. Applied to timber with figure-of-eight and circular movements.

**Sapwood**
New wood growing furthest from the centre of a tree, providing the least stable timber.

**Scotch glue**
The same as animal glue.

**SDS  Special Direct System**
A tool-free clamping system.

**Seasoning**
The process of removing moisture from the cell walls of wood.

**Second cut**
File with medium teeth.

**Set**
Saw teeth are alternately bent slightly to one side of the blade, then the other. The resulting cut (kerf) is wider than the blade itself.

**Shadow board**
A white-painted board fixed to the wall for hanging hand tools. The shape of each tool is outlined in a contrasting colour.

**Shiplap**
Prepared softwood boards that overlap each other when used horizontally. A rebate on the lower edge sits over the top edge of the next board. Often used for cladding timber sheds.

**Shoe**
The heads on a cramp that exert pressure on a work piece. One may be fixed at the end, while the other is adjustable.

**Shooting board**
A jig for planing edges or end grain of timber accurately. It consists of two boards glued together, the upper one narrower than the other. The side of the plane runs on the lower board, trimming the work piece that sits on the upper level.

**Shoulder**
The squared end on either one or both sides of a tenon or tongue.

**Single-cut**
Teeth slope in one direction across a file.

**Smooth cut**
File with fine teeth for the smoothest cut.

**Socket**
The space between a pair of pins in a dovetail joint.

**Sole**
The machined face of a spokeshave or plane, which comes into contact with the timber. A spokeshave will have either a flat or curved sole.

**Solvent**
The liquid in which a substance can be dissolved to create a solution.

**Spline**
A thin rectangular strip of veneer, plywood or timber used to strengthen a joint, glued into a slot cut by a fine saw.

**spm**
Strokes per minute

**Stile**
The vertical sides of a frame.

**Stock (1)**
On a square, the component into which the blade is fixed; on a gauge, the hardwood component through which the stem slides.

**Stock (2)**
Prepared timber, planed all round and ready to be worked.

**Stroke length**
The distance a jigsaw or reciprocating saw blade moves in and out.

**Strop**
Piece of leather used for producing a razor edge on a chisel or gouge, by rubbing the tool along it.

**Swing**
The biggest diameter timber blank that can be rotated without hitting the bed on a lathe.

**Tack cloth**
A fabric cloth impregnated with resin to collect dust particles from a surface.

**Tailstock**
Cast-iron assembly at the opposite end of the lathe to the headstock. Slides along the bed and locks to support the spindle when turning between centres.

**Tang**
The tapered end of a chisel blade, file or rasp, designed to be driven into a handle.

**Taper-ground**
The blade on some handsaws reduces in thickness from bottom to top, so reducing friction as it cuts.

**TCT (tungsten-carbide tipped)**
Circular saw-blade teeth and router bits are usually tipped, remaining sharp longer than high-speed steel (HSS) versions. Better for cutting man-made materials.

**Tearout**
Wood fibres tend to lift and break when planing timber in the wrong direction, or against the grain.

**Temper**
The process of hardening the cutting edge of a tool by heating and cooling the steel.

**Tenon**
Rectangular end of a rail cut to fit snugly into a mortise.

**Throat capacity**
The distance from the centre of the adjuster shoe to the neck or bar of the cramp.

**Through-and-through sawing**
When a log is sliced with a series of parallel cuts, leaving only the centre boards quartersawn.

**Tongue and groove**
Prepared softwood boards that interlock, with a projecting tongue along one edge and matching groove along the other. Also called matchboard.

**Tool rest**
A cast-iron support bar on which turning tools are held while turning. Slides along the bed and can be adjusted for height and angle.

**Torque**
The twisting force when driving a screw. Measured in Nm with power tools.

**tpi**
Teeth per inch (25 mm).

**Tracking**
The lateral movement of the belt across the rollers on a belt sander.

**Trenching**
A housing cut across the grain to a set depth. A number cuts are made with the saw blade, moving the work piece each time until the required width is reached.

**Trunnion**
A casting on which the band-saw table is mounted, enabling it to tilt. Usually incorporates a protractor scale to set the angle accurately.

**v**
Volt

**w**
Watt

**Waney edge**
The natural edge of a plank, which may still have a covering of bark.

**Winding sticks**
A pair of identical hardwood strips with parallel edges. Placed at opposite ends of a board, they are used to check for twist by sighting along one strip and aligning it with the other. Coloured edges make this easier.

# Index

# Acknowledgements

## Author acknowledgements

The Author would like to thank the following individuals for their help with this book: David and Shirley Askham; Lucy Coad (www.squarepiano.co.uk); Andy King; Steve Maskery; Dave Roberts; David Savage (www.finefurnituremaker.com); Stephen Simmons.

The Author would also like to thank the following companies: **Avon Plywood** (www.avonplywood.ltd.uk); **Axminster Power Tool Centre** (www.axminster.co.uk); **Bahco Tools** (www.bahco.com); **Black & Decker** (www.blackanddecker.co.uk); **Bosch** (www.boschpowertools.co.uk); **BriMarc Associates Ltd** (www.brimarc.com); **Chestnut Products** (www.chestnutproducts.co.uk); **Classic Hand Tools** (www.classichandtools.com); **DeWalt** (www.dewalt.com) **Fein** (www.feinmultimaster.co.uk); **Hammer** (www.ukhammer.co.uk); **Hegner** (www.hegner.co.uk) **JET** (www.jettools.com); **Leigh** (www.leighjigs.com); **Lie-Nielsen Toolworks Inc** (www.lie-nielsen.com); **Makita** (www.makita.com); **Metabo** (www.metabo.com); **Milwaukee** (www.milwaukeetool.com); **Pennyfarthing Tools** (www.pennyfarthingtools.co.uk); **Record Power** (www.recordpower.co.uk); **Rustins** (www.rustins.co.uk); **Ryobi** (www.ryobitools.com); **Screwfix Direct** (www.screwfix.com); **Stanley** (www.stanleytools.com); **Trend** (www.trendmachinery.co.uk); **Triton** (www.tritontools.com); **Veritas** (www.leevalley.com); **Woodrat** (www.woodrat.com).

## Picture acknowledgements

**Commissioned photography ©Octopus Publishing Group Ltd**/Colin Bowling

All other photography **©Octopus Publishing Group Ltd**, except: **David Askham** 18, 50, 51 bottom centre, 52 top, 53 top left, 53 top right, 53 centre right. **Axminster Power Tool Centre** 67 centre, 73 top, 137, 137 centre, 137 bottom, 142, 146 top left, 146 top right, 157 top, 172 bottom right; / Fein 123 bottom; / Irwin Industrial Tools 112 top; /Jet Machinery 57 centre, 147 centre, 162 top, 164 bottom, 165 top, 168 bottom. **Bahco Tools** 89 top centre, 101 top. **Black & Decker** 130 top 47, 65 centre right. **BriMarc Associates Ltd** 140 top; /Leigh Industries Ltd 140 centre; /Nobex Champion 91. **Corbis UK Ltd**/Wayne Lawler; Ecoscene 10 top left; /Marcelo Sayao/epa 10 centre left. **Phil Davy** 6, 11, 13 top, 13 bottom, 14, 15 top, 15 bottom, 31 right centre bottom, 63 bottom, 80 top, 80 bottom centre, 80 bottom, 80 top centre, 130 centre. **Dewalt Power Tools** 121 top, 122 top, 125 centre, 129 centre bottom, 132 bottom, 134 bottom, 147 bottom, 148, 149 top, 149 centre, 149 bottom. **Getty Images**/Marcus Lyon 10 bottom left. **Hammer UK Ltd** 57 bottom, 156, 167 top. **Hegner UK Ltd** 155 top, 155 bottom. **Jacqui Hurst** 62 bottom left. **Lie-Nielsen Toolworks** 94 centre. **Makita Power Tools** 120 centre, 125 top, 129 top, 147 top, 151 top right, 151 centre right, 151 top right, 151 bottom right, 158. **Metabo (UK) Ltd** 121 bottom, 122 bottom, 126, 150, 152 top, 152 bottom right, 152 bottom left, 153 top, 153 centre, 153 bottom, 166, 167 centre, 167 bottom. **Milwaukee Electrical Tools** 121 centre, 132 top, 132 centre. **NTPL**/Dennis Gilbert 51 bottom right; /Nadia Mackenzie 52 bottom. **PP Mobler** 38. **Record Power** 28 bottom Robert Bosch Ltd 107 picture 1, 122 centre, 129 centre top, 131, 135 top. **Ryobi Technologies (UK) Ltd** 123 top, 123 centre, 129 bottom. **Stanley UK** 108 centre top, 117 top, 117 centre. **Trend Machinery & Cutting Tools Ltd** 134 centre, 139. **Triton Workshop Systems** 141, 144, 145, 146 bottom, 160 bottom, 161 top, 168 top, 172 bottom left. **Victoria & Albert Museum**/V&A Images 51 bottom centre. **WoodRat Joining Machines** 140 bottom.

Executive Editor **Katy Denny**
Managing Editor **Clare Churly**
Design Manager **Tokiko Morishima**
Designer **Maggie Town and Beverly Price, One2six Creative Ltd**
Photographer **Colin Bowling**
Illustrator **John Lander**
Picture Library Assistant **Taura Riley**
Senior Production Controller **Manjit Sihra**